Lecture Notes in Computer Science 7449

Commenced Publication in 1973
Founding and Former Series Editors:
Gerhard Goos, Juris Hartmanis, and Jan van Lee

Simone Fischer-Hübner
Sokratis Katsikas   Gerald Quirchmayr (Eds.)

Trust, Privacy and Security in Digital Business

9th International Conference, TrustBus 2012
Vienna, Austria, September 3-7, 2012
Proceedings

 Springer

Volume Editors

Simone Fischer-Hübner
Karlstad University, Department of Computer Science
Universitetsgatan 2, 65188, Karlstad, Sweden
E-mail: simone.fischer-huebner@kau.se

Sokratis Katsikas
University of Piraeus, Department of Digital Systems
150 Androutsou St., 18532 Piraeus, Greece
E-mail: ska@unipi.gr

Gerald Quirchmayr
University of Vienna, Research Group Multimedia Information Systems
Liebiggasse 4, 1010 Wien, Austria
E-mail: gerald.quirchmayr@univie.ac.at

ISSN 0302-9743   e-ISSN 1611-3349
ISBN 978-3-642-32286-0   e-ISBN 978-3-642-32287-7
DOI 10.1007/978-3-642-32287-7
Springer Heidelberg Dordrecht London New York

Library of Congress Control Number: 2012943036

CR Subject Classification (1998): D.4.6, K.6.5, E.3, K.4.4, H.2.7, C.2, H.4, J.1

LNCS Sublibrary: SL 4 – Security and Cryptology

Typesetting: Camera-ready by author, data conversion by Scientific Publishing Services, Chennai, India

Printed on acid-free paper

Springer is part of Springer Science+Business Media (www.springer.com)

Preface

The advances in information and communication technologies have raised new opportunities for the implementation of novel applications and the provision of high-quality services over global networks. The aim is to utilize this "information society era" to improve the quality of life for all citizens, disseminating knowledge, strengthening social cohesion, generating earnings, and finally ensuring that organizations and public bodies remain competitive in the global electronic marketplace. Unfortunately, such a rapid technological evolution cannot be problem-free. Concerns are raised regarding the "lack of trust" in electronic procedures and the extent to which information security and user privacy can be ensured.

In answer to these concerns, the 9th International Conference on Trust, Privacy and Security in Digital Business (TrustBus 2012) was held in Vienna during September 4–6, 2012. TrustBus 2012 brought together researchers from different disciplines, developers, and users, all interested in the critical success factors of digital business systems, and provided an international forum for researchers and practitioners to exchange information regarding advancements in the state of the art and practice of trust and privacy in digital business.

TrustBus 2012 received 42 paper submissions, which were all reviewed by at least two, and most of them by three or four members of the international Program Committee (PC). Based on the reviews and discussions between PC Chairs and PC members, 16 full papers and three short papers were finally accepted for presentation at the conference. Topics addressed by the accepted papers published in the proceedings include Web security, secure management processes and procedures, access control, trust models, privacy policies and privacy-enhancing technologies, cryptographic solutions as well as secure services, databases, and data warehouses. An invited keynote talk was given by Sarah Spiekermann, Vienna University of Economics and Business, on "Privacy - A New Era?". Furthermore, TrustBus organized in 2012 for the first time a special session, in which EU FP7 research projects related to trust, privacy, and security presented their recent research results.

We would like to thank all authors, especially those who presented their work selected for the program, as well as all EU project presenters. Moreover, we are very grateful to all PC members and additional reviewers who contributed with thorough reviews and participated in PC discussions ensuring a high quality of all accepted papers. We also owe special thanks to Sarah Spiekermann for contributing with her keynote talk.

Last but not least, we gratefully acknowledge the valuable help by Costas Lambrinoudakis when preparing TrustBus 2012 and by the local DEXA organizer Gabriela Wagner for her outstanding support.

June 2012   Simone Fischer-Hübner
                                                                     Sokratis Katsikas
                                                                  Gerald Quirchmayr

Organization

General Chair

Quirchmayr, Gerald   University of Vienna, Austria

Program Committee Co-chairs

Fischer-Hübner, Simone   Karlstad University, Sweden
Katsikas, Sokratis   University of Piraeus, Greece

Program Committee

Acquisti, Alessandro	Carnegie Mellon University, USA
Agudo, Isaac	University of Malaga, Spain
Casassa Mont, Marco	HP Labs Bristol, UK
Chadwick, David	University of Kent, UK
Chu, Cheng-Kang	I2R, Singapore
Clarke, Nathan	Plymouth University, UK
Cuppens, Frederic	ENST Bretagne, France
De Capitani di Vimercati, Sabrina	University of Milan, Italy
Eloff, Jan	University of Pretoria, South Africa
Fernandez, Eduardo B.	Florida Atlantic University, USA
Fernandez-Gago, Carmen	University of Malaga, Spain
Foresti, Sara	University of Milan, Italy
Furnell, Steven	Plymouth University, UK
Fuss, Juergen	University of Applied Science in Hagenberg, Austria
Geneiatakis, Dimitris	University of Piraeus, Greece
Gonzalez-Nieto, Juan M.	Queensland University of Technology, Australia
Gritzalis, Dimitris	Athens University of Economics and Business, Greece
Gritzalis, Stefanos	University of the Aegean, Greece
Hansen, Marit	Independent Center for Privacy Protection, Germany
Jøsang, Audun	Oslo University, Norway
Kalloniatis, Christos	University of the Aegean, Greece
Karyda, Maria	University of the Aegean, Greece
Kesdogan, Dogan	University of Siegen, Germany
Kokolakis, Spyros	University of the Aegean, Greece
Lambrinoudakis, Costas	University of Piraeus, Greece

Lioy, Antonio   Politecnico di Torino, Italy
Lopez, Javier   University of Malaga, Spain
Markowitch, Olivier   Université Libre de Bruxelles, Belgium
Martinelli, Fabio   CNR, Italy
Matyas, Vashek   Masaryk University, Czech Republic
Mitchell, Chris   Royal Holloway, University of London, UK
Mouratidis, Haris   University of East London, UK
Rajarajan, Muttukrishnan   City University, UK
Okamoto, Eiji   University of Tsukuba, Japan
Olivier, Martin S.   University of Pretoria, South Africa
Oppliger, Rolf   eSecurity Technologies, Switzerland
Papadaki, Maria   Plymouth University, UK
Pashalidis, Andreas   Katholieke Universiteit Leuven, Belgium
Patel, Ahmed   Kingston University (UK) - University
                                         Kebangsaan, Malaysia
Pernul, Günther   University of Regensburg, Germany
Posegga, Joachim   University of Passau, Germany
Rannenberg, Kai   Goethe University of Frankfurt, Germany
Rizomiliotis, Panagiotis   University of the Aegean, Greece
Rudolph, Carsten   Fraunhofer Institute for Secure Information
                                         Technology, Germany
Ruland, Christoph   University of Siegen, Germany
Samarati, Pierangela   University of Milan, Italy
Schaumueller-Bichl, Ingrid   University of Applied Science in Hagenberg,
                                         Austria
Schunter, Matthias   Intel Labs, Germany
Soriano, Miguel   UPC, Spain
Theoharidou, Marianthi   Athens University of Economics and Business,
                                         Greece
Tsochou, Aggeliki   University of Piraeus, Greece
Teufel, Stephanie   University of Fribourg, Switzerland
Tjoa, A Min   Technical University of Vienna, Austria
Tomlinson, Allan   Royal Holloway, University of London, UK
Weipl, Edgar   SBA, Austria
Xenakis, Christos   University of Piraeus, Greece

Table of Contents

Applied Cryptography

Privacy

Secure Services, Databases and Data Warehouses

Presentation of EU Projects (Extended Abstracts)

How Much Network Security Must Be Visible in Web Browsers?

Tobias Hirsch[1], Luigi Lo Iacono[2], and Ina Wechsung[1]

[1] T-Labs, TU Berlin, Berlin, Germany
tobias.hirsch@qu.tu-berlin.de, ina.wechsung@telekom.de
[2] Cologne University of Applied Sciences, Cologne, Germany
luigi.lo_iacono@fh-koeln.de

Abstract. Visualizing security status information in web browsers has been a complex matter ever since. With novel security standards getting into wide spread use and entering the browser, this task becomes even more complex. This paper addresses this issue by analyzing the current state of the art in browser support for DNSSEC. As a result of this analysis, it is emphasized that the visual cues used for TLS and the ones for DNSSEC are not unambiguous and hence are more confusing than beneficial. An improvement is suggested, that relies on the idea of visualizing security services instead of security standard specifics. The paper contributes an icon set following this idea and presents evaluation results obtained by a user study.

Keywords: Web Browser, Security, TLS, DNSSEC, Visualization, Human Factors.

1 Introduction

Visualization of security information in browsers has always been an issue. Since the early days of *Secure Socket Layer* (SSL) [1] and its successor *Transport Layer Security* (TLS) [2], there have been a lot of misconceptions [3]. First, the underlying technical details are hard to abstract in something sensible for a common user and second, the strategy of presenting security status information in a way that enables the user to make informed decisions while keeping the right balance between the alert level and the appearance frequency is a challenging task. Annoying the user too much with such notifications will lead to disregard no matter if these messages contain any critical information [4].

With the wide-spread use of the *Domain Name System Security Extensions* (DNSSEC) [5] the door is opened for an additional security information source. First browsers include some form of DNSSEC support either natively or via extensions. Since the developed approaches differ substantially from each other a discussion on the best way of deploying DNSSEC in the browser from an user experience viewpoint has started [6]. This paper contributes to this discussion by analyzing the current state of the art in browser support for DNSSEC. The goals are to identify the need for DNSSEC-related security information looped into

S. Fischer-Hübner, S. Katsikas, G. Quirchmayr (Eds.): TrustBus 2012, LNCS 7449, pp. 1–16, 2012.
© Springer-Verlag Berlin Heidelberg 2012

the browser and to find an answer to the more general question on whether the addition of further network security mechanisms in the browser needs individual visualizations in the user interface.

2   Foundations

When it comes to network security in the internet, the commonly deployed cryptographic protocol is *Transport Layer Security* (TLS) [2]. TLS encrypts the segments of network connections above the transport layer (i.e. TCP), using asymmetric cryptography for key exchange and security session setup, symmetric encryption for confidentiality, and message authentication codes for message integrity [7].

The *Domain Name System* (DNS) [8,9] is a crucial network service, which enables the use of spellable internet addresses instead of numerical ones. As illustrated in Fig. 1, the client applications refer to a local program provided by the underlying operating system–the so-called DNS resolver–with the request to translate the human spellable address into an IP address. The DNS resolver in turn forwards the request to a DNS server, which has been configured in the networking settings either manually or automatically (by the organization operating the access network). Since the human spellable addresses are organized in a hierarchical structure, a cascade of subsequent requests to specific DNS servers is launched, in order to obtain the corresponding IP address. The final response containing the IP address is then send back to the requesting client application, which uses it to start the communication to the targeted server.

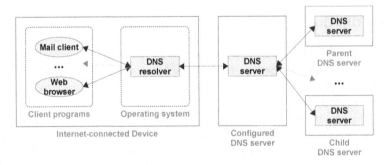

Fig. 1. Domain Name System (DNS)

Originally, DNS itself has no build-in security and, thus, was the vehicle for conducting various attacks in the past. Since the DNS responses are neither authenticated nor integrity protected, the core attack pattern is to implant falsified address information in order to direct clients to a different location than intended, which is often the basis for further attack steps. One example for such DNS spoofing attacks is known as *DNS Cache Poisoning* [10].

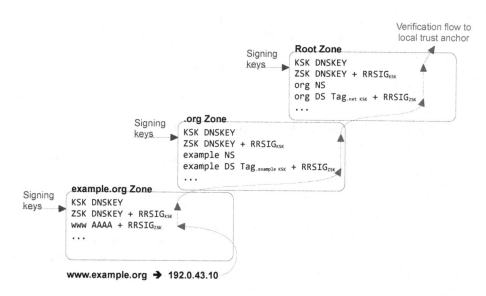

Fig. 2. DNSSEC chain of trust

The *Domain Name System Security Extensions* (DNSSEC) [5] adds an additional layer of protection to the network by guaranteeing that the information received from a DNS server has not been modified or tampered with. Technically this is realized by sealing the DNS entries by digital signatures. The hierarchical organization of the domain names is reused to build a chain of trust that flows from parent zone to child zone (see Fig. 2). Each zone has a cryptographic key pair. The zone's public signature verification key is published using DNS, while the private signing key is kept confidential. Higher-level zones sign the public keys of lower-level zones. A zone's private key is used to sign individual DNS data in that zone, creating digital signatures that are also published with DNS.

The security services provided by both protocols are compared in Tab. 1. TLS applies the security services confidentiality and message integrity to the application layer protocol, i.e. HTTP in the context of this paper. The HTTP messages are encrypted and assigned with a protection to detect manipulations. Before these measures are applied, a security session is established between the browser and the server, for which the authenticity of the server is checked by a certificate validation. DNSSEC also provides message integrity and source authentication.

Table 1. TLS and DNSSEC security servives

Security Service	TLS	DNSSEC
Confidentiality	yes	no
Message integrity	yes	yes
Source authentication	yes	yes
Authenticated denial of existence	no	yes

These security services are not targeted to HTTP, however, but to the DNS response instead. The same is true for authenticated denial of existence, which ensures that responses denying the existence of any entry can be validated, in order to prevent advisories to forge a response denying the existence of an existent domain name.

3   DNSSEC Entering the Web Browser

The differences between TLS and DNSSEC have encouraged to add visual DNSSEC information in the browser user interface. Analyzed using a layered approach, however, DNSSEC mechanisms, policies and enforcements are located at the operating system level (see Fig. 1). Each application that needs to access the internet can benefit from the DNSSEC security services in a transparent manner. If a connection to a specific remote host is requested and the signature of the DNS entry can not be verified, the connection is not established and the application is left with an appropriate error message. This is the standard case, if a DNSSEC validating resolver is accessible.

Still, there are many attempts to loop DNSSEC into the application layer. Most recently and prominently, the web browser has been targeted as information point and beneficiary of DNSSEC status information. In the following subsections, the current state of the art in browser-support for DNSSEC is analyzed in terms of the conducted browser integration and the developed visualizations.

3.1   DNSSEC Validator

The *DNSSEC Validator* (`http://www.dnssec-validator.cz/`) is an extension available for Mozilla Firefox and Google Chrome. It integrates a small icon into the browser's address bar (on the left in Firefox and on the right in Chrome), which displays a key in four distinct states as shown in Fig. 3. The upper-left red key is shown to the user when the DNS response is signed, but the signature verification detects a manipulation or the IP address of the loaded web page does not match with one obtained from the validated DNS response. The upper-right orange key tells that DNSSEC is present, but the validity of the signature is broken due to e.g. an expired key. If DNSSEC is used and the signature verification has been performed successfully, then the lower-right green key is shown. If DNSSEC is not deployed, then the grey key with the red do-not-enter sign gets displayed.

Fig. 3. DNSSEC visualization of DNSSEC Validator extension in Firefox

The DNSSEC verification results shown in Fig. 3 have been obtained by using the public DNSSEC validating resolver provided by the *Domain Name System Operations Analysis and Research Center* (DNS-OARC, `https://www.dns-oarc.net/oarc/services/odvr`). Interestingly, the domains belonging to the .gov TLD are not validated correctly, although these domains are secured by DNSSEC, as can be explored by the various available DNSSEC tools such as e.g. the one available online from `dnsviz.net`.

Attention must be paid due to the extensions behaving differently in both supported browsers. This is due to a technical reason and cause by Chrome providing no API for retrieving the IP address of the loaded page. Since Firefox does provide such an API, the extension validates whether the IP address of the loaded page corresponds with one IP address in the DNS response. If this is not the case the red key is shown.

Having such a check might be helpful to discover certain type of attacks, but it also produces false-positives in cases in which the DNS entries point to load balancing servers routing the user to a nearby content distribution location, such as occurring in the example illustrated in Fig. 4.

Fig. 4. Distinct validation results in Chrome and Firefox on the same host name

Note further, that the connection to the remote system is established although the DNSSEC response is manipulated. Since DNSSEC Validator serves passive security information only, it does not prevent the browser from accessing spoofed sites.

3.2 MyDnssec

An equivalent approach is taken by the project *MyDnssec* (`http://cs.mty.itesm.mx/dnssecmx/`). It developed a plugin for Internet Explorer and a few mobile apps to validate DNSSEC. An identical set of colored key icons is used to display the distinct evaluation results, but with a distinct semantic attached to some of the keys. The grey key does only appear in newly opened empty browsing tabs. The orange key is used to signal that the domain is not signed. The green and red keys are used to tell whether the validation processed successfully or not respectively. The key icon appears in the status bar at the bottom of the browser window, there being most possibly detached from the domain name printed in the address bar.

3.3 Extended DNSSEC Validator

The Firefox extension named *Extended DNSSEC Validator* (`https://os3sec.org/`) follows a different goal when integrating DNSSEC in the browser. It implements the IETF internet draft on the *DNS-Based Authentication of Named*

Entities (DANE) and combines it with TLS [11,12]. The DANE draft specifies how to store a web server's public key into the secured DNS (in the so-called TLSA record). This allows owners of DNSSEC enabled domains to securely deploy self-signed certificates or provide additional trust in their CA-signed certificates, adding a further information source certifying the authenticity of a server's public key. The extension performs the validation steps and displays the obtained results (see Fig. 5), but does not integrate with the TLS server certificate validation logic implemented in Firefox.

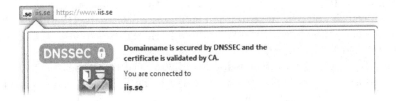

Fig. 5. DNSSEC visualization of Firefox extension Extended DNSSEC Validator

The visualization approach of the Extended DNSSEC Validator extends the standard TLS information dialog (see Fig. 5). It adds three colored icons including the protocol name and a padlock to notify the user about the validation results. A grey icon stands for non-usage of DNSSEC. A green icon means that the DNSSEC validation has been performed successfully and a red icon tells if some error occurred during the verification process.

3.4   Google Chrome

Chrome has a build in support for DNSSEC since version 14. It does not go for an separate presentation of DNSSEC validation results as the extensions described so far, but follows the approach to couple DNSSEC with TLS. For performance reasons, however, Chrome does not implement the out-of-band scheme specified in the DANE draft [12]. It uses an in-band approach instead, which adds the exchange of the DNSSEC chain of trust within the TLS handshake. Google implemented the scheme that is based on the TLSA record being an extension of the TLS certificate. If the extension with the OID `1.3.6.1.4.1.11129.2.1.4` is present, Chrome verifies the contained TLSA entry by own means. For this, it includes the public signature verification key of the DNS root zone (`http://src.chromium.org/svn/trunk/src/net/base/dnssec_chain_verifier.cc`). The result of the DNSSEC validation is then fed into the TLS server certificate validation logic.

A practical problem with this approach lies in the fact, that DNSSEC signatures are of short lifetime. This means, that the certificate needs to be updated as often as the DNSSEC entries are resigned. As a consequence, this is only feasible for self-signed certificates, since they do not involve a third party for the repeated certificate issuing. A second TLS in-band approach uses the IETF standard which specifies generic extension mechanisms for various TLS protocols [13]. Here, the TLSA record is assigned to the `extension_data` field of the extension defined for the `Server Hello` message. This decouples the DNSSEC chain from the TLS server certificate, but requires changes to the TLS protocol implementation in the server software.

Fig. 6. Chrome DNSSEC support: self-signed certificate carrying DNSSEC entry

A noticeable change in Chrome's TLS certificate validation logic is that if a self-signed certificate contains a TLSA extension and it includes a valid entry, then the TLS connection to the server is established automatically, without involving a trust decision by the user (see Fig. 6). This validation procedure is problematic, since self-signed certificates can not be distinguished any more from CA-signed certificates. Moreover, an adversary could sign a domain with DNSSEC and set up a self-signed certificate to automatically obtain a green lock icon possibly for a domain name confusingly similar to another site [14].

Fig. 7. Chrome's notification when not all content is sent via TLS

In another constellation, in which a CA-signed certificate is used, but not all of the page contents is send via the TLS-protected channel, Chrome uses the visualization depicted in Fig. 7 to warn the user about this inconsistency [6].

3.5 Summary

Letting aside all the discovered practical issues and the ones stemming from the specific implementation, from this analysis, one main issue becomes immediately visible, from which the following questions can be crafted. If there is more than one network security mechanism accessible for the browser, does each one need to have its own visualization concept and area?

Having distinct visualization areas, one for each network security mechanism may become confusing and in some cases even contradicting (see Fig. 7).

In another case in which the DNS entry of a remote host is protected by a DNSSEC signature but it does not provide a TLS-secured channel, the visualization of the DNSSEC Validator might lead some users to think that the communication to this host is encrypted since a green key is shown (see lower-right of Fig. 3). So, independent of the question whether DNSSEC verification results should be visible in the browser user interface or not, our suggestion is to visualize the security status obtained from one or more network security mechanisms in one single area, abstracting from the specific security mechanism and focusing on the provided security services.

4   Security Services Visualization

Based on these observations and the idea of focusing on the visualization of security services established between two connected hosts, a set of icons has been developed, which is proposed as a common set that any network-related security mechanism can potentially make use of instead of coming along with an own view.

When referring back to the security services each of the focused protocols offers (see Tab. 1), it becomes obvious that some of the services are much too technical in nature in order to be presented to a common user. The core security services which are required in the context of communications in the web have therefore been reduced to confidentiality and source authentication.

Message integrity is an important security services and a must have property in cryptographic protocols. Message integrity and symmetric key encryption need to go together, in order to prevent certain types of attacks. This cryptographic detail is, however, not of importance for common users. Their interests lay in the confidentiality of the exchanged messages in the first place. The integrity of the message is seen as given as well, if the confidentiality is given.

The same is true for the source authentication and authenticated denial of existence services. The security service authenticated denial of existence provided by DNSSEC is important from a technical viewpoint to fend from DoS attacks. From an usability perspective, this service can be abstracted to a detail that is crucial to decide on the authenticity of a DNS response. Thus, a common user will not be able to understand this technical notions and should therefore obtain the result of the authentication check only.

For these core security services, we developed a set of icons which provide a visual cue for each service (see Tab. 2). The closed padlock tells that the connection to the remote server is confidential. In case the authentication of the server has been verified successfully, a green check mark is depicted together with a green color scheme surrounding the domain name. If the authentication failed, then a red do not enter sign is shown and the domain name is crossed out by a red line.

In order to be consistent and comprehensive, for the states in which no security is enabled, corresponding icons need to be part of the icon set as well (see Tab. 3). An open padlock symbolizes an open non-confidential communication channel

Table 2. Provided security services

Security Service	Pictogram
Confidentiality	🔒
Source authentication passed	✓ www.example.com
Source authentication failed	⊖ www.example.com

and a grey question mark tells that no server authentication took place and that the identity of the server is unknown.

Table 3. Missing security services

Security Service	Pictogram
No Confidentiality	🔓
No Source authentication	? www.example.com

To demonstrate how these pictograms can be used and how they relate to settings in which multiple network security mechanisms are available, the combinations of all deployment scenarios based on TLS and DNSSEC are shown in Fig. 8. In case no security is available, the icon printed in the first row is shown to the user. The icon combines the open padlock and the question mark to notify about the missing confidentiality and source authentication. If a TLS-protected connection is established, depending on the kind of certificate four different states must be distinguished and visualized. If the authenticity of the server has been validated successfully, then the first icon is displayed, telling that the communication is confidential and the source has been authenticated. If the authentication failed for some reason, but the user still established the connection by clicking through active security warnings, then the third pictogram is shown. It notifies about the confidential connection and the non-authenticated server. A closed padlock and question mark highlighted in orange is used to indicate a self-signed certificate, in case the user trusted it only temporary. The last icon considers the case in which the page content is only partly transmitted confidential. Thus, independent on whether the server has been authenticated automatically or via user intervention, if the exchanged content is only partly encrypted, the open padlock is shown combined with the additional warning that the server behaves in a not trustworthy manner. If DNSSEC is present and the authenticity of the DNS response could been validated the green check mark is shown, but since DNSSEC does not provide confidentiality, the padlock remains open. Accordingly, when the DNSSEC authentication fails, the red do not enter sign will be visible. When both schemes are in use, the visualization is the same as shown for the TLS only case. Both mechanisms would then work jointly in order to establish a confidential and/or source authenticated channel.

The result set from a user's perspective remains the same, with the hope, that the security validation logic can decide on a larger percentage of the requests by itself, without the need for active user involvement.

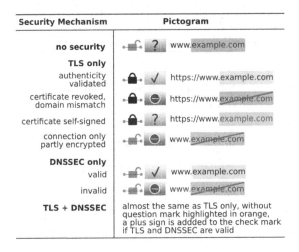

Fig. 8. Combined security services view for different security scenarios

By evaluating the possible combinations and their possible states depicted in Fig. 8, one can note that there are some settings which are equivalent from a security service viewpoint. By this, one benefit of the proposed approach becomes visible. It does not make a difference for the user what mechanism provides a particular security service. Thus, the technical details remain hidden and the focus is on the results of the security setup in terms of enabled security services. The various security protocols can benefit from each other, so that having them somehow within the browser would certainly help in building more robust and effective validation procedures. With the proposed approach, the visualization would not be influenced by the underlying constellation. This would provide the user with a visualization which is stable in terms of position, icon set and semantics of the provided icons.

5   User Study

To assess first insights into user perception regarding the developed icon set, a user study has been conducted. As stated above, one assumption is that the DNSSEC visualization in the form of an extra sign showing a key with different background colors, will be confusing, misleading or not be associated with the underlying meaning (authenticity of website). The indicators present the two security services authenticity and confidentiality simultaneously. It was expected, that this simultaneous presentation will make users more aware of the differences of these services and will thus promote a better understanding of the underlying concepts. Accordingly, the aim of the study was twofold: first, to determine whether users recognize and understand the proposed indicators and second, to compare the developed indicators with the available approaches. In order to limit the amount of questions, this study has been focused on one particular browser (Firefox) and one particular DNSSEC extension (DNSSEC Validator).

5.1　Participants

Twelve participants (5 female, 7 male, average age = 31 years) voluntarily took part in the study. Most of them were colleagues and students of the Quality and Usability Lab at the TU Berlin recruited via email. All of them were regularly Firefox users.

5.2　Test Design and Test Material

We used seven security scenarios in the study (see Fig. 9). For each scenario a pictogram was set up, displaying available and proposed security indicators. The proposed pictograms were edited into webpage screenshots of three different websites: the German Amazon homepage (www.amazon.de), the login page for the online banking service of Deutsche Bank (meine.deutsche-bank.de/trxm/db/) and the start/login page of the social network XING (www.xing.com/de). Accordingly, we followed a 7x2x3 factorial within the design (*security scenario* x *existing vs. proposed* x *content*) and prepared 42 target webpages. Additionally, we included 21 unmodified screenshots of webpages as distractors. The purpose was to avoid drawing the participants' attention to the pictograms, which were the only elements which changed in the screenshots for the three target websites. For each webpage we collected ratings on six 7-point scales. The end labels of the two scales relevant for the current study were *insecure* vs. *secure* and *untrustworthy* vs. *trustworthy*. Again four distractor scales were included (un-/aesthetic, conventional/novel, confusing/clear, un-/reliable). The aim was once more to prevent participants focusing on possible security aspects on the webpage due to the repeated presentation of the same content. The test was implemented and executed using PsychoPy v1.73 (http://www.psychopy.org/) on a MacBook Pro 13" and lasted about 30 minutes for each test. After the test an interview was conducted using a self-constructed interview guideline. The pictograms of the Firefox extension *DNSSEC Validator* and the proposed pictograms has been shown to study participants in addition. They were asked if they had recognized the pictograms during the test. For each pictogram the participants were asked which meaning they assign to it. The answers were then sorted into three different categories: *correct, unclear* and *wrong*. The category correct was only chosen if the participant clearly stated the underlying security service or the appropriate behavior (e.g., "This is a fake site", "I would not proceed" for the do-not-enter sign). Category wrong was chosen if the participant explicit assigned another meaning than the intended one (e.g., "encrypted connection" for the key pictogram). If the participant made ambiguous or imprecise statements (e.g., only saying "safe", "insecure") or told us that he or she is very unsure or do not know the meaning category unclear was chosen.

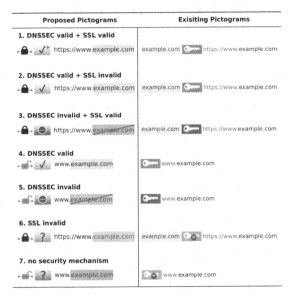

Fig. 9. Tested icons for seven security scenarios used in user study, *TLS invalid* means self-signed certificates here

5.3 Procedure

At first, the participants were asked to fill in a short demographic questionnaire. After that they were seated in front of the MacBook Pro where the instructions were presented. They were asked to look at 63 screenshots of webpages in Firefox 10.0.2. After each screenshot the ratings were collected. They could proceed from one screenshot to the next page by pressing the space key. The screenshots were presented in randomized order. Following the test, the subjects were interviewed by the experimenter.

5.4 Results

Regarding the ratings on the security scale a repeated measure ANOVA (Analysis Of Variance) showed no difference between the proposed vs. the existing pictograms: $F(1, 11) = 2.75$, $p = .126$, $part.\,eta^2 = .200$. Also for the trustworthiness ratings no differences were observed: $F(1, 11) = 4.68$, $p = .054$, $part.\,eta^2 = .298$. However, ratings for the seven security scenarios differed significantly for trustworthiness, $F(1.40, 15.41) = 10.19, p = .003, part.\,eta^2 = .481$, as well as for security, $F(1.26, 14.85) = 10.50, p = .004, part.\,eta^2 = .488$ (see

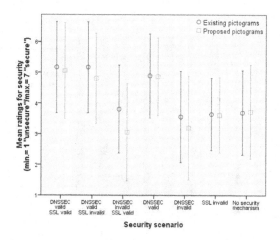

Fig. 10. Ratings for security. Error bar display one standard deviation.

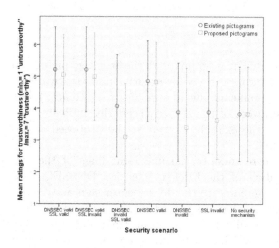

Fig. 11. Ratings for trustworthiness. Error bar display one standard deviation.

Fig. 10 and 11). Neither an interaction effect between proposed vs. existing pictograms and security scenario nor an main effect for content was shown.

In the interview conducted after the study two participants stated that they did not recognize the pictograms during the test. Regarding the understanding of the pictograms a Chi-square test showed significant differences, $\chi^2(16, N = 108) = 39.1$, $p < .001$. As shown in Fig. 12 the meaning of the padlocks and the do-not-enter sign was understood best. 5 out of 12 participants wrongly interpreted the key symbol of the Firefox extension DNSSEC Validator as a confidentiality indicator.

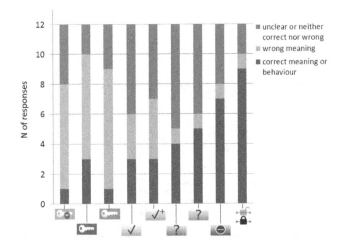

Fig. 12. Understanding of pictograms

5.5 Discussion

Between the proposed pictograms and the existing pictograms no differences were observed regarding ratings for security and trustworthiness. Still for the security scenarios significant effects were observed. Hence, the results imply that participants were aware of the security scenarios indicated by the pictograms. But each version—the existing as well as the proposed ones—indicated these scenario equally well.

However, the correctness of the understandings of the pictograms implied that the key symbols of the Firefox extension DNSSEC Validator are rather weak understood compared to the do not enter sign and the padlocks.

Content having no effect on the ratings might be due to the non-interactive test setting. It is plausible to assume that if participants were asked to actually enter their login or bank data their awareness regarding possible security threats would have been higher. Thus, further user studies have to be performed in order to validate the results using distinct test methods. Within another study, e.g., participants could be introduced to the security services confidentiality and authenticity beforehand and rate a set of pictograms regarding the status of these security services afterwards or design their own set of icons.

6 Conclusions

With new internet security mechanisms coming into wide-spread use, their integration into the application layer needs to be considered. With DNSSEC there is now one tool joining in alongside TLS. Several approaches have been developed to make use of DNSSEC in the browser. Some follow a orthogonal path to TLS and introduce an additional visual cue representing the DNSSEC verification result. Others try to combine both protocols in order to enhance the process of validating the authenticity of a remote server and make it more reliable.

The results obtained from this work advocate that in terms of DNSSEC it seems that bothering a common user with the task of monitoring an additional visual notifications and taking appropriate actions where required will most properly have no effect, as has been shown by other studies for other types of security warnings [4,3]. From a security and usability perspective it is therefore best to have the network stack perform the DNSSEC validations and then take the decision automatically to either establish a connection to the remote system or not. If the DNSSEC verification fails the channel will not be opened and the browser will react as in other network connection problem cases including not responding or not existing servers (see Fig. 13). This is the default behavior of any internetworked application if the local DNS resolver or the configured DNS server perform a DNSSEC validation.

Fig. 13. Web server not accessed due to false DNSSEC signature

The case is different, if DNSSEC is used in conjunction with TLS in order to increase the confidence in the authenticity of the remote server. The available approaches currently have their shortcomings. The Extended DNSSEC Validator prototype implements the DANE specification, but does not do anything with the obtained result but displaying it as a passive security information to the user.

Chrome follows an alternative path, which is not in conformance with the current DANE draft specification, since it uses an in-band approach for efficiency reasons. However, the validation result obtained from verifying the signed DNS response is injected into the TLS validation procedure. It has been adapted to trust self-signed certificates right away without any user action if such a certificate is contained in a corresponding valid DNSSEC chain of trust.

Independent of the implementation details, the approach of joining the security validation results in order to obtain a combined result may lead to more robust validation procedures. The way this is currently implemented in Chrome points into the right direction. The treatment of self-signed certificates for which a valid DNSSEC chain of trust exists, however, seems to be wrongly weighted. Further research is required to better understand the interplay of both protocols.

The conducted user study showed that the proposed security service oriented pictograms do not have the expected impact on the perceived security and trustworthiness of websites compared to the existing pictograms. Still, this result may be rooted in the test design. Thus, further user studies have to be performed in order to validate the results using distinct test methods.

References

1. Freier, A., Karlton, P., Kocher, P.: The Secure Sockets Layer (SSL) Protocol Version 3.0. RFC 6101, Internet Engineering Task Force (August 2011),
   http://www.rfc-editor.org/rfc/rfc6101.txt
2. Dierks, T., Rescorla, E.: The Transport Layer Security (TLS) Protocol Version 1.2. RFC 5246, Internet Engineering Task Force (August 2008),
   http://www.rfc-editor.org/rfc/rfc5246.txt
3. Sunshine, J., Egelman, S., Almuhimedi, H., Atri, N., Cranor, L.F.: Crying wolf: An empirical study of ssl warning effectiveness. In: Usenix Security (2009)
4. Egelman, S., Cranor, L.F., Hong, J.: You've been warned: an empirical study of the effectiveness of web browser phishing warnings. In: Proceedings of the Twenty-Sixth Annual SIGCHI Conference on Human Factors in Computing Systems, CHI 2008, pp. 1065–1074. ACM, New York (2008)
5. Eastlake, D.: Domain Name System Security Extensions. RFC 2535, Internet Engineering Task Force (March 1999), http://www.rfc-editor.org/rfc/rfc2535.txt
6. Internet Society: What is the correct "user experience" for DNSSEC in a web browser? Technical report (January 2012),
   http://www.internetsociety.org/deploy360/blog/2012/01/what-is-the-correct-user-experience-for-dnssec-in-a-web-browser/
7. Menezes, A.J., Vanstone, S.A., Van Oorschot, P.C.: Handbook of Applied Cryptography, 1st edn. CRC Press, Inc. (1996)
8. Mockapetris, P.: Domain names - concepts and facilities. RFC 1034, Internet Engineering Task Force (November 1987),
   http://www.rfc-editor.org/rfc/rfc1034.txt
9. Mockapetris, P.: Domain names - implementation and specification. RFC 1035, Internet Engineering Task Force (November 1987),
   http://www.rfc-editor.org/rfc/rfc1035.txt
10. Kaminsky, D.: It's the end of the cache as we know it. In: Black Ops. (2008)
11. Lexis, P.: Implementing a DANE validator. Technical report, University of Amsterdam (February 2012),
    http://staff.science.uva.nl/~delaat/rp/2011-2012/p29/report.pdf
12. Hoffman, P., Schlyter, J.: The DNS-Based Authentication of Named Entities (DANE) Protocol for Transport Layer Security (TLS). Internet-draft, Internet Engineering Task Force (February 2012),
    http://www.ietf.org/id/draft-ietf-dane-protocol-17.txt
13. Blake-Wilson, S., Nystrom, M., Hopwood, D., Mikkelsen, J., Wright, T.: Transport Layer Security (TLS) Extensions. RFC 4366, Internet Engineering Task Force (April 2006), http://www.rfc-editor.org/rfc/rfc4366.txt
14. Langley, A.: DNSSEC authenticated HTTPS in Chrome. Technical report (June 2011), http://www.imperialviolet.org/2011/06/16/dnssecchrome.html

A User-Level Authentication Scheme
to Mitigate Web Session-Based Vulnerabilities

Bastian Braun[1], Stefan Kucher[1], Martin Johns[2], and Joachim Posegga[1]

[1] Institute of IT-Security and Security Law (ISL)
University of Passau, Germany
{bb,jp}@sec.uni-passau.de, stefan.kucher@web.de
[2] SAP Research
martin.johns@sap.com

Abstract. After the initial login, web browsers authenticate to web applications by sending the session credentials with every request. Several attacks exist which exploit conceptual deficiencies of this scheme, e.g. Cross-Site Request Forgery, Session Hijacking, Session Fixation, and Clickjacking. We analyze these attacks and identify their common root causes in the browser authentication scheme and the missing user context. These root causes allow the attacker to mislead the browser and misuse the user's session context. Based on this result, we present a user authentication scheme that prohibits the exploitation of the analyzed vulnerabilities. Our mechanism works by binding image data to individual sessions and requiring submission of this data along with security-critical HTTP requests. This way, an attacker's exploitation chances are limited to a theoretically arbitrary low probability to guess the correct session image.

1 Introduction

In order to provide personalized services in the World Wide Web, remote applications must identify and authenticate their users. Upon signing up, users generally choose a username and a password that can be used as a shared secret to establish future sessions. After the authentication of the user, the web application assigns a unique temporary token to the user. This token is stored in the browser and subsequently used by the browser and the application to tell this user and others apart. Several attacks target the browser or the token to hijack established sessions. Clickjacking and Cross-Site Request Forgery mislead the victim's browser to send requests that are determined by the attacker. Session Hijacking and Session Fixation aim at sharing the token with the attacker.

In this paper, we introduce a method to authenticate security-sensitive operations. Our approach, named *Session Imagination*, can be applied to existing web applications and mitigates the above mentioned attacks. Specifically, we apply the two steps of identification and authentication to established sessions. After login, the user is equipped with a shared secret that is not stored in his browser. The former universal token then serves as the identification that is complemented

S. Fischer-Hübner, S. Katsikas, G. Quirchmayr (Eds.): TrustBus 2012, LNCS 7449, pp. 17–29, 2012.
© Springer-Verlag Berlin Heidelberg 2012

by the shared secret as the authentication for security critical operations. The shared secret can not be stolen by an attacker, and the browser can not be lured into misusing the secret.

Our contribution is twofold: we identify the above mentioned attacks' common root causes and provide an applicable solution that implements the well-known and approved concept of identification and authentication to web sessions. This solution remedies basic deficiencies of current web session implementations. We give details about the authentication scheme and its implementation, evaluate the approach, and show that the protection goals are achieved.

In the next section, we explain our solution's background in more detail. We give an overview of authentication in the web and how the focused attacks work. Then, we explore the attacks' common root causes. In Sec. 3, the actual solution, Session Imagination, is presented. We shed light on the user authentication scheme and provide evaluation of the scheme in terms of overhead, usability, and applicability. Then, we show that Session Imagination raises the bar for all four attacks though it can not yet completely prevent all of them. Sec. 4 presents related work before we conclude in Sec. 5.

2   Background

In this section, we explain details of authentication, particularly in web applications, and attacks on authentication and authenticated sessions. We show that these attacks share some common root causes.

2.1   Authentication

Authentication can happen based on something one knows, something one holds, who one is, what one does, or where one is. The most widespread approach is based on knowledge. A shared secret is established between the authenticating system and the legitimate user. The user provides this secret together with his identification (i.e. the claim who he is) in order to authenticate. The security of this approach lies in the fact that the shared piece of information remains secret. Thus, an entity which can provide the secret must be legitimate. Usually, the identification is called 'username' and the shared secret is the 'password' or 'PIN'.

2.2   Authentication Tracking in the Web

HTTP was designed to be a stateless protocol. Therefore, web applications have to implement their own session tracking on the application layer. For this purpose, session identifiers (SIDs) are used. Every HTTP request that carries the same SID is recognized by the application to belong to the same user session. In general, authentication tracking in web applications is tied to the application's session tracking, i.e., after a successful logon the user's session is marked to be authenticated on the server-side. In consequence, the SID becomes the user's de-facto authentication credential as long as the session is valid.

2.3   Web Session-Based Attacks

The vast majority of all existing web applications utilize HTTP cookies for SID transport. This means that the SID, i.e., the user's credential, is locally stored by the browser and automatically added to all HTTP requests which match the cookie's domain value. Several attacks are known that exploit this mechanism.

Session Hijacking: Session Hijacking denotes a class of attacks that strive to take over an existing session. As pointed out in Sec. 2.2, the session token allows access to individualised services. Thus, an attacker aims at knowing the SID. A promising variant is called *Session Hijacking via Cross-Site Scripting (XSS)*. The attacker first performs a XSS attack to steal the user's session ID and finally obtains access to the web application's internal area in his victim's name. The XSS attack is executed with maliciously injected JavaScript code that reads the stored cookies and transmits them to the attacker's site.

Session Fixation: Session Fixation attacks are similar to Session Hijacking attacks. A Session Fixation attacker places an unauthenticated token at the victim's browser, waits until it gets authenticated (i.e. the user logs in), and finally hijacks the session with the known token [8]. The first step, placing the cookie at the victim's browser, can be taken by several approaches [19]. A web application is vulnerable to Session Fixation attacks if it does not renew SIDs after user authentication. So, the attacker can reuse the known SID after the victim logged in.

Cross-Site Request Forgery (CSRF): An attacker can even perform some actions on behalf of a victim without ever getting any knowledge of the SID. He inserts a crafted link into some website that makes the browser send a request to the target web application. For example, the attacker might put http://www.yourbank.com/transfer.php?from=your_acc&to=my_acc into an image (<img>) tag on any website. Upon visiting this website, the user's browser tries to retrieve a picture and sends the crafted request to the banking website. The attack is successful if the victim is logged into his account at 'yourbank' at the same time. His browser will attach the SID cookie to the request and legitimate the money transfer.

Clickjacking: A Clickjacking attack [15] exploits the fact that the users' perception may vary from the page rendering outcome by the browser. In this attack scenario, the victim is a user that has an account at the target web application. To perform an attack, the attacker prepares a web page that makes the user perform actions on the target web application.

Technically, there are several ways the attacker can take [13]. First, he can load the target web application in a transparent *integrated frame (iframe)* [21] and place it as an additional layer in front of the visible underlying page while at same time luring the victim into clicking on a particular area by design of his own page. The attacker can make the user perform arbitrary actions as long as these are invokable by mouse clicks. Second, the attacker can include a button from the target web application in his own context. Therefore, he crafts an iframe that contains just the respective button as the only visible part of the target web page. This way, he changes the context of the triggered functionality. The victim might suppose to invoke a completely different action at a different web application.

In summary, Clickjacking attacks rely on a gap between a session context as it is perceived by the victim and the actual technical session context in the browser.

2.4   The Attacks' Root Causes

The previously described attacks share common root causes:

First, session authentication means authentication performed by the browser. For the user's perception, only one authentication step happens, namely the login where he provides his username and password. The rest of the session handling is transparent to the user. As explained above, HTTP does not have a session feature and, thus, session handling has to be implemented using session identifiers on the application layer. This fallback solution provides authentication of the browser with every request instead of authentication of the user as it would be required. The following example illustrates this fact: One person logs into his account on a web page, then leaves his computer to have a coffee. Every other person could now interact with the web application on behalf of the user logged in because the browser will do transparent authentication. So, as long as the browser maintains the session ID, all requests are authenticated. The same person accesses a terminal next to the coffee maker. He visits the same web application but he will not be able to access his account without another login though he already authenticated towards this web application.

Second, on the opposite side, the server can not distinguish different contexts of a request. On the server side, incoming requests generated by a JavaScript command, an image tag, or the click of a user respectively are all alike. The requests do not contain evidence that they are intended by the user. The server can not decide whether the user is aware of the action that is caused by a request.

To sum up, the common root causes of Session Hijacking, CSRF, Clickjacking, and Session Fixation are in fact *browser authentication* instead of *user authentication* along with the server's unability to determine a request's initiation context.

Browser-Level and User-Level Authentication: The authentication of HTTP requests can be divided into two classes: browser-level and user-level authentication.

Browser-level authentication is the current practice in web applications, meaning that after the user provided his credentials for login, the authentication token is cached and subsequent requests are implicitly applied by automatically sending the authentication token. In this case, the browser performs authentication on behalf of the user because the user logged in to the personalised service. Examples of implicit, e.g. browser-level, authentication are the above mentioned cookies, client-side SSL authentication, HTTP authentication (basic and digest), and authentication based on the client's IP address.

The other principle is user-level authentication. In this case, another authentication step for a user's requests is added. We require the user's explicit consent to a user-level authentication step such that this step can not be taken by the browser only but additional action by and knowledge of the user is required. Examples of explicit, user-level authentication are re-entering the username and password and passcodes received as text messages.

We identified two attack vectors emerging from browser-level authentication. CSRF and Clickjacking attacks make the browser send a request and authenticate on behalf of the user even though the authenticated user does not acknowledge. This problem is known as the 'confused deputy problem' [3]. The browser stores all secret information that is needed to authenticate the requests. The underlying assumption becomes evident in the attack scenarios: All requests are supposed to be only initiated by deliberate user clicks or by the browser that fetches regular content. This assumption stems from the early days of the World Wide Web where web applications were not personalized. The addition of web sessions and cookies turned this established assumption to a security risk. The web application can not decide whether the user deliberately initiated the requests. Uncommon request sequences may indicate CSRF attacks, Clickjacking attacks simulate regular user sessions and are harder to detect.

While CSRF and Clickjacking are based on requests initiated by the victim's browser and without his consent, there is another attack vector that exploits the fact that browser-stored information can be easily transferred. Session Hijacking and Session Fixation attacks strive to impersonate the user from different machines towards the web application. Both attacks share the same goal, namely the attacker and the victim share the same SID and are thus indistinguishable from the web application's point of view.

Both attack vectors are based on the same conceptual deficiency: Due to browser-level authentication, no user input is needed to supply evidence that the authenticated user intends the requested action. On the opposite, request authentication including user interaction prevents the attack vectors and remedies the conceptual deficiency.

3   Session Imagination

To mitigate the vulnerabilities described in Sec. 2.3, we implemented a new approach for user-level authentication, named *Session Imagination*. Thereby, we focused on overcoming the vulnerabilities' root causes (see Sec. 2.4). In this section, we will describe our solution that aims at mitigating CSRF, Clickjacking, Session Hijacking, and Session Fixation attacks. Session Imagination separates identification and authentication in web sessions and relies on visual authentication tokens which can be easily remembered and recognized by the user while the authentication token is not stored in the browser.

We model the attacker to be a regular web participant. He can send messages, access web applications and set up his own web sites. However, he does neither control the other user's machine or platform nor those of the web application nor the communication infrastructure between them.

3.1   Protection Goals

Our goal is to protect a web application and its users against the attacks described in Sec. 2.3. Protection means that an attacker's chances to reach his goals are limited to an upper bound of probability. The actual upper bound may be configurable. The attacker must not be able to increase this probability. For the sake of completeness, we must say that we aim at securing authentication tracking and do not consider an attacker who owns the login credentials. For example, a phishing attacker gaining knowledge of username and password can still use a protected web application in the victim's name.

3.2   The User-Level Authentication Scheme

Session Imagination uses images as per-session user-level authentication tokens. That means that every user is assigned an image upon login. This image is displayed once immediately after login (cf. Fig. 1).

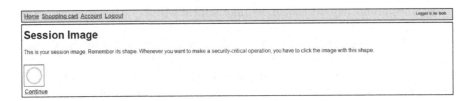

Fig. 1. A fresh session image is given immediately after login. This image has to be remembered throughout the session and identified among a set of images to legitimate security-critical requests.

It is then used together with a conventional session ID in a cookie to authenticate security-critical requests. For example, in an online shop, a set of critical actions is defined, e.g. sending an order or changing the shipping address. Upon requesting such an action, the user has to choose the right image among a given set before the action is executed (cf. Fig. 2). In our example implementation, we used circles, triangles, hexagons, arrows, squares, and ellipses as images. One could also use more usual images like animals, shoes, or hats. We call this intermediate step the 'challenge'. A brief overview of Session Imagination steps is given in Fig. 3.

For every new challenge, the images' shape is slightly varied. That does not affect the user's ability to distinguish the right image from the others but makes simple image recognition, e.g. by automatic hashing, harder. As an example, consider the images in Fig. 4 which represent the same six "classes" as those given in Fig. 2. Differences between two images of the same class can occur in terms of orientation (where appropriate), line color, and fill color. If pictures of animals or items serve as session secret, similar classes can be used. Users are expected to be able to distinguish cats from dogs etc.

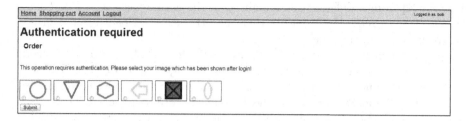

Fig. 2. Before a critical operation is executed, the respective request has to be authenticated. Therefore, the user has to identify the correct session image.

The next point of image recognisability is the *Uniform Resource Identifier (URI)*. The provided images could be identified by their file names, e.g. `circle1.png`. Given that, an attacker can conclude the image shape from the name which can be stolen by a XSS attack in conjunction with the session cookie. So, we implemented random names for all provided images. The names are re-generated with every response. They serve as one-time passwords that the user does not have to remember because he can identify the correct password by the corresponding image which is valid for the whole session.

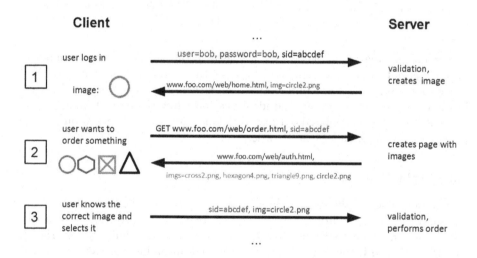

Fig. 3. An overview of authentication steps related to Session Imagination. We used descriptive file names for the pictures for the sake of clarity.

In the run of a XSS attack, the attacker could record the user's click and use a canvas element [20] to prepare an exact copy of the session image. The attacker can choose size 0 x 0 to avoid that the attack is detected by the victim. Next, the canvas is serialized and transmitted to the attacker's domain, e.g. by a hidden form or as a GET parameter. As a countermeasure, the images are integrated as iframes [21] from a different subdomain than the actual web page. The *Same-Origin Policy (SOP)* [16] prevents that the attacker's payload injected in the web page can read the image data.

Finally, the order of images must change with every challenge to avoid recognisability by position, e.g. "always the left most image". In particular, Clickjacking attacks are much easier if the sequence of images is predictable. The examples given in Fig. 2 and Fig. 4 illustrate how the images are re-arranged. The classes that are used in both examples are the same which is necessary to prevent intersection attacks. Otherwise, the attacker could prompt several challenges and compute the intersection. The remaining set must contain the correct class because the user must always be able to choose the correct image. This way, the attacker could reduce the number of candidates with every new challenge.

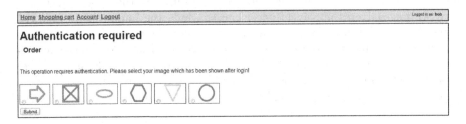

Fig. 4. The actual shapes of the session images vary. This does not lower identifiability by users but prohibits image recognition by hashing.

Session Imagination implements a user-level authentication scheme where the browser is not able to authenticate high-security requests transparently. The conventional separation of identification and authentication is restored. The SID in the cookie serves as a temporal identification while the correct image is the authentication. As we pointed out in Sec. 2.4, a user-level authentication scheme prevents all attacks under consideration.

3.3   Evaluation

The performance evaluation of Session Imagination can be restricted to the measurement of the additional steps required for the authentication of security-critical actions. The restriction to security-critical actions limits the overhead. In our prototype implementation, we considered an online shop as a use case. Putting items to the cart was possible without additional efforts while checking out and changing account information was classified as security-critical. So, for an average shopping trip, only one additional step is necessary.

Next, we come back to the protection goals named in Sec. 3.1. We will show that Session Imagination is able to overcome all of the respective vulnerabilities and, thus, meet the goals. This is achieved by the introduction of identification and authentication for requests to overcome the conceptual deficiency of SID-based authentication.

Session Hijacking and Session Fixation: Session Hijacking and Session Fixation attacks both aim to steal the established session context. Session Imagination does not prevent stealing or setting the session ID. So, we consider the case that the attacker already owns the correct SID. Then, he can act on behalf of his victim unless he faces a challenge where his only chance is guessing the right image. A Session Hijacking attack that makes use of XSS does not increase the attacker's probability. The payload can not access the images because they are served as iframes from a different domain. The right image is not stored on the victim's machine such that the attacker can not steal or set the right image in the same way as the respective cookie.

CSRF: A CSRF attacker can make the victim send a request for a security-critical operation. Though the attacker can generally not read back the application's response, he might know the application and can thus predict the form of the next request. This would be the answer to the challenge. At this point, the attacker not only has to guess the right image among the given ones but he has to guess the right image name which is a dynamic and random string of variable length. This is due to the fact that this string is used as a response parameter to decide whether the user clicked the right image and the attacker can not read the webpage to learn the provided names. In this scenario, the attacker's chances are lower than guessing the right image among the provided ones.

Clickjacking: A Clickjacking attack prohibits the victim's context awareness which is crucial for passing the challenges.

If the attack starts before user authentication, the attacker would have to include the target web application's user login while pretending to log in on the attacker's site. Moreover, the attacker would have to make the victim provide his credentials of the target web application. We consider this to be infeasible.

If the victim is already logged in at the target web application, the attack must fail because the attacker would have to make the victim deliberately click on the session image of another web application. This task can be rendered impossible if the session images contain their web application's context, like the company's logo. If the attacker overlays the images with his own images to hide the context, the attack fails because the attacker can not link the user's session image with the respective attacker image. So, the user ends up clicking an arbitrary image which is equal to guessing the image.

To sum up, in all scenarios, the attacker can not increase his chance higher than the probability to guess the correct image.

Relation to Picture-Based Authentication: Approaches based on password pictures differ in major aspects from our approach. First, we implement a secret on a session basis. The user thus does not have to remember another persistent password in the form of picture categories. Case studies on the long-term memorability of graphical passwords do not apply to our approach. Moreover, an attacker gaining knowledge of the user's session image can not use this after the user logs out and in again in our approach. Second, the user is not free to choose the picture. This fact avoids that the attacker can take advantage of familiarity with the victim to guess the correct image (e.g. the respective user loves cats).

Relation to CAPTCHAs: A CAPTCHA [1] denotes a "Completely Automated Public Turing test to tell Computers and Humans Apart". It is meant to provide a task that can be easily solved by a human but is hard to solve for a computer. However, a CAPTCHA contains all information that is needed to solve the task while the task consists in extracting this information. This would allow an attacker to hijack a session after stealing the session ID.

Relation to Other User-Level Authentication Schemes: The most widespread approach to make sure that the user is willing to perform the particular action is to require username and password entry again. This, however, is less secure compared to Session Imagination. First, the credentials entry form can be easily spoofed by an attacker (XSS, phishing) which makes the victim provide his confidential login data to the attacker. Second, username and password can be easily stored in the browser. This makes the browser again the storage point of all information needed to hijack sessions. The other common approach is to enter passcodes that have been received via text message. This approach has similar security properties as Session Imagination, e.g. guessing is still theoretically possible and an attacker owning the victim's platform will still succeed. However, this procedure induces additional cost and requires an additional device with GSM connectivity. Due to this fact, mobile and smartphones are excluded from accessing the respective web application. Session Imagination does not require GSM availability and can be used with a single device.

Usability: In order to assess the usability of Session Imagination, we conducted a survey. Therefore, we set up an online shop equipped with Session Imagination. 40 users had to provide the correct session image to check out and enter or change the shipping address. We found that 95% of them have never forgotten the correct session image. Next, we asked the test people whether they prefer another password entry (17, 5%), passcodes via SMS (22, 5%), or Session Imagination (47, 5%). The remaining 12, 5% do not like any of these. Nevertheless, 92, 5% would accept additional effort if this protects them from fraud. 47, 5% consider 2-5 challenges acceptable in the course of an online shopping trip where 45% tolerate only 1 challenge. Overall, we can say that a vast majority of all testers accept Session Imagination challenges and prefer this procedure to the alternative approaches.

Decreasing the Attacker's Chances: In our prototype implementation, we presented six images to the user, i.e. an attacker has a chance of 16.67% to guess the right image. More images can reduce the attacker's chances and increase security. As an alternative, a big picture could be presented where the user has to click a certain area to authenticate. The security level then depends on the number of areas. Further, aligned style sheets allow the provider to include many pictures while only some of them are visible to the user. This allows to increase security without lowering usability.

4   Related Work

There is related work in many areas. Session Hijacking prevention either prohibits script access to session cookies [12,4] or the execution of unauthorized
script code [11]. Session Fixation protection strives to renew the SID after authentication [8,19,5]. Server-side CSRF protection validates the transmitted ref-
erer [2] or request-specific nonces [7]. Client-side approaches strip off authentication information from suspicious requests [6,17]. Clickjacking [14,15] attacks
can be partially thwarted by HTTP headers [9,10].

However, all these approaches target only one of the attacks respectively, e.g.
they protect against CSRF attacks but can not thwart Clickjacking or combinations of CSRF and XSS [7]. Moreover, some of the standard defenses turned
out to not provide the aimed protection level [22,18].

To the best of our knowledge, there is no web-based approach with the same
protection as Session Imagination.

5   Conclusion

In this paper, we have thoroughly examined fundamental deficiencies in today's
web session management. We have explained how sessions are established and
handled between client and server. We have identified the common root causes
of four widespread vulnerabilities, Session Hijacking with Cross-Site Scripting,
Session Fixation, Cross-Site Request Forgery, and Clickjacking. The root causes
have been found in the use of browser-level authentication schemes and the
missing user context on server-side.

Based on these insights, we have proposed a user-level authentication scheme,
named Session Imagination. It makes use of images as session-based secrets that
are shared between the user and the web application. We have shown its effectiveness in the sense that it mitigates the above mentioned vulnerabilities. The
attacker's chances can be expressed as the probability to guess the correct session
image. At the same time, this probability can be set by design to an arbitrary
low value by providing a considerable number of images. The limit depends on
the actual design of the user interface. We have shown its usability in a survey
which confirms advantages in terms of user friendliness, universal applicability,
cost, and security over the two state-of-the-art approaches. Session Imagination
is applicable with reasonable efforts to new and existing web applications. It is
technology-independent and does not create new requirements on the client-side.

In sum, we provide a solution that does not tamper with the symptoms of
some vulnerability but resolves the underlying problem of web session-based
deficiencies. In the course of this, we achieved the mitigation of at least four
vulnerabilites that are exploited in practice.

Acknowledgments. We thank Daniel Schreckling for important advices
on the prototype and fruitful discussions on open attack vectors. This
work was in parts supported by the EU Project WebSand (FP7-256964),
https://www.websand.eu. The support is gratefully acknowledged.

References

1. Von Ahn, L., Blum, M., Hopper, N.J., Langford, J.: CAPTCHA: Using Hard AI Problems for Security. In: Biham, E. (ed.) EUROCRYPT 2003. LNCS, vol. 2656, pp. 294–311. Springer, Heidelberg (2003)
2. Barth, A., Jackson, C., Mitchell, J.C.: Robust Defenses for Cross-Site Request Forgery. In: CCS 2009 (2009)
3. Hardy, N.: The Confused Deputy (or why capabilities might have been invented). SIGOPS Oper. Syst. Rev. 22, 36–38 (1988)
4. Johns, M.: SessionSafe: Implementing XSS Immune Session Handling. In: Gollmann, D., Meier, J., Sabelfeld, A. (eds.) ESORICS 2006. LNCS, vol. 4189, pp. 444–460. Springer, Heidelberg (2006)
5. Johns, M., Braun, B., Schrank, M., Posegga, J.: Reliable Protection Against Session Fixation Attacks. In: Proceedings of ACM SAC (2011)
6. Johns, M., Winter, J.: RequestRodeo: Client Side Protection against Session Riding. In: OWASP Europe 2006 (May 2006)
7. Jovanovic, N., Kruegel, C., Kirda, E.: Preventing cross site request forgery attacks. In: Proceedings of Securecomm 2006 (2006)
8. Kolsek, M.: Session Fixation Vulnerability in Web-based Applications. Whitepaper, Acros Security (December 2002),
http://www.acrossecurity.com/papers/session_fixation.pdf
9. Microsoft. X-Frame-Options (May 20, 2011),
http://blogs.msdn.com/b/ie/archive/2009/01/27/ie8-security-part-vii-clickjacking-defenses.aspx
10. Mozilla. X-Frame-Options response header (May 20, 2011),
https://developer.mozilla.org/en/the_x-frame-options_response_header
11. Mozilla. Csp (content security policy). Mozilla Developer Network (March 2009),
https://developer.mozilla.org/en/Security/CSP
12. MSDN. Mitigating Cross-site Scripting With HTTP-only Cookies (June 08, 2012),
http://msdn.microsoft.com/en-us/library/ms533046VS.85.aspx
13. Niemietz, M.: UI Redressing: Attacks and Countermeasures Revisited. In: CONFidence 2011 (2011)
14. Hansen, R.: Clickjacking (May 20, 2011),
http://ha.ckers.org/blog/20080915/clickjacking/
15. Hansen, R., Grossman, J.: Clickjacking (May 20, 2011),
http://www.sectheory.com/clickjacking.htm
16. Ruderman, J.: The Same Origin Policy (August 2001),
https://developer.mozilla.org/En/Same_origin_policy_for_JavaScript
(June 08, 2012)
17. De Ryck, P., Desmet, L., Heyman, T., Piessens, F., Joosen, W.: CsFire: Transparent Client-Side Mitigation of Malicious Cross-Domain Requests. In: Massacci, F., Wallach, D., Zannone, N. (eds.) ESSoS 2010. LNCS, vol. 5965, pp. 18–34. Springer, Heidelberg (2010)
18. Rydstedt, G., Bursztein, E., Boneh, D., Jackson, C.: Busting Frame Busting: a Study of Clickjacking Vulnerabilities on Popular Sites. In: Proceedings of W2SP 2010 (2010)
19. Schrank, M., Braun, B., Johns, M., Posegga, J.: Session Fixation - the Forgotten Vulnerability? In: Proceedings of GI Sicherheit 2010 (2010)

20. W3C. HTML5 - The canvas element (September 24, 2011),
    `http://www.w3.org/TR/html5/the-canvas-element.html`
21. W3C. HTML5 - The iframe element (August 29, 2011),
    `http://www.w3.org/TR/html5/the-iframe-element.html#the-iframe-element`
22. Zhou, Y., Evans, D.: Why Aren't HTTP-only Cookies More Widely Deployed? In: Proceedings of W2SP 2010 (2010)

Access Control Configuration for J2EE Web Applications: A Formal Perspective*

Matteo Maria Casalino[1,2], Romuald Thion[2], Mohand-Said Hacid[2]

[1] SAP Research Sophia-Antipolis, 805 Avenue Dr M. Donat, 06250 Mougins, France
`matteo.maria.casalino@sap.com`
[2] Université de Lyon, Université C. Bernard Lyon 1, LIRIS CNRS UMR5205, France
`{romuald.thion,mohand-said.hacid}@liris.cnrs.fr`

Abstract. Business services are increasingly dependent upon Web applications. Whereas URL-based access control is one of the most prominent and pervasive security mechanism in use, failure to restrict URL accesses is still a major security risk. This paper aims at mitigating this risk by giving a formal semantics for access control constraints standardized in the J2EE Java Servlet Specification, arguably one of the most common framework for web applications. A decision engine and a comparison algorithm for change impact analysis of access control configurations are developed on top of this formal building block.

1 Introduction

The security of web applications has become increasingly important, since organizations have employed them more and more extensively as a lightweight front-end for business services. The J2EE Java Servlet Specification (JSS) [1] standardizes the interface between the J2EE web front-end components and the containers specifying, among others, how containers shall enforce *declarative security* constraints, part of the web applications' configuration.

Failure to restrict URL accesses and security misconfigurations are considered as top ten Web application security risks by OWASP[1]. Unfortunately, the declarative security semantics of the JSS is described in English prose, which can cause errors due to misinterpretation. Such errors may lead to non-compliant containers' implementations or to vulnerabilities in access control configurations. Misconfiguration vulnerabilities [2] prove that even small counter-intuitive fragments of the specification are among the causes of serious security breaches.

Significance of access control issues in web applications motivate the need for formal verification tools that help system administrators ensure the correct behaviour of the policies they define. Interesting analysis tasks include determining whether a given access request is permitted or evaluating the impact of a change within a configuration without running the container. We contribute to solve these problems by defining a formal semantics for JSS declarative

---

* This work is partially supported by the FP7-ICT-2009.1.4 Project PoSecCo (no. 257129, `www.posecco.eu`)
[1] `https://www.owasp.org/index.php/Top_10_2010`

S. Fischer-Hübner, S. Katsikas, G. Quirchmayr (Eds.): TrustBus 2012, LNCS 7449, pp. 30–35, 2012.

security (Section 2), from which we
provide a query engine to evaluate access control requests and a comparison algorithm for configurations w.r.t.
their permissiveness (Section 3). Figure 1 depicts the J2EE framework on
the right and the related analysis tool,
our contribution, on the left.

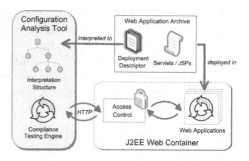

Section 4 compares our contributions to related research on access
control. Section 5 concludes the paper
and outlines future work.

Fig. 1. J2EE framework and proposed contribution

2 Semantics of Security Constraints

J2EE declarative security [1] defines an access control policy language, where
subjects and *resources* are respectively roles and URL patterns. Access control
is configured by associating, in the so-called *security constraints*, URL patterns
and HTTP methods with the set of roles allowed to access them. Entire URL
hierarchies can be specified as URL patterns ending with the '/*' wildcard.

In order to have access granted, a user must be member of *at least one of
the roles* named in the security constraint that matches to her/his HTTP request. An empty role set means that *nobody* can access the associated resources.
Unauthenticated access is allowed by default to unconstrained URL patterns.

In case the same URL pattern and HTTP method occur in different security
constraints, they have to be composed. If two non-empty role sets are composed,
the result is their union. In contrast, if one of the sets of roles is empty, their
composition is empty. Constraints on more specific URL patterns (e.g. /a/b)
always override more general ones (e.g. /a/*). Finally, if some HTTP methods
are explicitly mentioned in a web resource collection, all the other methods are
unconstrained, whereas, if none is named, every method is implicitly constrained.
Verb tampering attacks [2] exploit this behaviour to bypass the access control
check in wrongly-configured web applications.

In this section we define a structure, called *Web application Access Control
Tree* (WACT), suitable to represent security constraints and we provide an operator which captures the aforementioned rules for combining security constraints.

Our structure is built as the result of interpreting security constraints. The
complete grammar and further details on the parser can be found in the extended version of this paper [3]. In the latest revision (3.0) of the JSS, security
constraints are more complex, as HTTP methods can be explicitly *omitted*. Yet,
if the set of HTTP methods is finite, the semantics is comparable to the one
introduced above, which refers to version 2.5 of the JSS. As such, encompassing
this extension would merely result in engineering a more complex parser, which is
of scarce interest. Investigating the implications of explicit prohibitions, without
any assumption on the finiteness of HTTP methods, is left to future work.

As already mentioned, roles are grouped into sets. Furthermore, an order of permissiveness is implicit: the largest is a role set, the more users can access the associated resources. Let the finite set $\mathcal{R}$ denote the domain of all the roles defined for a web application. We define the role lattice $\mathcal{R}^*$ as the complete lattice given by the powerset of the role domain, ordered by set inclusion, and containing the top element $\top \notin \wp(\mathcal{R})$, to take the case of unauthenticated users into account. We denote by $\leq_R$ the partial order between sets of roles.

Definition 1 (Role Lattice). *The complete role lattice is* $\mathcal{R}^* = \langle \wp(\mathcal{R}) \cup \{\top\}, \leq_R \rangle$, *where* $R_A \leq_R R_B$ *iff* $R_B = \top$ *or* $R_A \subseteq R_B$.

Notice that the top element $\top$ semantically corresponds to the default *allow all* authorization which is implicitly associated with any unconstrained web resource. In contrast, the bottom element $\emptyset$ represents the *deny all* constraint.

We define URLs as sequences of symbols in $\mathcal{S}$ which may end with a special symbol in $\mathcal{E} = \{\epsilon, *\}$, where $\mathcal{S} \cap \mathcal{E} = \emptyset$. Formally, a URL $u \in \mathcal{U}$ is either (i) the empty sequence $u = \langle \rangle$, or (ii) the sequence $u = \langle s_0, \ldots, s_n \rangle$, with $n > 0, s_0, \ldots, s_n \in \mathcal{S}$, or (iii) the sequence $u = \langle s_0, \ldots, s_n, s_e \rangle$, with $n > 0, s_0, \ldots, s_n \in \mathcal{S}, s_e \in \mathcal{E} = \{\epsilon, *\}$. For a given URL $u = \langle s_0, \ldots, s_n \rangle$ its *length*, written $|u|$, equals $n + 1$, the length of the empty URL being 0. The *l*-long *prefix* of u, written $u^{\leq l}$, is the sequence $\langle s_0, \ldots, s_{l-1} \rangle$, with $u^{\leq 0} = \langle \rangle$, and the ith symbol s_i in u is written u_i. The concatenation of two URLs u, v is the URL $u \oplus v = \langle u_0, \ldots, u_{|u|}, v_0, \ldots, v_{|v|} \rangle$, and it is defined if and only if $u_{|u|} \in \mathcal{S}$.

URL patterns have an intrinsic hierarchical structure, which is crucial to determine which constraints apply to a given request. We therefore structure URLs in trees, where each node's parent is the node's prefix.

Definition 2 (URL Tree). *A URL tree is a partially ordered set* $\langle U, \prec \rangle$ *where:*

(i) $U \subseteq \mathcal{U}$;
(ii) the empty URL always belongs to U: $\langle \rangle \in U$;
(iii) U is prefix-closed: $u \in U$ *and* $|u| > 0 \Rightarrow u^{\leq |u|-1} \in U$;
(iv) $u \prec v$ *iff* $|u| \leq |v|$ *and* $u = v^{\leq |u|}$.

The WACT structure maps then nodes of URL trees to the authorized roles.

Definition 3 (Web application Access Control Tree). *Let $\mathcal{M}$ be the (finite) domain of HTTP methods. A WACT is a pair $t = \langle U, \alpha \rangle$, where U is a URL tree according to Def. 2 and $\alpha : U \times \mathcal{M} \to \mathcal{R}^*$ is a partial function giving the set of roles allowed on a pair $\langle u, m \rangle$. The set of all WACTs is denoted by $\mathcal{T}$.*

Finally, the *composition* of two WACTs $\langle U_1, \alpha_1 \rangle \dot\cup \langle U_2, \alpha_2 \rangle$ is the WACT $\langle U_1 \cup U_2, \alpha \rangle$ where α is defined by (1).

$$\alpha(u,m) = \begin{cases} \alpha_1(u,m) \otimes \alpha_2(u,m) & \text{if } \langle u,m \rangle \in \text{dom}(\alpha_1) \cap \text{dom}(\alpha_2) \\ \alpha_1(u,m) & \text{if } \langle u,m \rangle \in \text{dom}(\alpha_1) \setminus \text{dom}(\alpha_2) \\ \alpha_2(u,m) & \text{if } \langle u,m \rangle \in \text{dom}(\alpha_2) \setminus \text{dom}(\alpha_1) \end{cases} \quad (1)$$

$$R_A \otimes R_B = \begin{cases} \emptyset & \text{if } R_A = \emptyset \text{ or } R_B = \emptyset \\ R_A \bigsqcup R_B & \text{otherwise.} \end{cases} \quad (2)$$

If both trees define a set of roles for a common pair $\langle u, m \rangle$, their role sets are merged through the $\otimes : \mathcal{R}^* \times \mathcal{R}^* \to \mathcal{R}^*$ operator defined in terms of the role lattice's least upper bound $\bigsqcup$ (2).

3 Applications

According to the JSS [1, Sec. 12.8.3], an access request corresponds to a triple $\langle u, m, R \rangle \in \mathcal{U} \times \mathcal{M} \times \mathcal{R}^*$ composed by a URL identifying the requested resource, a HTTP method and an element of the role lattice representing the set of roles assigned to the user who submitted the request. We compute access control decisions, i.e., $\{false, true\}$ answers to requests, by means of two functions: ρ computes the set of roles needed to access URL u with method m, and Δ determines whether the roles associated with the incoming request are sufficient.

For every URL tree U, we denote the set of $*$-predecessors of $u \in U$ by $u_* \downarrow$. The elements of this set are all the immediate successors of the ancestors of u, ending with the symbol $* \in \mathcal{E}$. Formally, $u_* \downarrow = \{ w \oplus \langle * \rangle \mid w \prec u \wedge w \oplus \langle * \rangle \in U \}$. This behaviour captures the *best match* algorithm of [1, Sec. 12.8.3], which may be informally summarized by *"most specific URL pattern takes precedence"*.

Definition 4 (Effective Roles). *Given a WACT $t = \langle U, \alpha \rangle$ the set of effective roles for each couple $\langle u, m \rangle \in \mathcal{U} \times \mathcal{M}$ is given by the function $\rho_{\langle U, \alpha \rangle} : \mathcal{U} \times \mathcal{M} \to \mathcal{R}^*$*

$$
\rho_{\langle U, \alpha \rangle}(u, m) = \begin{cases} \alpha(u, m) & \text{if } \langle u, m \rangle \in \mathrm{dom}(\alpha) \\ \alpha(w, m) & \text{else if } \{w\} = \max(u_* \downarrow) \wedge \langle w, m \rangle \in \mathrm{dom}(\alpha) \\ \top & \text{otherwise.} \end{cases} \quad (3)
$$

Equation (3) assumes that the function max, which maps a set of URLs to the subset having maximum length, applied to $u_* \downarrow$ is a set of at most one element: this is proved in [3], together with the other results of this section.

The decision function Δ is defined from ρ: access to $\langle u, m \rangle$ is granted either if the user is unauthenticated and the resource accessible to unauthenticated users or if the user endorses at least one role in the set of effective roles of $\langle u, m \rangle$.

Definition 5 (Decision Function). *For every $t = \langle U, \alpha \rangle \in \mathcal{T}$ the access control decision function $\Delta_t : \mathcal{U} \times \mathcal{M} \times \mathcal{R}^* \to \{false, true\}$ is defined as follows:*

$$
\begin{aligned}
\Delta_t(u, m, \top) &= true & \text{iff} \quad \rho_t(u, m) = \top \\
\Delta_t(u, m, R) &= true & \text{iff} \quad \rho_t(u, m) \bigcap R \neq \emptyset \\
\Delta_t(u, m, R) &= false & \text{otherwise.}
\end{aligned} \quad (4)
$$

It's worth noting that Δ encodes the entire access control behaviour of a web application, independently from its container. As such, it can be leveraged to perform a static analysis of the security configuration at either design or development time. Furthermore, the formal definition of Δ can be used as a reference to verify the compliance of the decision function implemented in existing J2EE containers w.r.t. the JSS; a test methodology (as shown in Fig. 1) being as follows.

First, a set of configurations is generated, exploring the interesting corner cases of the language. Each configuration is deployed in the container under scrutiny and parsed in a WACT structure t. HTTP requests are then issued to the server and answers are compared to the value of Δ_t for every triple $\langle u, m, R \rangle$.

The impact of changes into security constraints is another relevant piece of information to be known prior to deploying a web application. For instance, one may wish to verify that a new constraint leads to a more restrictive policy. For this purpose, we define a relation between WACTs according to their permissiveness and show that this order is compatible with access control decisions. A WACT t_1 is less permissive than t_2, written $t_1 \leq_T t_2$ if for any node in the tree and any method, the set of effective roles of t_1 is included in that of t_2.

Definition 6 (Comparison of WACTs). *Let* $t_1 = \langle U_1, \alpha_1 \rangle$ *and* $t_2 = \langle U_2, \alpha_2 \rangle$

$$t_1 \leq_T t_2 \; \textit{iff} \; \forall u \in U_1 \cup U_2, m \in \mathcal{M} : \rho_{t_1}(u, m) \leq_R \rho_{t_2}(u, m). \tag{5}$$

Proposition 1 ensures the semantic consistency of $\leq_T$ with respect to Δ.

Proposition 1. $t_1 \leq_T t_2 \; \textit{iff} \; \forall u, m, R : \Delta_{t_1}(u, m, R) \Rightarrow \Delta_{t_2}(u, m, R)$.

4 Related Work

XACML is an industry-promoted standard able to capture a broad class of access control requirements, which comes with an informal evaluation semantics. Several formal semantics have been given to core concepts of XACML using for instance process algebra [4], description logics [5], or compositional semantics [6].

It is tempting to translate J2EE security constraints into XACML and then rely on cited formalisms. Unfortunately, some of the selected subsets of the XACML language are incomparable and it seems there is no consensual agreement on its formal semantics (see related work of [6] for discussion and examples). Moreover, we argue that a direct semantics for J2EE security constraints from its specification provides valuable insights to the policy developers.

Instead of working on a language like XACML which suffers from a lack of formal foundations, researchers have proposed access control languages with formal semantics. For instance, the authors of [7] provide a model with identity attributes and service negotiation capabilities as key features. Similarly, a model of attribute-based access control, particularly well suited to open environments, is proposed in [8]. In this paper we face another challenge: in order to support querying and comparison of concrete configurations, we do not design a language from scratch and give its formal semantics *a priori*, instead we analyse an existing language and give its semantics *a posteriori*. As the semantics of J2EE security constraints is quite specific, it is not clear whether the language can be translated into another one or not. For instance, the Malgrave System [9] is a powerful change impact assessment tool based on a restricted sub-language of XACML. However, hierarchical resources, which are the core of J2EE security constraints and very common in web oriented models, are not supported.

Related work on J2EE access control configurations analysis [10] stems from premises analogous to ours. However, this approach rather focuses on checking the consistency of access control configurations w.r.t. the implementation of J2EE components of the business tier, in order, e.g., to detect accesses to EJB fields or methods that are inconsistent with the access control policy. Our work on declarative security is complementary: our formalization supports other reasoning tasks, such as the comparison of different configurations.

5 Conclusion

In this paper we have proposed a formal role-based access control framework for hierarchical resources, able to effectively capture the semantics of the declarative security fragment of the J2EE Java Servlet Specification.

We highlighted several capabilities of the framework, namely answering to access control requests and comparing the permissiveness of security constraints. Such tools can help web developers understand the security of their applications to prevent misconfiguration vulnerabilities. To this regard, we envision to provide an environment from which configurations will be canonically generated, complemented with algorithms to detect anomalies which may reflect authoring mistakes (e.g., non-monotonicity of permissiveness along URLs paths).

Another opportunity for future work consists in extending the model to support the analysis of more access control languages, for instance allowing increased expressivity for the rules' resource selectors (e.g., by means of regular languages) and supporting generic hierarchies of subjects and resources.

References

1. Coward, D., Yoshida, Y.: Java servlet specification, version 2.4. Technical report. Sun Microsystems, Inc. (November 2003)
2. NIST, http://web.nvd.nist.gov/view/vuln/detail?vulnId=CVE-2010-0738
3. Casalino, M.M., Thion, R., Hacid, M.S.: Access control configuration for j2ee web applications: A formal perspective (extended research report) (June 2012), http://liris.cnrs.fr/publis/?id=5601
4. Bryans, J.: Reasoning about xacml policies using csp. In: SWS 2005, pp. 28–35. ACM, New York (2005)
5. Kolovski, V., Hendler, J., Parsia, B.: Analyzing web access control policies. In: WWW 2007, pp. 677–686. ACM, New York (2007)
6. Ramli, C.D.P.K., Nielson, H.R., Nielson, F.: The logic of xacml - extended. CoRR abs/1110.3706 (2011)
7. Bertino, E., Squicciarini, A.C., Paloscia, I., Martino, L.: Ws-ac: A fine grained access control system for web services. World Wide Web 9, 143–171 (2006)
8. Yuan, E., Tong, J.: Attributed based access control (abac) for web services. In: ICWS 2005, pp. 561–569. IEEE Computer Society, Washington, DC (2005)
9. Fisler, K., Krishnamurthi, S., Meyerovich, L.A., Tschantz, M.C.: Verification and change-impact analysis of access-control policies. In: ICSE, pp. 196–205. ACM (2005)
10. Naumovich, G., Centonze, P.: Static analysis of role-based access control in j2ee applications. SIGSOFT Softw. Eng. Notes 29, 1–10 (2004)

Cloud Separation: Stuck Inside the Cloud

Waldo Delport and Martin S. Olivier

Information and Computer Security Architectures Research Group
Department of Computer Science
University of Pretoria
South Africa
{wdelport,molivier}@cs.up.ac.za

Abstract. When something erroneous happens happens in digital environment, a Digital Forensic Investigations (DFIs) can be used to gather information about the event. When conducting a DFI, Digital Forensic Procedures (DFPs) are followed. DFPs provide steps to follow to ensure the successful completion of the DFI. One of the steps in a DFP is to isolate possible evidence in order to protect the evidence from contamination and tampering. The introduction of Cloud computing complicated the isolation process because there is a shared layer between users. This means that the methods used to isolate evidence must be adapted and reworked to work in the Cloud environment. In some cases new procedures need to be introduced to address the isolation problem.

In this article we introduce the idea of Cloud separation to isolate a part of the Cloud. We argue that the separation process consists of methods to move instances, as well as methods to divide the Cloud. The paper also introduces methods to accomplish the movement of instances and the division of the Cloud. The paper reports on the finding of testing the dividing methods on different Cloud operating systems in experimental conditions. The experimental outcome was that some of the methods are not applicable to Cloud separation and the methods to be used will depend on the circumstances of the DFI. Out of the experiment some lessons were learnt which should be considered when conducting Cloud separation.

Keywords: Cloud Computing, Digital Forensic, Digital Forensics Process, Isolation.

1   Introduction

Cloud Computing is a fast growing industry and is becoming part of most enterprises [1]. Cloud computing builds on advances in both the network industry and in virtualization [2]. As network infrastructure becomes faster and more reliable, it is also becoming better able to handle large volumes of data, fast and reliably. Virtualization also enables virtual resources to be provided. The process of creating and maintaining virtual resources is being simplified and optimized. Cloud Computing enables a provider to provide virtual resources over the network [4].

S. Fischer-Hübner, S. Katsikas, G. Quirchmayr (Eds.): TrustBus 2012, LNCS 7449, pp. 36–49, 2012.

When something erroneous happens an investigation may be required. In the Cloud Computing environment the resources are virtual and most interactions with the Cloud are digital in nature [5]. When conducting an investigation on digital artifacts, a Digital Forensic Investigation (DFI) may need to be performed [6]. When conducting a DFI, a Digital Forensic Procedure (DFP) is followed [7], which enables admissible evidence to be gathered from the investigation. In the virtual Cloud environment a DFP is followed to conduct an investigation.

In previous work we introduced a Distributed Instance System (DiS) environment, in which multiple instances form a single resource [8]. This is accomplished when multiple instances work together to achieve a common goal. The previous work introduced conditions for isolating single instances to protect the evidence. When working within a DiS environment it is preferable to isolate all the instances at once in order to protect the evidence from tampering and contamination.

In this paper we propose methods to isolate a set of DiS instances. This set of isolated instances can then be used in a Digital Forensic Investigation.

We look into a subset of the proposed methods and provide feedback on them. The results were gathered from empirical experimentation using different Cloud operating systems.

The remainder of the paper is structured as follows: in section 2 cloud computing is explained. Section 3 explains the Digital Forensic Procedure (DFP) followed when conducting a DFI. The reasons for Cloud isolation are given in section 4. The methods that can be used for Cloud separation are introduced in section 5. In section 6 considerations are introduced when conducting Cloud separation on different Cloud models. Experimental results are reported in section 7.

2   Cloud Computing

Cloud Computing builds on different forms of distributed computing tying together distributed computing and virtualization [1]. Cloud Computing enables a service provider to provide a flexible, cost effective and on-demand infrastructure to its clients, freeing clients from running their own infrastructure. In a Cloud environment, an instance is typically accepted to be a virtual system resource, established within that Cloud. Multiple instances can also form one logical instance and can be contained within a single node. The Cloud itself consists of multiple nodes. The Cloud can be described by service and deployment models, where the service models describe what service the Cloud offers and the deployment models specify the physical deployment of the Cloud. There are three types of Cloud Computing service models, namely the Infrastructure as a Service (IaaS), Platform as a Service (PaaS) and Software as a Service (SaaS) models [9]. Each of the service models will be explained below.

The first service model is *Infrastructure as a Service*. The users of a Cloud infrastructure are provided a virtual computer which can be interacted with, usually through the Internet [3]. This virtual computer needs to be set up and maintained by the user and can also be referred to as an instance. If the requirements of the user change in terms of computational power or storage space, it is an easy process to change the scope of the instance to accommodate the new requirements of the user. If a new instance is required, the task of starting up an instance is trivial. The service provider is responsible for maintaining the Confidentiality, Integrity and Availability (CIA) of the instances on a hardware level. The user is responsible for protecting the CIA on a higher level, e.g. the content of files and the operating system [10].

The second service model is *Platform as a Service*, where the user is provided with a platform that is maintained by the Cloud service provider [9]. The platform is an instance that was created with a specific focus by the service provider. The user must then configure the application on the platform. The service provider may also provide the necessary tools to successfully build upon the platform.

The last service model is *Software as a Service*, where software is made available through the use of Clouds. The application and the data of the application are seen as the resources on the Cloud [11]. The user pays to get access to an application that can be customised according to the requirements of the user. The user has no concerns related to the underlying hardware and software below the application of interest.

As mentioned, the Cloud has different deployment models. There are four deployment models for Clouds. They are Public, Private, Hybrid and Community models [5]. In a *Public* Cloud, the infrastructure is owned by a Cloud service provider and the service provider will sell resources of the Cloud to other companies and the public. The service provider is responsible for managing the Cloud.

In a *Private* Cloud, the Cloud infrastructure is for the exclusive use of one company, therefore the company owns the Cloud and uses the resources. The Cloud infrastructure can be on company property or may be located elsewhere. The company, or a contracted company, is responsible for maintaining the Cloud.

If the Cloud infrastructure is for the use of several companies, it can be seen as a *Community* Cloud. The companies own the Cloud and use the resources collectively, forming a community with shared interests. The Cloud infrastructure can be on one of the companies' properties or may be located elsewhere. The companies, or a contracted company, would be responsible for maintaining the Cloud.

The *Hybrid* model is a combination of at least two of the above models. Each of the models used is still a separate entity in the Hybrid Cloud. This is normally used for load balancing.

Cloud Computing is growing and is estimated to become a billion dollar industry this year 2012 [12]. The reason for this is that some of the largest IT related companies have implemented or are implementing Cloud Computing. Some of these large companies are Google, Microsoft, IBM and Amazon [10] [3]. These companies state that they will provide CIA to their customers by using various techniques.

3   Digital Forensics Process

In order to obtain admissible evidence a well-defined forensic process needs to be followed. Cohen [7] proposes a model for the digital forensic investigation that consists of seven phases, namely the Identification, Collection, Transportation, Storage, Examination and Traces, Presentation and Destruction phases. The *Examination and Traces* phase consists of four subcategories: Analysis, Interpretation, Attribution and Reconstruction [7].

Although not previously mentioned, documentation is a continuous process that needs to take place in all phases of the digital examination [6] [7]. One of the main aids to help preserve the integrity of the evidence is documentation. The documentation should at least include the name of the evidence and the place where the evidence is gathered. It should also include the processes followed in identifying, retrieving, storing and transporting the evidence. The documentation should also mention the chain of custody when the examination was in progress. There have been several cases where the outcome of the case was influenced by the documentation.

There are alternative DFPs to Cohen's proposed model for digital forensic investigation. The other models include most of these phases or a combination thereof. One such prominent DFP was defined by the National Institute of Justice (NIJ) [6]. The phases defined are Collection, Examination, Analysis and Reporting. The two processes include the same set of underlying steps. Cohen's process is subdivided into more steps. This enables a more systematic flow of events.

The process of isolation forms part of a DFP [8], and is especially important in the collection phase. Examples of isolation methods used in DFPs are when seized cell phones are placed inside a Faraday bag [13] and when conducting hard drive forensics on a hard drive, a write blocker is used to enable a write-free read [14]. The isolation helps protect the possible evidence from contamination and loss of continuity.

4   Cloud Isolation

Previous work has been done on isolating single instances [15] [8]. We proposed conditions that we argue need to be met in order to identify instances as successfully isolated. The conditions are, the instance's physical location is known, the instance is protected from outside interference (Incoming Blocking), the instance is blocked from communicating with the outside word (Outgoing Blocking), possible evidence from the instance can be gathered (Collection), the possible evidence is not contaminated by the isolation process (Non-Contamination), information unrelated to the incident is not part of isolation (Separation). The conditions can be expanded to the isolation of a sub-part of the Cloud.

Gathering evidence is one of the aims of a DFI. If there is suspicion that the evidence is invalid by any means it will not be able to serve as admissible evidence. In order to add to the evidence's admissibility, the evidence needs to be protected from contamination and tampering. The need for isolation in the Cloud environment becomes apparent when taking the evidence's admissibility into account.

In order to isolate a Cloud we isolate a sub-part of the Cloud. This is done to keep the isolated part of the Cloud in a Cloud environment [15] [8]. In this paper the focus is not on isolating a single instance or a small sub-set of instances but rather a part of the Cloud. This sub-Cloud will have the normal functionality of a Cloud. The instances running on the Cloud will not be aware of the change of Cloud to sub-Cloud. This separation is done to tie together cooperating instances and to exclude unrelated instances. The separation also aids in the admissibility of the evidence. Once the Cloud is separated the DFI is done on the isolated part of the Cloud without any disruption of service to the other clients of the Cloud provider.

5   Cloud Separation

Cloud separation can be argued as a vital part of a DFI on Clouds since, as stated above, the isolation process can aid the admissibility of the evidence. The Cloud separation forms part of the Collection phase of a DFI, the separation is done to prepare the Cloud for an the investigation. We argued that the conditions for isolation as stated in section 4 need to be met in order to state that the separation was done successfully. After careful consideration while creating the condition we discovered the notion of Cloud separation can be separated into moving the instances and dividing the Cloud.

Moving the instance involves relocating the instances from one node to another. This moving of instances should move all the involved instances to a certain part of the Cloud and all non-related instances to another part of the Cloud. The movement is done as a starting point to do the isolation explained in section 4. The movement can be done using one of several methods, the fist option is that the instances can be moved from one Cloud to another directly. The second option is to move the instances to an external Cloud and then from there to the other Cloud. The third option is to move the instance to an external Cloud, then move it two one or more other external Clouds and finally move it to the other Cloud. The fourth option is to use the Cloud operating system to move the instances. The last option is to just identify the nodes which contains suspect instances but we do not move them.

The division of the Cloud is done to complete the isolation. This division can be done in several ways: the first option is to separate the nodes by creating two separate networks from one network, the second option is to create two virtual networks on one logical network and the third option is to create sub-clouds inside the actual Cloud. The last option for Cloud division is using the movement methods to move the instances to a Cloud dedicated for the DFI. The movement and division methods together form the Cloud separation. This means different Cloud movement and division methods can be used together in different combinations depending on the specific requirements. The remainder of this section will expand on the movement and dividing methods.

When using the first option to move instances, from one cloud to the another, it can be done using two different methods. The first method is to mirror an external Cloud then send instances from the main Cloud to the external Cloud. The external Cloud is thus not external but a controlled Cloud that was setup to accept instances. An overview is given in Figure 1. Some Cloud operating systems have the functionality to send instances from their Cloud to another Cloud. This functionality will be used to transfer the instances. It must be known how the instances are sent and what is required while sending it. This will make it possible to mirror one of these external Clouds and receive instances from the main Cloud. The advantage of this method is that instances can see this movement as a normal Cloud operation activity. A second method is when the Cloud operating system allows the sending and receiving of instances. The Cloud operating system is used as an aid in the movement of the instances. An example of a Cloud operating system that can send and receive instances is VMWare [16].

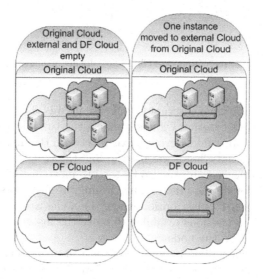

Fig. 1. Moving an instance from one Cloud to another

When using an external Cloud in the process of moving instances, the same methods as suggested above, can be used. The instances are sent to an external Cloud. This external Cloud can accept instances from the main cloud and can be assessed by the DFI team. Once the instance is on the external Cloud it is sent to the controlled Cloud. Cloud operating systems like Nimbula and VMWare can send instances to external Clouds. This external Cloud can be hosted by other companies or be another Cloud owned by a company. Figure 2 explains the steps. Automated methods can be used to move these instances. In the case where there are no automated methods, one of the methods proposed to move an instance can be used [15].

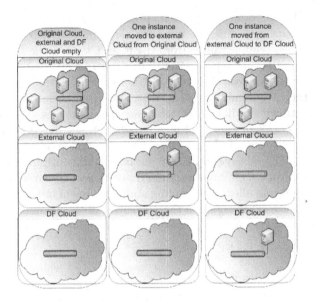

Fig. 2. Moving an instance from one Cloud to another using an external Cloud

The option where multiple external Clouds are used is the same as the above but there exist multiple external Clouds between the two Clouds. This method can be employed when no middle ground exists between the main Cloud and the other Cloud. The external Clouds are used to link the two Clouds.

The Cloud operating system can also be used to move instances. Some Cloud operating systems provide the functionality to migrate instances while they are running between nodes. The last option where the nodes are only identified will be used if there are no methods available to move the instances, or if there are only suspect instances on the node.

The first option when dividing the Cloud is using the self-healing characteristic of Clouds that will be used to create two Clouds. If a node or nodes malfunction in Nimbula the Cloud itself will continue to operate. In this option the first step is to identify the nodes that need to form part of the new Cloud. The second step is to move all non-related nodes from these Clouds. The next step will be explained by means of an example: if the Cloud has six nodes and three of them need to move to the new Cloud, the process is as follows: Connect two switches to each other, the one has all the nodes connected to it. Systematically move the suspect nodes' network wire/VLAN one by one to the other switch. Once all the suspect nodes are connected to the other switch the connection between the two switches is broken. Then the Cloud operating system will create a new Cloud using the self-healing ability. The process is illustrated in figure 3.

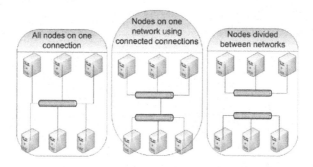

Fig. 3. Creating two Clouds from a single Cloud

The second option for Cloud dividing is to create two Clouds on one network. A high level overview is given in figure 4. This category can be separated on the notion of knowing which node belongs to which Cloud or not knowing which node belongs to which Cloud. Each Cloud runs its own Cloud operating system that will control it. There are different methods to create two Clouds on the same network. One option is to create separate Subnet masks for each instance of the Cloud [2]. This will enable the installation and operation of each Cloud on a separate Subnet mask. A possible alternative option is to use a Cloud operating system that enables the selection of the controlling node, and by using this strategy, a new master is set up on the network and some nodes are allocated to it.

The third option to divide the Cloud, is to create sub-Clouds. The Cloud is logically broken up into separate parts. The same Cloud operating system controls them. The sub-Cloud is a fully functional Cloud and it just runs on the main Cloud but is interacted with as if it is a normal Cloud. Some Cloud operating systems allow for the creation of sub-clouds inside the Cloud itself. It is used to sell a Cloud to the service provider's customers. To do this a sub-cloud is created on the main Cloud and then instances are moved to the sub-cloud. This sub-Clouds is implemented on the same hardware as the base Cloud. The moving functionality is provided by the Cloud operating system. Figure 5 shows the main Cloud's hardware and the virtual Clouds created on that hardware.

The last option to divide the Cloud is to use any of the instance movement methods to move instances to an already divided Cloud. This Cloud can be a Cloud prep to do Cloud forensics. The Cloud can also be located on the Cloud providers premises or an external Cloud on the DFI teams premises.

While conducting the separation all steps must be documented as part of the DFI, this created a audit trail which can be used to prove the viability of the methods followed.

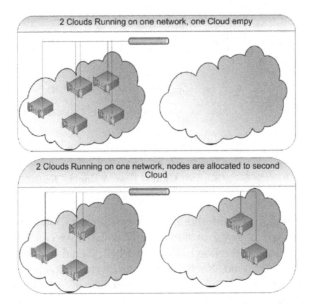

Fig. 4. Creating two Clouds on one network

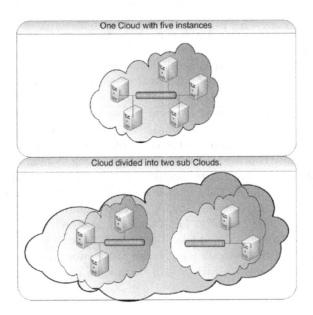

Fig. 5. Creating two sub-Clouds

6   Cloud Separation on Different Types of Clouds

In the previous section we introduced methods for Cloud separation. As stated in section 2 Clouds can be divided into different service and deployment models, which have different impacts on isolation. Some considerations need to be taken into account when conducting Cloud separation for the different models. The important consideration is the Confidentiality, Integrity and Availability (CIA) of instances.

The difference between service models is in who owns what part of the instance. The instance can usually be divided into the hardware, the hypervisor, the operating system, applications and data. In an IaaS model, the service provider is responsible for the hardware and hypervisor whereas the client is responsible for the rest. If the service provider is requesting the DFI it must get the cooperation of the client to gather evidence from the operating system, applications and other data residing on the system. If the client is requesting a DFI they must get the cooperation from the service provider in gathering evidence form the hardware. The client and service provider are both responsible for the availability of the system. It is easily possible for clients to have multiple instances working together without the knowledge of the service provider.

In a PaaS model the service provider is responsible for the hardware, hypervisor, operating system and some applications. The client is responsible for applications and data on the system. The service provider must ensure that high availability is maintained. The client can provide evidence from their own applications and stored data. It is possible, but more unlikely than in IaaS, to have cooperating instances.

When conducting a DFI on a SaaS the service provider is responsible for the hardware, hypervisor, operating system and applications. The client is responsible for configurations of applications and data on the system. The service provider must ensure high availability of the systems. Clients are only responsible for their data. It is very unlikely for a client to have cooperating instances.

For the purpose of this paper we will only look at public and private development models, and we argue that hybrid and community development models have the same considerations as public and private development models. When conducting Cloud separation on a public development model the Cloud service provider is responsible for protecting the CIA of their clients. When separating a part of the Cloud it must be confirmed that only data related to suspect instances are separated. The separation must also protect the admissibility of the evidence. All unrelated instances should not be affected by the separation and must thus stay available. If the service provider is conducting the DFI the provider must protect the privacy of its clients and inform its clients of the investigation. If an external company is conducting the DFI the company must protect the privacy of the service provider and its clients.

When conducting Cloud separation on a private development model all data should belong to one company. The separation is done to protect the admissibility of the evidence. If the owners of the Cloud are responsible for conducting the investigation, the main focus is not on protecting the privacy of the information. If an external company is responsible for conducting the investigation the separation should also protect the privacy of the owner's data. The owner is responsible for deciding the importance of the availability of the Cloud.

It can be argued that Cloud separation is valid for IaaS and PaaS models. Cloud separation can be an integral part of a DFI on a public Cloud but can also be important in a DFI on a private Cloud.

7   Experimentation

In this section our experimentation results are given. The experiment was limited to the dividing methods, moving an instance can be done by the Cloud operating system making it part of normal Cloud operation or if there is no functionality by using one of the methods proposed in the paper by Delport et al [15]. In the experiment we tested two dividing methods, the methods were: creating two Clouds using the network hardware and creating sub-Clouds. The experiment used VMware and Nimbula Director. This was done to get some comparison between the methods' feasibility. The reasons why VMware and Nimbule were chosen is that VMware is a widely used platform to provide Cloud resources and Nimbula focuses on providing private Cloud infrastructure. This gives us better coverage for both public and private Cloud computing.

In order to create sub-Clouds one needs more than one layer of abstraction. In the experiment VMware was used to create the sub-Clouds. There were two base nodes running VMware, which are known as ESXi hosts. These nodes have Intel i5 processors and 2GB DDR3 memory. On each of the hosts two other ESXi hosts were created. The virtualized ESXi hosts were used to form a Cloud on each main host. A vCenter management instance was created on each virtual Cloud. VCenter is used to control the Cloud [16]. Two instances running CentOS 6.0 minimal were also created on the virtual Cloud. The layout then is vCenter running on Windows 2008 server and two CentOS minimal instances running on two ESXi hosts. The ESXi hosts are running as virtual machines on a base ESXi host.

The setup and maintenance of this experiment was relatively easy. The Clouds where stable and there were no apparent problems with the recursive virtualization. In the testing environment there was some loss of performance: this occurred because some resources are used to run the other virtual hosts and another reason is that there are two controlling layers.

To test the performance loss a single sub-Cloud was created on a Dell PowerEdge R710 with two i7 processors and 97GB of memory. On this node the performance decrease was not noticeable. The performance drawback should not be noticeable on most of the powerful infrastructure used by most Cloud Providers. The instances might notice the loss in performance on the node and might start self defense mechanisms, while this can be done the performance on the Cloud environment is inherently unstable because of resource over committing that is part of most Cloud environment [16].

VMware also aids in creating sub-Clouds. VMWare allows the movement of instances from the main Cloud to the virtual Cloud and from the virtual Cloud to the main Cloud. The user must link the virtual Cloud's vCenter to the underlying infrastructure. This allows the user to move instances between the layers of virtualization. The drawback is that there is a connection created from the virtual Cloud to the underlying Cloud. This can be used to tamper with evidence. The advantage is that a virtual Cloud can be created at a later stage and instances moved to it from the main Cloud. Once a digital investigation is required the instances can be moved to sub-Clouds, one for uninvolved instances and one for suspected instances. If instances are no longer suspected in the suspect Cloud it can be moved to the other Cloud.

An experiment using Nimbula director was conducted to create sub-Clouds. The Cloud consisted of three nodes, on each two virtual nodes were created. It was possible to access each of the sub-Clouds separately. The problem was that the virtual node should be on a virtual network. If they are not on a virtual network they cannot communicate with the other virtual nodes. It was possible to create instances on the virtual nodes. Because of a limitation in Nimbula instances can not be moved from the main Cloud to the sub-Cloud directly. The movement methods proposed in previous work needs to be used to move the instances to the sub-Cloud.

The next experiment created two Clouds using network hardware. This experiment was done using Nimbula director and using six nodes with 2GB of RAM and 15 processors. The experiment was done as described in section 4. Access was lost to the Control centre of Nimbula on the one part but the instances were still running. A possible problem is that the control centre holds information about all running instances. If the Cloud is broken up the control centre loses communication with the other instances that are running on the other part of the Cloud. They will show as being in an error state. The instances can then be "deleted" from the control centre as they are not applicable to it. The problem continues because the Clouds cannot be joined later. There are two control centres running each with its one instance. In the experiments' experimental conditions it seemed impossible to join the Cloud back together. Although connection was lost with the control centre the Cloud still functioned proving that the self-healing characteristics of Nimbula are intact.

The last experiment was done using VMware to create two Clouds using the network hardware. The same procedures were followed as for Nimbula. The experiment was successful although a few problems occurred and configuration changes were needed. The problems were in vCentre assuming that host failure occurred and it tried to relaunch the lost instances. This happened because high availability was enabled on the cluster, the job of HA is to recover lost instances. It failed because the instance storage was on the direct attached storage. On the other part of the Cloud a new vCentre needed to be created because there was no management over the new cluster.

From the experimentation it can be seen that the method where a sub-Cloud is created using network hardware is then not advisable as it would require a lot

Table 1. Experiment Summary

	vmWare	Nimbula	SAN	DAS
Cloud seperation using sub-Clouds	✓	X	✓	✓
Cloud separation using Network Hardware	✓	X	X	✓

of re-setup to put the Cloud together again, it is advised against the use of this method. The other experiment shows it is more reliable to have sub-clouds for cloud separation. Table 1 contains a summary of the experimentation.

From the experiment the following lessons were learnt: Performance is affected on less powerful Clouds, HA needs to be turned off before starting with Cloud separation, recombining the Cloud after the DFI can be hard to impossible.

An overall possible problem that must be considered with all methods for Cloud separation is where the instances storage is located. As a basic example the storage can either be on a SAN or the DAS. Creating sub-Clouds when using a SAN is not possible as connection to the SAN may also be lost. Creating a sub-Cloud can still be done when using a SAN because the nodes can still communicate with the SAN. Both methods are applicable when using DAS. Another problem with SAN's is that multiple instances share the resource, this can be avoided by using a SAN dedicated for the storage of suspect instances. Another problem is the IP address of the instance.

When moving an Instance the IP of that instance should be constant to correlate the IP with gathered network evidence. In the experiments the instances had static IP's which did not change if the instances moved. If a dedicated firewall is used to assign the IP the IP should stay the same if he instances moves. When the IP of the instance is manage by the node it's residing on the IP might change if the instances is moved to aid in correlation of evidence the IP before and after the move must be noted.

8   Conclusion

As Cloud computing grows it will become easier for individuals to create DiS resources. If the DiS resource is used in a form of a crime, methods must exist to start a DFI on the DiS without disruption the other users of the Cloud.

In this paper we introduced the notion of Cloud separation, which consists of moving instances and dividing the Cloud. We explained methods to move instances around in the Cloud as-well as moving instances out of the Cloud. We also explained the methods that can be used to divide the Cloud.

We conducted experimentation on the division methods and discovered that the methods used will depend on the circumstances of the DFI. We saw that the method that uses the network hardware to create two Clouds might not be desirable to use and the method to create sub-Clouds might be a valid choice.

Future work includes testing the methods on more Cloud operating systems to better test all the methods and discover some pitfalls. If we discover that the methods do not work on all platforms we plan to find other methods that will work on specific platform. There is also a a need to investigate the performance loss when conducting a DFI.

References

1. Vouk, M.A.: Cloud computing - issues, research and implementations. In: 30th International Conference on Information Technology Interfaces, ITI 2008, pp. 31–40 (June 2008)
2. Barrett, D., King, T.: Computer networking illuminated. Jones and Bartlett illuminated series. Jones and Bartlett (2005)
3. Biggs, S., Vidalis, S.: Cloud computing: The impact on digital forensic investigations. In: International Conference for Internet Technology and Secured Transactions, ICITST 2009, pp. 1–6 (November 2009)
4. Foster, I., Zhao, Y., Raicu, I., Lu, S.: Cloud computing and grid computing 360-degree compared. In: Grid Computing Environments Workshop, GCE 2008, pp. 1–10 (November 2008)
5. Mell, P., Grance, T.: The NIST Definition of Cloud Computing, Recommendations of the National Institute of Standards and Technolog. Technical report, National Institute of Standards and Technology (2011)
6. Ashcroft, J.: Electronic Crime Scene Investigation: A Guide for First Responders. Technical Working Group for Electronic Crime Scene Investigation (July 2001)
7. Cohen, F.: Digital Forensic Evidence Examination, 2nd edn. Fed Cohen & Associates, Livermore (2010)
8. Delport, W., Olivier, M.S.: Isolation, stuck inside the cloud. In: Eighth Annual IFIP WG 11.9 International Conference on Digital Forensics (in Press, 2012)
9. Binnig, C., Kossmann, D., Kraska, T., Loesing, S.: How is the weather tomorrow?: towards a benchmark for the cloud. In: Proceedings of the Second International Workshop on Testing Database Systems, DBTest 2009, pp. 1–9. ACM, New York (2009)
10. Lu, R., Lin, X., Liangand, X., Shen, X.: Secure provenance: the essential of bread and butter of data forensics in cloud computing. In: Proceedings of the 5th ACM Symposium on Information, Computer and Communications Security, ASIACCS 2010, pp. 282–292. ACM, New York (2010)
11. Nitu, I.: Configurability in SaaS (software as a service) applications. In: Proceedings of the 2nd India software engineering conference, ISEC 2009, pp. 19–26. ACM, New York (2009)
12. Ruan, K., Carthy, J., Kechadi, T., Crosbie, M.: Cloud forensics: An overview. In: IFIP International Conference on Digital Forensics, p. 7 (2011)
13. Lim, N., Khoo, A.: Forensics of computers and handheld devices: identical or fraternal twins? Commun. ACM 52, 132–135 (2009)
14. Lyle, J.R.: A strategy for testing hardware write block devices. Digital Investigation 3(suppl.), 3–9 (2006); The Proceedings of the 6th Annual Digital Forensic Research Workshop (DFRWS 2006)
15. Delport, W., Olivier, M.S., Köhn, M.: Isolating a cloud instance for a digital forensic investigation. In: 2011 Information Security for South Africa (ISSA 2011) Conference (2011)
16. Vmware inc. Computer Program. vSphere 5.0 (2011), http://www.vmware.com (accessed May 26, 2012)

Proposed Control Procedure to Mitigate the Risks of Strategic Information Outflow in the Recruitment Process

Kashif Syed[1], Pavol Zavarsky[2], Dale Lindskog[2], Ron Ruhl[2], and Shaun Aghili[2]

[1] Risk and Compliance Department, Regional Municipality of Wood Buffalo
9909 Franklin Avenue, Fort McMurray, AB, Canada T9H 2K4
[2] Information Systems Security Management, Concordia University College of Alberta
7128 Ada Boulevard, Edmonton, AB, Canada T5B 4E4
kashif.syed@woodbuffalo.ab.ca,
{pavol.zavarsky,ron.ruhl,dale.lindskog,
shaun.aghili}@concordia.ab.ca

Abstract. This research paper focuses on the security of strategic information during the hiring process. Information control and communication channel vulnerabilities are identified through the process-based risk assessment and human factor analysis. A control procedure is proposed to address these security concerns through system design and information flow improvements in the recruitment process. This proposed control procedure can also serve as a base model for different human resource functions to integrate and create uniformity in risk mitigation to maximize and streamline the management's efforts and resources in managing the information related risks in different human resource processes.

Keywords: Recruitment, Strategic information, Risk assessment, Human factor analysis.

1 Introduction

In recent years, human resource management has evolved as a strategic partner in the development of a corporate policy, vision and culture that guides an organization to succeed in the ever changing business environment. Recruitment is the first step in the hiring process, as it unwraps the different security issues in terms of information exchange between prospective employees and the hiring organization.

Recruitment professionals are restricted by different privacy and confidentiality laws and regulations (ex: Personal Information Protection and Electronic Document Act (PIPEDA) in Canada, Directive 2002/58/EC (the E-Privacy Directive) in European Union, or Privacy Act of 2005 in United States of America) to protect privacy and security of the personal information of employees, prospective job applicants and customers. Protection of an organization's strategic information resources are in the hands of upper management with high potential of information leakage to unintended recipients. Information exchange is an integral part of the recruitment process

S. Fischer-Hübner, S. Katsikas, G. Quirchmayr (Eds.): TrustBus 2012, LNCS 7449, pp. 50–64, 2012.

at all levels and a slight mishandling of enterprise strategic information during the interview and hiring may result in lost competitive advantage, often accentuated by sharp declines in stock prices as a result of lost investor confidence. Strategic Information leakage cases are common headlines in the business world. However, it is difficult to point out an information leakage case in the recruitment process partially, because of the complexity of the whole process of recruitment.

This paper explains the various stages of the hiring process. We use a combination of process based risk assessment techniques and human factor analysis to identify the possible routes of information leakage and its significance in business context.

Process-based risk assessment technique was originally developed by Khanmohammadi and Houmb (2010) and was effectively used as a risk assessment model in a financial environment in order to identify the cumulative risk on the basis of process instead based on assets and vulnerabilities [1]. In this research, we use this risk assessment technique to avoid the risk of duplication of risk with the same assets duplicated in different stages of the recruitment process. A process-based risk assessment technique also provides a more strategic approach to assess the risks associated with the recruitment processes with an integration of both tangible and intangible assets.

Human Factor Analysis is used as a technique to uncover the multidimensional nature of human capital in the risk scenario. Human Factor Analysis was developed by Shappell and Wiegmann (2000) to a trend that suggested some form of human error as a primary factor in 80% of all flight accidents in the Navy and Marine Corps [2]. In this paper, this technique is used to discover the soft sides of management systems in order to better understand the dynamics of human behaviour affecting organizations in both individual and corporate capacity. Human capital is the biggest source of risk in a corporate culture, and at the same time the most capable tool to mitigate the risks. In this research paper, we use this technique to uncover the human factors that are responsible for risk generation and also identify the relationship of corporate policies and organizational culture to minimize the risk of security breaches in the recruitment process.

A control procedure is proposed to address information security concerns identified in the hiring process. This proposed control procedure is based on the Guide for Applying the Risk Management Framework to Federal Information System (800-37 rev. 1) published by the National Institute of standards and Technology (NIST), and customized it to accommodate the special requirements of the recruitment function [3].

2   Methodology

This research is based on secondary data from three major sources: a) Human Resource Management (HRM) literature; b) Industry best recruitment practices; c) NIST SP 800-37 Guide for Applying the Risk Management Framework to Federal Information Systems. Risk assessment is based on the recruitment process instead of assets alone to identify the overall impact at the corporate level in case of any exploitation of identified vulnerabilities in the recruitment process. This technique is very useful to identify the impact of risks in all-inclusive ways. Hiring processes involve many different stakeholders at different levels of the recruitment process. The underlying objectives are also diversified in their own parameters. Recruitment is also a very significant promotional component of any organization's marketing mix and many times this approach goes too far without even understanding the inherent risks of the information outflow without even identifying it.

Human factor risk analysis identifies risks associated with the human nature, especially under the banner of the organizational culture. Human factor risk analysis findings are helpful in the identification of various policy vulnerabilities contributing to the enterprise risk level.

The proposed control procedure is primarily based on the combination of basic principles of System Development Life Cycle (SDLC) and NIST publication 800-37 Revision 1. It is a general model of best practices for the recruitment process that can be customized as per business and industry needs. Clearly defined stages in SDLC approach are best suited for the dynamic and ongoing nature of the recruitment process to establish specific and understandable deliverables for every stage. This control procedure is focused on the resultant product of total risk associated with recruitment process rather than focusing on individual risks in different stages of recruitment process. The control procedure is easy to implement, while supporting an integrated security system to monitor the overall information security of an organization. This control procedure serves as a base line security and provides flexibility for organizations to customize it as per their unique business needs for optimal security.

This proposed control procedure serves will address security components at different stages of the hiring process. The recruitment process is very dynamic, because of the involvement of different departments to complement specific business requirements. The proposed control procedure can also serve as a base model for different human resource functions to integrate and create uniformity in risk mitigation to maximize and streamline the management's efforts and resources in managing the information related risks in different human resource processes.

3   Risk Assessment of the Hiring Process

Different stages of recruitment process were studied in isolation and their interrelationship discussed in order to assess the overall impact of embedded risks at the corporate level in the recruitment process.

Process-based risk assessment is performed to identify the security risks in the recruitment process. Information plays an integral role in all stages of the recruitment process and information classification, flow and storage are key areas in terms of security. Figure 1 illustrates the normal flow of activities in the recruitment process in a broad scale for an overall recruitment process. Using the previously discussed model of Khanmohamadi and Houmb, risks are identified at the recruitment process level [1]. This technique is an effective assessment of risk in the recruitment process, because it concentrates on the value of a business process in relation to the overall corporate objectives, instead of asset value, irrespective of its direct and indirect impact on the business process. This technique also provides insights in further risk evaluation for risk prioritization and devising strategies for in depth control measures.

Fig. 1. Recruitment Process in Information Security Perspective

As per Table 1, the recruitment sub process is comprised of six stages as follows:

1. *Job Analysis*: This refers to a sub-process to collect information about a certain job and involves information sharing at different levels conducted by the human resource department. Sometimes an external entity also participates in this process. The information (highly confidential in terms of work processes, skill inventories and assets {Physical, technical and information}) is collected through direct observations, interviews or surveys and after that this information is used to develop job specification and job descriptions. The information collection method is vulnerable, because the confidentiality of this information is the cornerstone of the recruitment process as it also involves compensation related issues. Every collection method needs special consideration to protect and secure the flow of information. Storage of this confidential information is also a concern, because of the processing of this confidential data at different levels and the impact of different technologies rooted in the storage systems. This process is further complicated further, if external partnerships are in place to assist the human resource department.

2. *Job Specifications and Descriptions*: Different departments are often involved in the job description stage and work in collaboration with the human resource department and any external sources, if used. Job specifications are also used for human resource planning purposes and are also part of the competency dictionaries. On the other hand, job descriptions involve all the information related to assets and procedures pertaining to the particular job. This information is shared across functional departments for the integration of business processes. Organizations with different geographical presence with decentralized recruitment systems also share information across different recruitment offices for streamlining businesses and human resource processes. External staffing agencies also need this information to develop appropriate job advertisements.

Table 1. Examples of Vulnerabilities, Threats and Risks in Recruitment Process

Recruitment Sub-process	Vulnerabilities	Threats	Risks
Job analysis	Organizational design, information collection techniques and process	Incorrect decisions about information classification	Insider and collusion risks of confidential information leakage
Job specifications and job descriptions	Communication channel, storage technologies and information classification process	Role ambiguities, inappropriate access controls	Corporate information theft both from internal and external sources
Job advertisement	Communication medium , technologies and inter-departmental conflicts	Disclosure of confidential information	Leakage of confidential information
Data collection	Technology platform, communication channels, information sharing with a third party	Social engineering, steganography, malicious code with information submission	Application and software attacks, creation of backdoor for sensitive information collection
Screening process	Reference checks, information disclosure to third parties, physical presence of candidates in organizational premises	Information disclosure to third party and social engineering	Confidential information leakage to third party or prospect employees
Selection process	Design of interview, type of interview questions, human judgment process	Human error risks, poorly designed questions containing strategic information	Corporate espionage or trespass, loss competitive advantage

3. *Job Advertisements*: Development of job postings and job advertisements (directed towards external candidates) is often an exercise in artistic prose in order to create a positive image of the enterprise.

However, many times the thrust of getting attention from qualified candidates make advertisement writers cross a fine line by disclosing strategic information about the enterprise. Any disclosure of strategic direction, assets or technologies can be potentially significant in terms of losing competitive advantage. Development of job advertisements is often the primary responsibility of the human resource department; but in many organizations the respective department also participate in the creation of job advertisement. A lot of C- level executives believe, that the department where the vacancy is open, should have more authority and role to play to maximize future efficiency and effectiveness issues. This approach leads to some interdepartmental conflict. As a result, the integrity of the recruitment process is compromised.

Another very important consideration is the choice of the medium used to transmit these "Help Wanted" messages. Conventional methods like newspaper advertisements, employment magazines and job ads in professional or trade publications are still very popular because of convenience and simplicity. Internet job boards, internet job portals and social media are also used because of reach and cost efficiency advantages. Internet job advertisements are similar with paper advertisements in presentation, content and message but the underlying technologies and web connectivity to unlimited users translate electronic side more vulnerable. The World Wide Web provides the opportunity to reach clients at mass scale levels but at the same time opens some hidden doors for intruders to satisfy their malicious intents.

At the advertisement stage, external agencies play a very important role when internal human resource departments lack required hiring competencies. To take maximum advantage of the external recruitment source, organizations should share job & company related information diligently to clarify the job requirements but not disclose private strategic information or any confidential information that is not relevant to the recruitment process. Important considerations should also be made towards the audit of business processes and technologies used by the external partner to make sure that the information is safe and only mutually decided information is publicized.

4. *Data collection*: Once job advertisements are up and noticed, prospect candidates start inquiring information through different channels. In order to properly explain and direct applicants on to the right process of recruitment, selected individuals from the human resource department offer application support. Prospect candidates ask for clarifications about job and company and the help staff responds these questions tactfully. Information disclosure by poorly trained human resource staff may lead to leakage of sensitive information either intentionally or unintentionally.

Furthermore, paper applications, electronic mail and web job portals are very common delivery methods used for information receipt from candidates. Some organizations also organize career fair to collect applications in house and offer assistance for application process in a prearranged schedule. This is a great opportunity for applicants to get a feel of the company, because they get first look at the company's culture and resources. Organizations also use career fairs as a tool for marketing their name to attract qualified applicants. This opportunity could be an excellent opportunity for social engineering in case of poor controls and monitoring of all visitors. Application submitted through electronic mail may contain embedded malware designed to damage a system, create a back door for intruders to hack databases, email accounts or other information-based assets for malicious purposes. Steganography can also be used to transmit important strategic documents outside of the enterprise without authorization for fraudulent activities.

5. *Screening Process*: The screening stage involves different activities reliant on the nature of the vacancy and the recruitment strategy. Basic requirement match is done either manually or electronically to create a list of qualified candidates for selection considerations. Reference checks should be the first major screening step for organizations. The nature and extent of reference checks depend upon the criticality and significance of the advertised position. Many organizations do not have the required resources, time and skills to conduct enhanced reference

checks. As a result, professional companies are used to conduct reference checking. As such, organizations have to clearly define the depth and scope of the reference checks and share enough information with external agencies to enable these reference checking entities to understand the nature of the job and its requirements. Information sharing at this stage also poses serious challenges in case of ambiguity of the roles in recruitment process between the external entity and the parent organization. Many jobs also require security checks through regional law enforcement agencies.

Initial interviews are also a part of screening process to establish an understanding of a 'right fit' concept. These interviews also provide an opportunity to candidates to ask question about the job and the company in order to make better judgement for their carer. This interview is also an activity that can be done in house or outside agencies can also conduct initial interview as part of the screening process.

6. *Selection process*: This is the last and the most crucial part of recruitment in security perspective. Job related testing like competency, personality, cognitive ability or any special knowledge test is a part of this phase. Normally the assessment center is organized in house to accommodate special consideration of the job or organization. These assessment centers are very extensive in nature and may last for days. Interviews are the most common and popular selection tool. Panel interviews and serial interviews are more vulnerable, because of the number of individuals involved in this sub-process of the recruitment process. Any unstructured question can provoke a discussion that can lead to unintentional or intentional information leakage. Many organizations also conduct a series of questions with different departments involved in these interviews. The interviews conducted by the executives are more susceptible because of less formal training of interviewing and ignorance of security issues by the interviewers. Recruitment agencies or professionals are also a part of selection interviews in special cases or special skills requirements. Free flow of information is the life blood of the interview; but, unstructured interviews coupled with a lack of interviewing skills may sometimes lead to information leakage that can be used in corporate espionage.

Risk of corporate espionage through information leakage in the recruitment process is possible at any stage. Information movement, control and storage are challenges for management. Communication vulnerabilities lead us to analyze the soft side of management. In next section human factors contributing towards risks are discussed.

4   Human Factor Analysis of the Recruitment Process

Human resources are the driving force of all business processes and as a result all vulnerabilities and risks are only materialized with malicious human resource intent. It is important to understand the factors contribute towards the lack of awareness of vulnerabilities and threats in the recruitment process. In this section, we analyze the factors possibly directly contributing towards poor organizational alignment and possible negative aspiration that can lead to information security breaches for personal gains or a simple retaliation against the organizational policies.

We divided the identified factors affecting human performance into three broad groups (Fig 2) based on their source. Organizational, group and personal groups contain factors that play a significant role in the security perceptions of individual and also direct their actions in corporate settings.

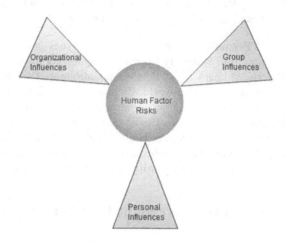

Fig. 2. Human Factor Risk Groups

1. Organizational Influences: This group represents all policies and regulations of an organization for the control of business processes. It includes resource allocations, human resources and technological assets and governance structure. All organizational policies can have either positive or negative impact on human resources depending upon the organizational structure, corporate culture and socio-demographic characteristics affecting the job satisfaction. Organizational policies also contribute towards the organizational commitment or the negative consequences of unsatisfied customer both internal and external. Organizational structure and corporate strategy set the tone of management control to optimize the organizational resources for corporate gain. Various organizational factors may lead to employee disgruntlement. Conflict or ambiguities are the result product of poor combination of corporate strategy, organizational design and human resource strategy. Inappropriate Job design is another major source of employee dissatisfaction with the organization in terms of low motivation and morale. Enforcement of policies without proper education and training may negatively affect employees' commitment and result is retaliations in many forms including security or information leakage.

2. Group Influences: Organizations are a combination of vision, resources and direction towards an agreed upon objective. Human interactions are not only important in team work but are also the core of the soft side of the management process. Social interaction among coworkers is not limited to the confines of an organization; it actually has more impact outside our job roles. Power structure in group dynamics is also a key factor in creating an atmosphere of sharing and belongingness with the organization. Every group or team also has an informal power structure that even influence more than the formal hierarchy structure. Intragroup and intergroup conflicts can result in low motivation, productivity and low organizational bond. So-cioeconomic factors are the building block of these informal groups and affect heavily by the organizational culture. These informal groups or leaders emit negative energy if the organizational structure is not aligned with the corporate strategy. This disorientation of human capital can lead to the possibility of exploitation of resources in many manners including information outflow to unintended recipients.

3. Personal Influences: Personal circumstances of employees are often beyond the control of an organization; but, indirectly impact the organizational success or failure through employees' personal characters. Personal situations are the leading source of fraud and misconduct in the corporate world. Employees with differing personal objectives than that of the organization may be motivated to take a route against the hiring enterprise. Human capital is one of most complicated components of the risk management process of every organization. Human factors contributing towards risks should be carefully monitored and comprehensively evaluated form a risk perspective through a combined effort of corporate security and human resource department

5   Security Control Procedure in the Recruitment Process

Risk assessment and human factor analysis has defined the strategic risk in the hiring process and a need of an integrated control procedure.

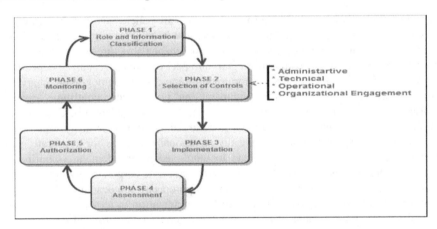

Fig. 3. Proposed Security Control Procedure in the Recruitment Process

Coordination of information security into system architecture and system development life cycle will provide a real risk monitoring approach to ensure smooth recruitment processes with proper risk mitigation strategies in place for the protection of information and information assets. Role based security controls and policies enable recruitment teams to have timely access to the information for decision making process without compromising cross functional controls.

This control procedure is primarily based on NIST special publication 800-37 Revision 1 and customized to accommodate the recruitment process in system development life cycle approach. The following steps provide a logical sequence in accordance with the recruitment process (including sub-processes) to mitigate information security risks in a comprehensive and efficient approach.

5.1   Phase 1: Role and Information Classification

Role and Information classification should be done at the start of the recruitment process to assist in designing the decision making process and validate the integrity of the recruitment process.

The involvement of cross functional teams in the recruitment process at different stages also extends the need of role clarification for efficiency of communication channels and security control. Information classification serves as a baseline for security control development. Correct classification of recruitment data would provide necessary platform to apply proper access control. Table 2 provides a summary of role classification guidelines. A summary of the guidelines for information classification is in Table 3.

Table 2. Guidelines for Role Classification

Executives C-Level leadership, ultimately responsible for strategic implication of human resource strategy. They deal in strategic direction and are the owner of high level policies. They should have access to all policy making tools and assets at high level.
Incharge/Project Manager Recruitment heads or human resource managers who own a particular recruitment project are responsible for decision making. They do share selective strategic information related to a particular recruitment project.
Liaison Staff Staff for other departments like Compensation, Organizational development and Human Resource Policy division that also assists in the development of recruitment process e-g Job evaluation. They should not have access to any strategic information related to recruitment projects.
Functional Staff Recruiters and talent acquisition officers/managers play the functional role of recruitment process like processing of information, creation of job postings and qualification assessment process. They only require access to the tactical policies and procedures to properly complete functional aspects of recruitment process.
Facilitators Recruitment assistants, reception staff and help desk fall into this category. They provide necessary information to prospect applicants to follow proper recruitment procedures. They should have limited access to information directly related to the particular job posting. They should know the proper protocol for accessing further information or to direct prospects for further information to appropriate staff.

Information classification should be based on the criticality and overall impact of information on strategic business processes which in turn translate these values into business success. Information classification should incorporate confidentiality, integrity and availability component in accordance to the corporate security policy. Top secret and confidential information should be treated as private strategic information and retained in separate server with high security.

Table 3. Guidelines for Information Classification (see also [4])

Public Information
Access: Public
Definition: information for public use
Confidentiality: Examples include company profile and   business summaries
Integrity: examples include job postings and job advertisements
Availability: examples include mission statements and job profiles
Internal Information
Access: Internal by incharge/project managers and functional staff
Definition: Operations may be disrupted in case of information leakage
Confidentiality: Examples include manpower   planning and non-public job descriptions
Integrity: Examples include non-public compensation and benefits data
Availability: Examples include benefit administration and reference checks
Confidential Information
Access: Internal by department executives and incharge/project managers
Definition: Risks of a high damage in case of information leakage
Confidentiality: Examples include information on patents, technology and   critical applications
Integrity: Examples include financial and research data
Availability: Examples include human information system, integrated business applications
Top Secret Information
Access: Internal by C-level executives only
Definition: Risks of catastrophic effects in case of information leakage
Confidentiality: Examples include business strategy, corporate mergers, etc.
Integrity: Examples include new market penetration, new product line, etc.
Availability: Examples include decision making,   stock offerings, etc.

Adequate information classification also suggests the type of resources needed to protect and safeguard information resources. Information classification is also significant in drawing the information security scope in relation to the overall security tolerance of the organization. Information classification process should not only consider information value in the recruitment process but special consideration should be made to understand the correlation of different business processes dependent on the information. Job analysis data should be classified for different human resource functions and job descriptions should only contain internal data for security purposes. Job advertisements and job postings should only consider public data to share with prospects. In the same account, interview questions should be based on job description only. Behavioral descriptive questions supplemented with situation-based question would minimize the chances of confidential information leakage very early in the interview design. This is the developmental phase in the organization's information system and initiation stage in the system development life cycle (SDLC).

5.2   Phase 2: Selection of Security Controls

The controls can be selected and tailored appropriately from the NIST control catalogue. The controls are divided into four separate categories to accurately safeguard information and information assets in the recruitment process. These controls should be customized to align with the organizational design and culture of the organization to gain better reception from employees. Administrative controls explain and provide guidelines to use technical control in the forms of policies and procedures. Technical controls are the means to use technology to enforce security policies. Awareness and training programs are the part of operational controls to ensure that the employees have understanding and skills to effectively use security controls. Organizational engagement is the result of the favourable organizational policies in building a security conscious culture.

Administrative controls include policies, procedures and physical protection. Policies and procedures for information classification and communication plans should be customized to be the specific requirements of an organization at the process and recruitment stage in relation to its environment for better coverage. These controls should also express the role and responsibilities in the capacity of information processing, sharing and storage mediums used in the recruitment process. Administrative controls also facilitate the use of appropriate technical controls to clarify ambiguities and conflict of interest. These controls should also capture role uncertainty through separation of duties. Document control and 'tailor-made' non-disclosure agreements should be used when external parties are involved in the recruitment process. Risk acceptance should be clearly stated and embedded in the roles specified and must be acknowledged in the security documents.

Technical controls include access controls, identification and authentication, as well as, communication protection. Access controls should be assigned on the basis of interim role of recruitment staff instead of positions or job titles [5]. Role based access control should be used with appropriate file sharing technology, especially when multiple user accessing the same file with different security levels for example job evaluation data or job specifications. Project management approach should be used in the design phase to implement access controls with the flexibility to accommodate multiple roles. Job specifications and Job description data should be kept in the main server with customized limited access to the recruitment team on the least privilege principle. "Two-factor" authentication process should accommodate multiple roles within different recruitment projects in sequence with the security level of information data in use. Communication from outside should be protected with firewalls, intrusion detection systems and anti Steganography tools should be used to protect servers containing recruitment data.

Awareness and training is an integral part of *operational controls* due to its enormous importance and significance. Success of administrative controls is hugely based on the understanding of the value of these controls. Technology is not self sufficient and proper training and understanding of technical controls plays a major role in effective implementation of controls. Security awareness should be focused on the development of the security culture at all levels of management. Security training should be a part of the orientation program for all new employees and refresher security courses should be a part of the regular training sessions. Security awareness should be the part of performance evaluation process.

Organizational commitment is one of the key components of organizational success. Proper awareness programs supported by favourable human resource and organizational policies will minimize the risk of human factor contribution towards risk. Equity, fairness and employee involvement in decision making would gear in the development of the positive organizational culture resulting in organizational commitment. This is the last part of developmental phase (as illustrated in Fig. 3) of information system and also final step in the initiation stage of SDLC.

5.3   Phase 3: Implementation of Security Controls

Implementation of security controls is the first stage in the implementation of information system security and part of the SDLC. Information security architecture is significant in order to establish and implement security controls for the correct security balance. Information security professionals in assistance with subject matter specialists should create a security design harmonized with the functional requirements of the recruitment process. In addition, security tools should be supported with adequate configuration management and change management processes. Role-based access controls should be used in different composition in all stages of recruitment to share selective information stored in a uniform location. At this stage, security designer should also understand and decide the most suitable technologies complacent to the security architecture for best utilization of the security system. Integration of security controls with other departments would be critical to understand the interdependencies of risk in information sharing and storage. Security design should also address the unique needs of information classification within the human resource department for different security levels. Assessment and assurance requirements are also set in this stage to ensure the quality and identification of any possible weaknesses in the system. A good understanding of the organizational culture is critical to identify the possible human risks contributing towards information security. Human resource policies should address factors contributing towards risks and minimize dissatisfaction among employees to enhance organizational commitment.

5.4   Phase 4: Assessment of Security Controls

The assessment phase provides the assurance that the security controls are appropriately in place and successfully protecting information and information assets. Security assessment plan should consider these following components; security policies, basic security mechanism and security tools. Assessments policies should also be based on the combination of defense in depth and need to know principle. Assessors should conduct assessments unbiased and without any organizational influence. Access control assessments should clearly examine and test the scope and extent of information share in different stages among different users. Assessment should also ensure that the access control is proper and integrated with the security structure and design across different division involved in the recruitment process. Internal networks containing job analysis data should be tested to ensure that there is no external access for the security of top secret and confidential data.

Internal and external assessment both provide assurance of greater degree because of different perspectives but external assessments should be in controlled environment to mitigate the inherent risk of this process. Configuration and customization of technical controls should be logged properly for future references. Separation of duty, education and understanding of controls should be part of the assessment process. This is part of information system development stage and SDLC implementation phase and leads us to the authorization stage.

5.5   Phase 5: Authorization of Security Controls

The authorization is based on the finding of assessment process. Ideally, organizations can predict and plan a strategy for the implementation of the controls in a streamlined fashion to accommodate any specific changes identified in the assessment process. Implementation strategy should outline the desired landmarks in the course consistent with the overall risk mitigation strategy across the organization. This stage also ensures that the level of residual risk is consistent with the risk tolerance of the organization. Risk acceptance should be clarified in different roles for accountability purposes. A detailed documented plan should describe the steps in implantation, different stages and ownership of responsibilities.

Prioritization in implantation strategy is dually based on the overall security policy and functional requirements of the recruitment process. Job evaluation data is used in different human resource functions and generated through a combined process and the implementation strategy should not counteract common controls already in place [6].

5.6   Phase 6: Monitoring of Security Controls

The monitoring is a continuous process and entails learning about the strengths and weaknesses of an organizational security plan. A SWOT analysis (Strength, Weakness, Opportunity, and Threat) provides a blend of the internal and external information for decision making in managing the security posture of an organization. A comprehensive security analysis comprising of administrative and technical controls should focus and uncover the business processes and their interdependencies to identify the actual potential of the risks. Monitoring plan should establish documentation procedures and change management steps to record all findings for future security analysis. Monitoring also provides an opportunity for the security professionals to understand the impact of how a change in controls can affect security environment of the organization.

This proposed control procedure is based on the concept that the risk generation are two folded; one is the business processes and the second is human factor. A combination of administrative and technical controls should protect the risks entrenched in the business process. Organizational policies and proper awareness and training programs should minimize the risks of human side of management.

6   Conclusion

This research paper revealed information security risks embedded in the current recruitment practices. Communication channel and access control issues threaten the unintended exposure of strategic information in the recruitment process. The authors proposed a control procedure based on risk management framework (RMF by NIST) to align the security and communication design with the recruitment process through the use of role based access and communication controls. This paper also provides an opportunity for information security analysts and human resource information specialists to efficiently implement information security controls without compromising the effectiveness of business process through process based security design in line with recruitment process of their organizations. Business process based security design can be extended to the other human resource functions and streamline the security structure for resource optimization.

References

1. Khanmohammadi, K., Houmb, S.H.: Business Process-based Information Security Risk Assessment. In: 4th International Conference on Network and System Security (2010), http://ieeexplore.ieee.org/xpl/freeabs_all.jsp?arnumber=5635519
2. Shappell, S.A.: The Human Factors Analysis and Classification System (HFACS), National Technical Information Service, Springfield, Virginia (2000), http://www.nifc.gov/fireInfo/fireInfo_documents/humanfactors_classAnly.pdf
3. NIST SP 800-53 Rev.3 Recommended Security Controls for Federal Information Systems and Organizations (2009), http://csrc.nist.gov/publications/nistpubs/800-53-Rev3/sp800-53-rev3-final_updated-errata_05-01-2010.pdf
4. FIPS PUB 199 Standards for Security Categorization of Federal Information and Information Systems (2004)
5. Solms, B.V.: Corporate Governance and Information Security. Computer and Security 20, 215–218 (2001)
6. NIST SP 800-53A Rev.1 Guide for Assessing the Security Controls in Federal Information Systems and Organizations, Building Effective Security Assessment Plans, http://csrc.nist.gov/publications/nistpubs/800-53A-rev1/sp800-53A-rev1-final.pdf
7. An Introduction to the Business Model for Information Security. Information Systems Audit and Control Association, ISACA (2009), http://www.isaca.org/Knowledge-Center/Research/Documents/Intro-Bus-Model-InfoSec-22Jan09-Research.pdf
8. Catano, V.M., et al.: Recruitment and Selection in Canada, 3rd edn., Toronto, Canada, pp. 3–11. Thomson Nelson (2005)
9. Flouris, T., Yilmaz, K.A.: The risk management framework to strategic human resource management. International Research Journal of Finance and Economics 36 (2010), http://www.eurojournals.com/irjfe_36_03.pdf
10. Rezende, R.V., Carvalho, C.S.: Selection of executives through in-house recruitment. In: Engineering Management Conference, Sao Paolo, pp. 356–359 (1994)
11. Dafoulas, G.A., Nikolau, A., Turega, M.: E-Service in the internet job market. In: 36th Hawaii International Conference on System Sciences (2003), http://www.hicss.hawaii.edu/HICSS36/HICSSpapers/DTESS04.pdf
12. Ruskova, N.: Decision Support System for Human Resource Appraisal and Selection. In: 1st International IEEE Symposium on Intelligent Systems, vol. 1, pp. 354–357 (2002)
13. Dart, D.: What Are the Real Costs of a Bad Hire? Ezine Articles, http://ezinearticles.com/?What-Are-The-Real-Costs-of-a-Bad-Hire?&id=6421866
14. Yager, F.: Costs of Hiring the Wrong Person Go beyond the Financial. eFinancialCareers (2011), http://news.efinancialcareers.com/News_ITEM/newsItemId-35369
15. Bardin, J.: The Brave New World of InfoSec, Moving to a Risk-Based Organization – NIST 800-37 Revision 1 (2010), http://blogs.csoonline.com/1188/moving_to_a_risk_based_organization_nist-800_37_rev_1
16. Barner, R.: Talent Wars in the Executive Suite. The Futurist 34(3), 35 (2000), http://www.allbusiness.com/management/534851-1.html

An Autonomous Social Web Privacy Infrastructure with Context-Aware Access Control

Michael Netter, Sabri Hassan, and Günther Pernul

Department of Information Systems
University of Regensburg
Regensburg, Germany
{michael.netter,sabri.hassan,
guenther.pernul}@wiwi.uni-regensburg.de

Abstract. The rise of online social networks (OSNs) has traditionally been accompanied by privacy concerns. These typically stem from facts: First, OSN service providers' access to large databases with millions of user profiles and their exploitation. Second, the user's inability to create and manage different identity facets and enforce access to the self as in the real world. In this paper, we argue in favor of a new paradigm, decoupling the management of social identities in OSNs from other social network services and providing access controls that take social contexts into consideration. For this purpose, we first propose Priamos, an architecture for privacy-preserving autonomous management of social identities and subsequently present one of its core components to realize context-aware access control. We have implemented a prototype to evaluate the feasibility of the proposed approach.

Keywords: Privacy, Online Social Networks, Context-Aware Access Control, Privacy-Preserving Social Identity Management.

1 Introduction

Over the last decade, the evolution of the WWW led to a significant growth of Online Social Networks (OSN). While Social Networks have always been an important part of daily life, the advent of Web 2.0 and its easy-to-use services increasingly shift social life to their online counterparts. OSNs provide an infrastructure for communication, information and self-expression as well as for building and maintaining relationships with other users.

However, the rise of OSN services has been accompanied by privacy concerns. Typically, two sources of privacy threats can be distinguished [21]: On the one hand, privacy threats stem from OSN service providers. Currently, the oligopolistic social web landscape leads to few OSN service providers possessing large databases with millions of user profiles. On the other hand, privacy concerns target the challenges of presenting different identity facets of the self in different social contexts and to keep those views consistent. While this bears

S. Fischer-Hübner, S. Katsikas, G. Quirchmayr (Eds.): TrustBus 2012, LNCS 7449, pp. 65–78, 2012.

resemblance to managing different appearances of the self in the real world, the inherent properties of mediated OSN communication (e.g. permanency and searchability of personal information) put privacy at risk. Although privacy controls are in place to restrict access to personal data today, users seem to be shortsighted concerning future issues of current behavior [20] [10].

To address the aforementioned privacy issues, different research areas evolved. One direction of research are decentralized OSNs that employ user-centric management of digital identities and create a provider-independent social network. While being a promising approach to enhance privacy and data ownership, current implementations such as Diasproa[1] lack user adoption due to high transaction costs of replicating existing identities [10] and strong lock-in effects of established centralized OSNs [5]. Another area of research aims at enhancing privacy within centralized OSNs, e.g. by proposing more fine-grained access controls to enable selective sharing of personal data. Ultimately however, their enforcement depends on the OSN service provider's willingness to adopt these approaches.

To overcome the aforementioned drawbacks, we present a new paradigm of managing social identities in an autonomous, provider-independent manner to enhance users' privacy. We envision identities being decoupled from other OSN services and managed in a user-controlled environment yet integrated into the existing social web landscape. To realize this vision, this paper introduces **Priamos**, an architecture for **P**rivacy-preserving autonomous **m**anagement **o**f **s**ocial identities and its components. One of the components, a context-aware access control component that facilitates selective sharing of personal information by considering contextual information, is presented in detail. Finally, we present a prototypical implementation of our solution.

This paper contributes to OSN privacy by (1) proposing an architecture for autonomous and privacy-preserving social identity management (PPSIdM), (2) enabling context-aware access control to imitate real world sharing of personal information, and (3) enforcing these access control decisions.

The remainder of this paper is structured as follows. After describing related work in Section 2, we present our autonomous social identity management architecture and its components in Section 3. In Section 4, we focus on one component and introduce a context-aware access control model. Section 5 shows the implementation of the proposed architecture. We conclude the paper in Section 6 with an outlook on future work.

2   Related Work

As shown in Section 1, two major research directions have evolved to face privacy challenges of centralized OSNs, namely decentralization and selective sharing of personal information.

Decentralization and cross-OSNs management of identities has been studied by various research groups [4], [15], [19]. Bortoli et al. [4] propose a web-based

---

[1] http://www.diasporaproject.org/

application for automatic social network integration, based on globally unique identifiers and semantic web technologies. The authors focus on the decentralized and boundary-crossing management of OSN identities. Similarly, the OpenPlatform proposed by Mostarda et al. [15] aims at improving OSN interoperability. The approach is based on OpenID[2] and uses connectors and converters to access the user's social graphs in different OSNs. The InterDataNet project [19] proposes a distributed data integration approach to support the management of digital profiles. The authors employ an overlay network to uniformly manage personal data in a trustworthy manner. Managing social identities in our autonomous architecture differs from the above systems in the following ways: First, we protect the user's privacy by preventing OSN service providers from getting access to personal data. Second, our architecture enables contextual sharing of personal information and enforcement of access control policies. Third, our approach is OSN agnostic and does not rely on connectors to integrate different OSNs.

Additionally, research [14] shows that selective and context-sensitive sharing of personal information is a key element to enhancing privacy in OSNs. Regarding this, the PrimeLife project [6] has developed two prototypes called Clique and Scramble!. Clique [3] is a prototypical OSN that implements the concept of audience segregation to facilitate the definition of fine-grained access control policies. The Firefox plugin Scramble! [2] is a cryptographic approach to define and enforce access control policies for personal data in OSNs. In contrast to the first prototype, we aim at enhancing privacy within the existing centralized OSN landscape while the second prototype differs from our approach as we aim at managing identities and access to personal information beyond OSN boundaries. To additionally improve selective sharing, OSN-specific access control models have been proposed [13], [7], [8], [1]. The D-FOAF architecture proposed in [13] relies on semantic web technologies and utilizes existing OSNs to define access rights based on the relationship between users, which are described by trust level and path length between requester and resource owner. Similar, the works by Carminati et al. [7], [8] employ semantic web technologies to create a Social Network Knowledge Base (SNKB) that contains OSN related information. Based thereupon, the authors propose a rule-based access control model that takes type, depth and trust level of a relationship into consideration. In [1], Ali et al. propose a social access control model in which objects and subjects are annotated with trust levels and authentication and access to objects is controlled by a trusted third party. Our context-aware access control mechanism differs from the aforementioned approaches in the following two ways: First, for defining contextual access constraints we only regard contextual information provided by the user (e.g. the trust he puts in a contact) to prevent spoofing. Second, unlike the aforementioned approaches that rely on OSN service providers to adapt their models and enforce access control policies, the user-controlled environment of Priamos ensures enforcement.

---

[2] http://www.openid.net/

3   Priamos Architecture

Based on the shortcomings of existing approaches, this section introduces Priamos, an architecture for privacy-preserving, autonomous social identity management. We first present the design characteristics that constitute the foundation of Priamos followed by an in-depth presentation of its components.

3.1   Design Characteristics

As aforementioned, neither solely decentralized OSNs (e.g. Diaspora) nor isolated extensions to centralized OSNs (e.g. fine-grained access control models) are sufficient for enhancing OSN privacy. Our analysis underlines these findings stating that a user-centric and user-controlled environment is essential to enforce the user's privacy preferences while integration into today's centralized OSN landscape is mandatory for user adoption, resulting in the following design characteristics. Firstly, **user-centric management of identities** is required to effectively model and enforce the user's sharing and privacy preferences. Currently, most OSN service providers only allow for creating a single identity profile, a paradigm that counters Nissenbaum's concept of acting in different social contexts using different identities [17]. Enabling the user to create multiple (potentially contradicting) identities and allowing for multiple attribute representation (attribute types can have multiple values) enables the user to map his real-world identities to the social web. Additionally, autonomous social identity management fosters identity portability and prevents OSN service providers from profiling [21]. Secondly, **fine-grained access controls** need to be capable of modeling the user's information sharing behavior of the real-world. Controlling access to a user's social identity requires to additionally take contextual properties such as tie strength and temporal restrictions of personal information into consideration. On the contrary, relationships in existing OSNs are initially flat and personal information is persistently stored [18].

Besides those two core characteristics, additional components of Priamos facilitate user awareness and decision making. As research [20] has shown that people are shortsighted about future conflicts of current disclosure of personal information, **logging and awareness** are key requirements of social identity management enabling the user to track previous information disclosure and facilitating the construction of non-conflicting identities. In addition, privacy-invading characteristics of OSN service provider mediated communication, such as persistence and searchability demand **user assistance** to support users in deciding which personal information to share with whom [18].

3.2   Priamos Components and Functionality

Based on the previous design characteristics, this section outlines our proposed autonomous social IdM architecture. Figure 1 provides a high level overview which can be divided into two major components: The Priamos Identity Management System (IdMS) and a local browser plugin on the contact's side. Together, both

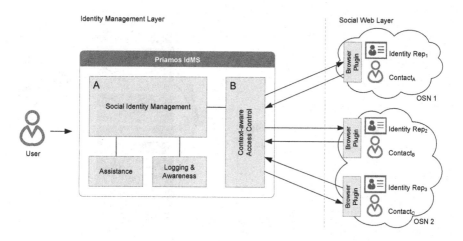

Fig. 1. Priamos architecture and components

components realize the concept of managing identities in a provider-independent manner while being integrated into the existing OSN landscape.

Priamos IdMS. The Priamos IdMS represents the central element of our architecture and aims at managing the user's social identities in a user-centric and provider-independent manner. It is designed to be either self-hosted or hosted by a trusted third party. Priamos consists of four components to address the design characteristics as presented in Section 3.1. Each of the components is discussed below.

Social Identity Management Component. The Social Identity Management component (component A in Figure 1) allows for creating personal attributes, which can be bundled to different identity facets. Each attribute value as well as each identity facet is accessible via a unique URL, realizing the concept of URL-based identities. Note that the proposed concept of privacy-preserving, user-centric social identity management and URL-based identities can easily be extended to other, non-OSN services that require access to the user's personal attributes (similar to OpenID, see Section 5 for implementation).

Context-Aware Access Control Component. Additionally, for each attribute fine-grained access control policies can be defined and enforced using the Context-aware Access Control component (component B in Figure 1), which is described in detail in Section 4. The combination of URL-based identities and context-based access control allows for an OSN-agnostic distribution of identities, as the identity representation solely depends on the requester's access rights.

Logging & Awareness Component. Building upon defined access policies as well as previous access requests of the user's contacts, the Logging & Awareness

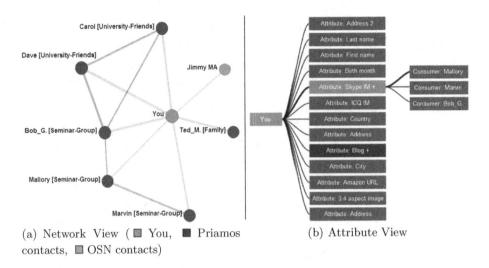

(a) Network View (■ You, ■ Priamos   (b) Attribute View
contacts, ■ OSN contacts)

Fig. 2. Visualization of personal data propagation

component aims at increasing the user's awareness and understanding of flow
and distribution of personal information using visualization techniques. Thereby,
it enables the user to construct future identities that do not confer with existing identities and keep a consistent self-image [12]. In Figure 2, the two main
visualization techniques of Priamos are depicted. Figure 2(a) depicts a graph-
based view on the user's network, showing Priamos contacts as well as contacts
from existing OSN that have been imported. The network view enables the user
to capture the relations between his contacts and thereby understand potential
flows of shared personal information. Besides, in Figure 2(b), a tree-like attribute
view is offered. Using this visualization, the contact's having access to the user's
personal information can be visualized on a per-attribute basis. This enables the
user to easily track which contacts have access to which attributes and thereby
facilitates transparency.

Assistance Component. Additionally, the Assistance component supports
the user in constructing and maintaining different social identities. This comprises means to automatically propose groups of semantically similar contacts
and thereby facilitate audience segregation and targeted sharing of personal information, which we have presented in [16].

Browser Plugin. In order to realize the concept of URL-based identities, the
browser plugin is an auxiliary tool that is preconfigured and provided by the Priamos user and installed at his contacts side. While a contact is surfing the web,
its goal is to detect identity URLs, to resolve their value and embed it on the fly
into the current website. It is designed to work completely in the background with
no user interaction required. Its design as a browser plugin makes this component
completely agnostic in terms of the visited website.

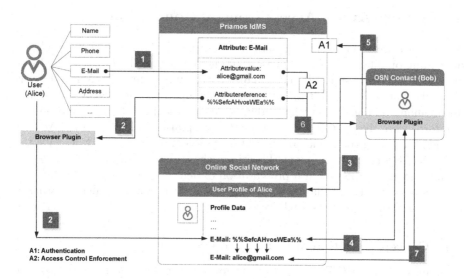

Fig. 3. Attribute definition and access workflow

3.3   Personal Attribute Definition and Access Workflow

This section outlines the workflow of defining and accessing personal information using the Priamos architecture. Prior to this, the user is able to import contacts from existing OSNs using a built-in connector. Subsequently, each of the user's contacts is provided with a preconfigured browser plugin, containing the required access tokens (see Section 5 for details). Thus, the initial distribution of access tokens is not within the scope of this work, but can easily managed by other communication channels such as E-Mail. Figure 3 depicts the workflow for a single personal attribute that is subsequently described. First, the user logs in his Priamos instance account to create a new attribute type (e.g. E-Mail), enters the corresponding value and assigns access rights for this attribute (1). Internally, a Base64-encoded URL, referencing the attribute value, is created. Next, the user employs a browser-based wizard that is included in the browser plugin to seamlessly add the attribute to his social network profile (e.g. on Facebook) which completes the user-related tasks (2). Eventually, one of the user's OSN contacts visits his social network profile (3). In the background, the browser plugin detects the encoded URL in the DOM[3] tree (4) and initiates an OAuth-based[4] authentication process with the user's Priamos instance (5). If successful, predefined access control policies for the request are evaluated and enforced (A2 in Figure 3). If access is granted, the attribute value is returned (6) and the BASE64-encoded URL in the DOM tree is replaced by the corresponding value (7). It is notable that Steps 4-7 require no interaction an thus are completely transparent to the contact.

---

[3] http://www.w3.org/DOM/
[4] http://oauth.net/

4   Context-Aware Access Control Component

As shown in Section 1, sharing personal information is highly contextual, i.e. depending on different factors such attending people and the user's goals. However, existing OSNs support contextualization only to a limited extent. To overcome these limitations, in this section we built upon the previously introduced autonomous and user-controlled architecture for social IdM and outline our *Context-aware Access Control component* (Component B in Figure 1). We first introduce a conceptualization of context for OSNs and subsequently describe the characteristics of the component. Therein, rather than aiming at a formal definition, we focus on the in-depth presentation of defining and applying contextual constraints with the ultimate goal to imitate the situation-dependent sharing of personal information of the real world.

4.1   Conceptualization of Context in OSNs

Defining context in OSNs is a prerequisite for a context-aware access control model, however to the best of our knowledge, no conceptualization of context for sharing personal information in OSNs exists. To define context in OSNs, we built upon the generic definition of Zimmermann et al. [22], introducing the contextual dimensions *Individuality, Activity, Location, Time*, and *Relations*.

In OSNs, we define *Individuality* to comprise information on the user's attributes, such as profile data, that create a desired identity facet. The *Activity* dimension comprises information on the user's goals. In OSNs common goals are, for instance, maintaining relationships and impression management. Both aforementioned contextual dimensions are covered by our user-centric social IdM component (see component A in Figure 1) by supporting users in shaping their online identities according to personal preferences (for instance by allowing for multiple attribute representation).

The three dimensions *Location, Time* and *Relations* contain contextual information helping a user to adapt the amount and type of personal information to be shared in a specific situation and thus are important sources for our context-aware access control component. The *Location* dimension describes the digital equivalent of a physical space in the real world, which is created by grouping people, a feature which is already available in many OSNs and therefore not described more detailed in the remainder. Besides, sharing personal information is often temporally bound to the situation a user is currently in. Thus, the *Time* dimension captures lifetime and temporal restrictions of information sharing. Finally, the *Relations* dimension describes users connections to other OSN users within a context. A relation can be characterized in terms of level of trust, describing the tie strength between the user and a contact.

4.2   Applying Contextual Constraints in Priamos

Based on *Time* and *Relations*, we introduce three types of contextual constraints for our access control component, whereas additional constraints can easily be added. Note that (as in the real world) people can store or simply remember personal information while available. Thus these constraints do not aim at preventing a contact from accessing and copying personal information while available but rather at increasing the transaction costs to do so.

Temporal Constraints (Time). In the real world, a situation exists only at a specific point in time and personal information shared in this situation is usually ephemeral [18]. In order to transfer this real world concept to OSNs, we introduce two types of temporal constraints: Expiry date and time period. While the former sets a specific date until which a personal attribute is accessible, the latter specifies a timeframe for granting access.

Quantitative Constraints (Relations). A common motivation for joining OSNs is to build new relationships but at the same time, users are afraid of stalking and cyberbulling [9]. To resolve this paradox, we propose to quantitatively constrain access to personal attributes by allowing the user to set the number of granted access requests per contact and per attribute before access is denied.

Social Constraints (Relations). In addition, the binary conception of friendship of most OSNs does not reflect the different tie strengths of relationships in the real world [18]. To overcome this shortcoming of flat relationships, we propose to assign a trust value (specified by the user and representing the tie strength) to each contact and constrain access to personal attributes based on this trust value.

4.3   Context-Aware Access Control in Priamos

To implement the previously defined contextual constraints, we adapt the Core RBAC standard [11] in Figure 4 using the notation of OSNs (e.g. contacts and personal attributes). For the sake of simplicity, we do not consider sessions and read access is the only operation available. A major difference to the Core RBAC model lies in the role-permissions assignment relationship. In the Core RBAC model, permissions are statically assigned to a role, i.e. each role member has the same permissions. Likewise, in our model each contact that is member of a role (corresponds to groups in OSNs) is assigned a set of permissions. However this set of permissions is additionally constrained by contextual parameters at runtime, arriving at a constrained permission set.

Contextual Constraint Specification. Contextual constraints are specified while defining access rights for personal attributes (Step 1 in Section 3.3 and implementation in Figure 5). We define three different sources of contextual information, whereupon access permissions can be further restricted, namely *Contacts*, *Roles*, and *Personal Attributes* (Figure 4). For each *Contact*, the user specifies a trust value (ranging from 0.0 - 1.0) that represents the tie strength of

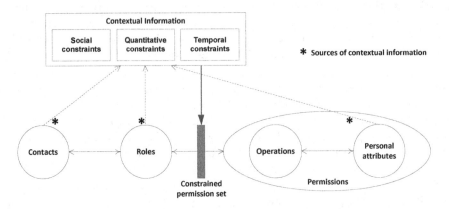

Fig. 4. Context-aware access control model, based on the Core RBAC model [11]

this relationship. Additionally, the minimum required trust value to access a single *Personal Attribute* (or a set of attributes representing an identity facet) can be assigned (**social constraints**). To improve usability, a default trust value can be assigned to a *Role* that is inherited by each role member if no separate trust value has been assigned. Besides, Priamos allows for specifying the maximum number of permitted access requests for each *Contact* and *Personal Attributes*, i.e. the visibility of an identity facet can be limited in terms of pageviews, e.g. to prevent stalking (**quantitative constraints**). Finally, **temporal constraints** can be specified for a single *Personal Attribute* or a whole identity facet. The user can set an availability period for personal attributes and specify an expiration date, after which access is denied.

Contextual Constraint Enforcement. To effectively enforce access control policies and contextual constraints, each contact must authenticate with the user's Priamos instance (A1 in Figure 3). We employ an OAuth-based authentication for our implementation (see Section 5) which is completely handled in the background by the browser plugin. After authentication, the contact's role is selected and the set of permissions is determined. Role assignment is a prerequisite for access, i.e. each contact must be member of a role to access personal attributes. For each of a contact's requests for personal attributes, contextual parameters are determined at request time (such as the contact's trust level and the attribute's minimum required trust level). Based thereupon, the set of permissions is additionally constrained if one or more requirements are not met. Access is granted if the constrained set of permissions is sufficient for accessing the requested attributes, otherwise access is denied.

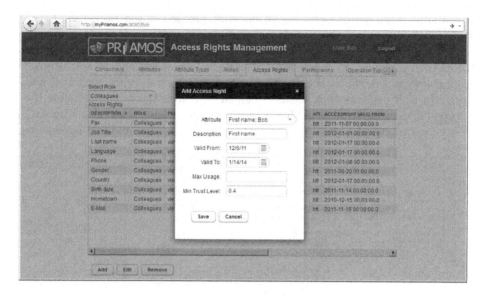

Fig. 5. Priamos IdMS implementation

5 Implementation

We have implemented the proposed Social IdMS with context-aware access control to evaluate the feasibility of our approach. As we envision our IdMS to be either self-hosted or by a trusted third party, it is designed as a Web Application Archive (WAR) File that can easily be deployed at any provider. Our implementation is based on Java EE 6. For the backend we have implemented RESTful webservices with OAuth authentication to access personal information. The client-side browser plugin is implemented for Firefox and integrates a Javascript-based OAuth client to communicate with the Priamos IdMS.

To demonstrate the functionality of our approach, consider a simplified scenario in which Bob employs his Priamos IdMS instance to create various identity facets for different user audiences. One of those audiences are Bob's four work colleagues (Alice, Carol, Dave and Ted) with whom he wants to share only parts of his personal information. Out of all his personal attributes Bob thus selects his *first name*, *last name* and *relationship status* as being visible for the role *work colleagues*. However, Bob additionally restricts access to his relationship status on the basis of a trust value using the Priamos context-aware access control component. Only colleagues with a minimum trust value of 0.8 shall be allowed to access his relationship status. Carol, Dave and Ted are Bob's trusted long-term work colleagues (trust value=1.0). Alice, however, only recently joined Bob's team and thus Bob assigns a lower trust value of 0.5 to her. After defining those constraints, a Base64-encoded URL value is added to Bob's Social Network Profile (e.g. his Facebook profile) using Priamos IdMS. Alice has installed the Priamos Browser-Plugin provided by Bob that contains the required OAuth tokens.

Eventually, Alice visits Bob's social network profile. In the background, the Browser-Plugin detects the Base64-encoded Identity URLs and sends an OAuth request to Bob's Priamos instance (Request in Listing 1.1). Priamos employs the OAuth consumer key and secret to authenticate Alice and to activate the *work colleague* role. Subsequently, the contextual constraints are evaluated and access to Bob's relationship status is denied as Alice's trust level is below the required minimum trust level of 0.8. Priamos' response (Response in Listing 1.1) thus contains only the remaining two attributes (Bobs' first and last name).

Identity request (OAuth)

```
GET /resources/Bob/attributes HTTP/1.1
Host: myPriamos.com:8080
Authorization: OAuth realm="http://myPriamos.com:8080/resources/Bob/attributes/",
    oauth_consumer_key="e856c3ec6c32b6b603c87c4286160657",
    oauth_token="4f9377815b41b34e7704038cc823d20e",
    oauth_nonce="9BiRV7",
    oauth_timestamp="1325521195",
    oauth_signature_method="HMAC-SHA1",
    oauth_version="1.0",
    oauth_signature="g0qaRUpJUaAHjvQCqkc0sLqFK9w"
```

Identity response (JSON format)

```
{ "oauth_consumer_key":"e856c3ec6c32b6b603c87c4286160657",
  "AttributeSet":[
  { "axSchemaURI":"http://axschema.org/namePerson/first",
    "value":"Bob",
    "label":"First name"
  },
  { "axSchemaURI":"http://axschema.org/namePerson/last",
    "value":"Dylan",
    "label":"Last name"}
  ]}
```

Listing 1.1. OAuth-based identity request and response

6   Conclusions

Currently, OSNs users are confronted with the dilemma that fully exploiting the benefits of OSNs requires to increasingly provide personal data to commercially-driven service providers and rely on their insufficient tools to manage identities consistently. To improve privacy, in this paper we argued for a paradigm shift where identity information is decoupled from other OSN services and managed in a user-controlled environment. Therefore, we introduced Priamos, an architecture for autonomous management of social identities, that (1) prevents centralized OSN providers from accessing personal information, (2) allows for more accurate sharing of personal information by considering context information and (3) enforcing these decisions. For the future, we envision OSN service providers to focus on value-added services to attract users and provide interfaces to seamlessly integrate their users' social identity management systems to access infrastructural services, such as for the purpose of user discovery. Moreover the use of such external social identity management systems allows individuals to use their personal data for multiple purposes and application domains beyond OSNs like expert search systems and collaboration platforms. With users being faced to deal with identity management tasks it seems that user privacy does not come without expenses. At least the effort users bring up on managing their identity is well spent considering that they remain in control of their data and that they are even able to use it for multiple purposes. With regard to the effort users have to spent usability aspects shift into focus. Ideally users should be given a hand to manage their identity in an intuitive and less time consuming manner whilst supporting them in access control decisions by the provision of tools that assist the user (e.g. by offering recommendations) and that have been crafted with usability aspects in mind. From a technical point, future work will focus on automatically adjusting the contacts' trust values over time and to support the user in defining an online situation by suggesting proper contacts and an appropriate identity facet addressing the need for usabillity enhancements.

Acknowledgments. The research leading to these results is partly funded by the European Union within the PADGETS project under grant agreement no. 248920. Any opinion, findings, and conclusions or recommendations expressed in this material are those of the authors and do not necessarily reflect the views of the European Union.

References

1. Ali, B., Villegas, W., Maheswaran, M.: A trust based approach for protecting user data in social networks. In: Proceedings of the 2007 Conference of the Center for Advanced Studies on Collaborative Research, pp. 288–293. ACM (2007)
2. Beato, F., Kohlweiss, M., Wouters, K.: Scramble! Your Social Network Data. In: Fischer-Hübner, S., Hopper, N. (eds.) PETS 2011. LNCS, vol. 6794, pp. 211–225. Springer, Heidelberg (2011)
3. van den Berg, B., Leenes, R.: Audience Segregation in Social Network Sites. In: Proceedings of the 2010 IEEE Second International Conference on Social Computing, SOCIALCOM 2010, pp. 1111–1116. IEEE Computer Society (2010)
4. Bortoli, S., Palpanas, T., Bouquet, P.: Decentralised social network management. International Journal of Web Based Communities 7(3), 276–297 (2011)
5. Boyd, D.: Taken Out of Context: American Teen Sociality in Networked Publics. Ph.D. thesis, University of California, Berkeley (2008)
6. Camenisch, J., Fischer-Hübner, S., Rannenberg, K. (eds.): Privacy and Identity Management for Life. Springer (2011)
7. Carminati, B., Ferrari, E., Heatherly, R., Kantarcioglu, M., Thuraisingham, B.: A semantic web based framework for social network access control. In: Proceedings of the 14th ACM Symposium on Access Control Models and Technologies, p. 177. ACM, New York (2009)
8. Carminati, B., Ferrari, E., Heatherly, R., Kantarcioglu, M., Thuraisingham, B.: Semantic web-based social network access control. Computers & Security 30(2-3), 108–115 (2011)
9. Doruer, N., Menevi, I., Eyyam, R.: What is the motivation for using Facebook? Procedia - Social and Behavioral Sciences 15, 2642–2646 (2011)
10. Edwards, L., Brown, I.: Data Control and Social Networking: Irreconcilable Ideas? Harboring Data: Information Security, Law, and the Corporation, 202–228 (2009)

11. Ferraiolo, D.F., Sandhu, R., Gavrila, S., Kuhn, D.R., Chandramouli, R.: Proposed NIST standard for role-based access control. ACM Transactions on Information and System Security 4(3), 224–274 (2001)
12. Goffman, E.: The Presentation of Self in Everyday Life. Anchor (1959)
13. Kruk, S.R., Grzonkowski, S., Gzella, A., Woroniecki, T., Choi, H.-C.: D-FOAF: Distributed Identity Management with Access Rights Delegation. In: Mizoguchi, R., Shi, Z.-Z., Giunchiglia, F. (eds.) ASWC 2006. LNCS, vol. 4185, pp. 140–154. Springer, Heidelberg (2006)
14. Leenes, R.: Context Is Everything Sociality and Privacy in Online Social Network Sites. In: Bezzi, M., Duquenoy, P., Fischer-Hübner, S., Hansen, M., Zhang, G. (eds.) Privacy and Identity. IFIP AICT, vol. 320, pp. 48–65. Springer, Heidelberg (2010)
15. Mostarda, M., Zani, F., Palmisano, D., Tripodi, S.: Towards an OpenID-based solution to the Social Network Interoperability problem. In: W3C Workshop on the Future of Social Networking (2009)
16. Netter, M., Riesner, M., Pernul, G.: Assisted Social Identity Management - Enhancing Privacy in the Social Web. In: Proceedings of the 10th International Conference on Wirtschaftsinformatik (2011)
17. Nissenbaum, H.: Privacy in Context: Technology, Policy, and the Integrity of Social Life. Stanford Law Books (2010)
18. Peterson, C.: Losing Face: An Environmental Analysis of Privacy on Facebook. SSRN eLibrary (2010)
19. Pettenati, M.C., Ciofi, L., Parlanti, D., Pirri, F., Giuli, D.: An Overlay Infrastructural Approach for a Web-Wide Trustworthy Identity and Profile Management. In: Salgarelli, L., Bianchi, G., Blefari-Melazzi, N. (eds.) Trustworthy Internet, pp. 43–58. Springer (2011)
20. Tufekci, Z.: Can You See Me Now? Audience and Disclosure Regulation in Online Social Network Sites. Bulletin of Science, Technology & Society 28(1), 20–36 (2008)
21. Ziegele, M., Quiring, O.: Privacy in Social Network Sites. In: Trepte, S., Reinecke, L. (eds.) Privacy Online. Perspectives on Privacy and Self-Disclosure in the Social Web, pp. 175–189. Springer (2011)
22. Zimmermann, A., Lorenz, A., Oppermann, R.: An Operational Definition of Context. In: Kokinov, B., Richardson, D.C., Roth-Berghofer, T.R., Vieu, L. (eds.) CONTEXT 2007. LNCS (LNAI), vol. 4635, pp. 558–571. Springer, Heidelberg (2007)

A Prototype for Enforcing Usage Control Policies Based on XACML*

Aliaksandr Lazouski, Fabio Martinelli, and Paolo Mori

Istituto di Informatica e Telematica
Consiglio Nazionale delle Ricerche
G. Moruzzi 1, Pisa, Italy
{aliaksandr.lazouski,fabio.martinelli,paolo.mori}@iit.cnr.it

Abstract. The OASIS XACML standard emerged as a pure declarative language allowing to express access control. Later, it was enriched with the concept of obligations which must be carried out when the access is granted or denied. In our previous work, we presented U-XACML, an extension of XACML that allows to express *Usage Control (UCON)*. In this paper we propose an architecture for the enforcement of U-XACML, a model for retrieving mutable attributes, and a proof-of-concept implementation of the authorization framework based on web-services.

1 Introduction

The *Usage Control (UCON)* model [4,5] extends traditional *Access Control* models to address the issues of modern distributed computing systems. UCON introduces new features in the decision process, such as the mutable attributes of subjects, objects, and environment, and the continuity of policy enforcement to guarantee that the right of a subject to use the resource holds while the access is in progress. Hence, this model can be successfully adopted in case of long-standing accesses to resources, because the access right is continuously re-evaluated during the usage of the resource and the access is interrupted as soon as this right does not hold any more. In recent years UCON has drawn a significant interest from the research community on formalization and enforcement of policies [10].

As an example, the UCON model can be successfully adopted to regulate the usage of virtual resource in the Cloud scenario, such as Virtual Machines running in Infrastructure as a Service (IaaS) Clouds. Usually, these resources are long-standing instances exposed to end-users through a proper interface. For example, a Software as a Service (SaaS) Cloud provider could implement his file storage service on top of IaaS services. In this case, the access of the file storage service provider to the IaaS service could last a very long period of time, even

---

* This work was supported by the EU FP7 projects *Open Computing Infrastructures for Elastic Services* (CONTRAIL) FP7-ICT 257438 and *Network of Excellence on Engineering Secure Future Internet Software Services and Systems* (NESSOS) FP7-ICT 256980.

S. Fischer-Hübner, S. Katsikas, G. Quirchmayr (Eds.): TrustBus 2012, LNCS 7449, pp. 79–92, 2012.

when the access right is not valid any more. Hence, traditional Access Control models, that aim to assure that only allowed principals are granted to access a resource [1] by performing the policy evaluation at the request time only, are not sufficient in this scenario.

In a previous work [2], we defined the U-XACML language, that is an extension of XACML [3] for expressing UCON policies. In this paper, we propose an authorization framework for the enforcement of Usage Control policies written in U-XACML and we present a proof-of-concept implementation of the proposed framework based on the web-service technology, along with some performance tests that show promising results. Also, we introduce the *attribute retrieval policy* for collecting fresh values of mutable attributes. This policy is separated from the Usage Control one because attribute retrieval is usually environment-dependent whereas the Usage Control policy is application-independent and encodes high-level security goals.

The paper is structured as follows. Section 2 gives basic notes on Usage Control, a running policy example, and describes the U-XACML language. Section 3 addresses the retrieval of mutable attributes. Section 4 describes the architecture of the prototype, its implementation details and the performance tests. Section 5 summarizes related work. Section 6 concludes the paper.

2 Usage Control

Figure 1 shows on the time axis the main difference between the traditional Access Control models and the UCON model [4,5]. The subject requests to execute a long-standing action over a resource by sending the *"tryaccess"* request. Access control models authorize the execution of the access at request time, i.e., before it starts. Assuming that the authorization framework allows to execute the access, it replies with the *"permitaccess"*. Traditional Access Control models do not perform any other check from this point on. The UCON model, instead, performs security checks after the access is started. The continuous policy enforcement starts when the system, which executes the access, notifies the authorization framework by sending the *"startaccess"* message. This message identifies that a new usage session has been created and the access is ongoing. Then, the authorization framework *continuously* re-evaluates the access decision. If the policy is not satisfied any more at some point of time, the authorization framework issues the *"revokeaccess"* and forces the system to terminate the access. If the policy always holds, the system notifies the authorization framework by sending the *"endaccess"* message when the action finishes its execution. Either the usage session is revoked or ended, Usage Control concludes by performing post attribute updates and post obligations specified by the policy.

Continuity of control is a specific feature of the Usage Control model intended to deal with mutable attributes of the requesting subject, of the accessed resource and of the execution environment. Attributes change values as a result of the access execution or caused by other uncontrollable factors. Continuous control implies that policies are re-evaluated each time the attributes change their values.

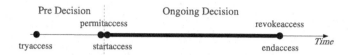

Fig. 1. Access and Usage Control

Access decisions in Usage Control are based on *authorizations* (predicates over subject and object attributes), *conditions* (predicates over environmental attributes), and *obligations* (actions that must be performed along with an ongoing access). Authorizations and conditions constrain behaviour of mutable attributes qualified in terms of time, e.g. "a subject reputation must be *always* above a given threshold during the access". The access evaluation is based only on the current values of attributes. This allows to define a mutable attribute as a *bag* in the XACML terms and model authorizations and conditions as the XACML's `<Condition>`. Obligations in Usage Control do not correspond exactly to the obligations in the XACML language. Also, attribute updates are not specified in XACML. These concepts should be added to the XACML language in order to support the full expressiveness of UCON.

2.1 Running Policy Example

Let us consider the following security policies explained in the natural language which govern operations on Virtual Machines (VM) in Cloud IaaS scenario and include both traditional Access Control and Usage Control:

– **Access Control authorizations (Usage Control pre authorizations):** A user is allowed to access to an endorsed VM, i.e., the VM certified by the producing authority;
– **Usage Control ongoing authorizations:** Users are allowed to run VMs as long as they have a high reputation and the balance of their e-wallet is positive;
– **Usage control ongoing obligations:** During the VM execution, the system sends notifications when the balance of user's e-wallet is below a threshold. These notifications repeat every 30 minutes unless the balance is recharged;
– **Usage control post updates:** If the VM execution was ended by the user, the reputation should be increased, while if the access was revoked by the authorization framework, the reputation should be decreased.

2.2 U-XACML Approach

Figure 2 shows the U-XACML policy schema that is obtained by enhancing the standard XACML language with the constructs to express when the conditions and obligations must be evaluated. To represent continuous control, U-XACML specifies when the access decision must be taken through the clause

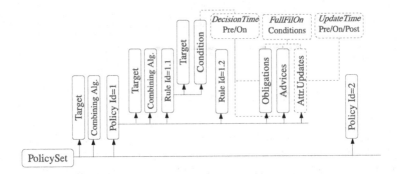

Fig. 2. U-XACML Policy Model

`DecisionTime` in the `<Condition>` elements (the admitted values are `pre` and `on` denoting, respectively, pre and ongoing decisions), and the `TriggerOn` clause in the `<Obligation>` elements. To represent attribute updates, we defined a new element, `<AttrUpdates>`, that contains a collection of single `<AttrUpdate>` elements to specify update actions. The time when the update is performed is stated by the element `UpdateTime` that has values of `pre`, `on` and `post` updates. For further details on the policy language, we refer the reader to [2].

3   Mutable Attributes Retrieval

Here and in the following, the meaning of the term "attribute" is the same as defined in UCON [4], i.e., properties paired to subjects, objects, or environment. The *role* or the *reputation* are examples of subject's attribute. The enforcement of Usage Control implies a policy re-evaluation each time when mutable attributes change their values. Catching all attribute changes is a challenging issue, usually impossible. We introduce a concept of *attribute retrieval policy* which specifies when to collect fresh attribute values and trigger the access re-evaluation.

Following the XACML approach, we propose an XML-based language to express retrieval policies. The `AttributeRetrieval` is a top-level element in the policy schema which aggregates `Target` and `Prerequisites` elements:

```
<xs:element name="AttributeRetrieval"/>
<xs:complexType name="AttributeRetrivalType"/>
    <xs:sequences><xs:element ref="Target"><xs:element ref="Prerequisites"></xs:sequences>
<xs:complexType>
```

The `Target` element specifies identifiers of mutable attributes which the retrieval policy is intended to collect. The `AttributeValue` element taken from the XACML policy schema, contains a literal value of an attribute identifier:

```
<xs:element name="Target"/>
<xs:complexType name="TargetType"/>
    <xs:sequences><xs:element ref="xacml:AttributeValue"></xs:sequences><xs:complexType>
```

The `Prerequisites` element includes a conjunctive sequence of conditions which must be satisfied before executing an attribute retrieval and the subsequent

```
<AttributeRetrieval>
 <Target><AttributeValue> u-xacml:subject:reputation </AttributeValue></Target>
 <Prerequisites>
  <Condition>
   <Apply FunctionId="dataTime-greater-then">
    <AttributeDesignator Category="environment" AttributeId="env:current-time"/>
    <Apply FunctionId="addTimeDuration">
     <AttributeDesignator Category="local" AttributeId="um:last-retrieval-time"/>
     <AttributeDesignator Category="configuration" AttributeId="time-between-queries"/>
    </Apply></Apply>
   </Condition>
 </Prerequisites>
</AttributeRetrieval>
```

Fig. 3. Attribute Retrieval Policy

re-evaluation of a usage policy. The prerequisites are done when *all* conditions
are evaluated to true:

```
<xs:element name="Prerequisites"/>
<xs:complexType name="PrerequisitesType"/>
  <xs:sequences><xs:element ref="xacml:Condition"></xs:sequences><xs:complexType>
```

The Condition element is taken from the XACML policy schema and it expresses a boolean function evaluating the environmental factors, configuration
settings and local variables.

Figure 3 shows an example of the retrieval policy which states that subject's reputation must be refreshed when x minutes passed since the last attribute retrieval,
where x is represented by the configuration setting time-between-queries. The
new attribute retrieval is performed when the current time is greater than the sum
of the time-between-queries with the time of the last retrieval, that is stored in
the local variable um:last-retrieval-time. This variable is updated every time
when a new value of the attribute is collected.

The attribute retrieval policy is enforced when the access is in progress. When
the conditions in the policy hold, the PIP is invoked to collect fresh attributes,
that are then pushed to the PDP for the access re-evaluation.

4   Prototype

This section presents the architecture and the implementation details of our
prototype of authorization framework supporting the enforcement of U-XACML
policies.

4.1   Architecture and Work-Flow Model

The authorization framework works by intercepting every access request (e.g.,
Virtual Machines creation, suspension, reactivation and disposal in the IaaS
Cloud scenario) determining whether the request is allowed in accordance with
security policies, and enforcing the access decision by executing or aborting the
request. While the access is in progress (e.g., a Virtual Machine is running) the

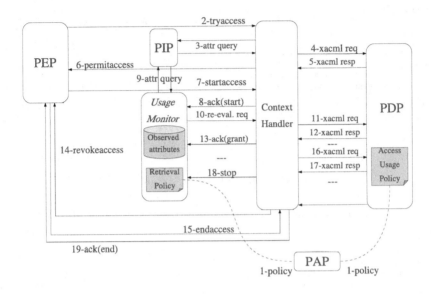

Fig. 4. U-XACML Policy Enforcement Architecture

authorization framework should be able to terminate the access and release the resource when the security policy is violated. Figure 4 shows the main components of the authorization framework's architecture. As most authorization systems [11,3], the main components are:

- *Policy Decision Point* (PDP) evaluates security policies based on the attribute values that have been included in the request;
- *Policy Enforcement Points* (PEPs) are embedded in the components of the framework that implement accesses to resources. They intercept access requests and grants or denies the access based on the decisions provided by the PDP. Moreover, PEPs are also in charge of interrupting access that are in progress to enforce a revocation decision provided by the PDP;
- *Policy Information Point* (PIP) manages *real attribute values*, and provides facilities for its storing, updating, retrieving, and delivery to the PDP;
- *Policy Administrative Point* (PAP) provides and manages security policies;
- *Context Handler* (CH) converts messages sent among components in the proper format. It is also the front-end of the authorization system, since it mediates the message exchanges with the PEPs;
- *Usage Monitor* (UM) is the main novelty with respect to the XACML architecture. This component implements the ongoing decision process by collecting fresh attribute values, and triggering the policy re-evaluation. The strategy that specifies when the new attribute values have to be collected is described by the attribute retrieval policy. The Usage Control policy re-evaluation is triggered only if the values of the attributes that have been collected are different from the ones stored in the UM cache.

The enforcement of access control is the same as described by XACML and without loss of generality we present here the simplest way to enforce it. Our authorization framework operates enforcing Usage Control policies as follows:

1. The PAP is exploited to create policies for Usage Control and attributes retrieval and makes them available for the PDP and the UM respectively;
2. The PEP intercepts the access request R_A and sends the "tryaccess" message to the CH;
3. The CH pulls from the PIP the attributes concerning the subject S_A and the resource O_A involved in R_A;
4. The CH constructs the XACML request exploiting R_A and the attributes retrieved in the previous step, and sends it to the PDP;
5. The PDP evaluates the security policy rules concerning traditional access control rules, and returns the XACML response to the CH;
6. The CH translates the PDP response and replies to the PEP. Let us assume that the response is "permitaccess". Hence, the PEP starts the access A;
7. The PEP notifies the CH that a new usage session was created and the access has started;
8. The CH activates a new instance of UM for A, and it forwards the request to this UM instance that, in turn, starts the continuous policy enforcement by monitoring the attributes related to S_A and O_A;
9. The UM enforces the retrieval policies related to the attributes of S_A and O_A to decide when fresh values must be pulled from the PIP;
10. If the observed values are different form the cached ones, the UM triggers the policy re-evaluation sending the request to the CH (go to the next step). Instead, if no changes in the attribute values are detected, the UM repeats the previous step by enforcing the attribute retrieval policy again and deciding when fresh attributes values must be pulled from the PIP;
11. The CH constructs the XACML request to re-evaluate the right of executing A and sends it to the PDP;
12. The PDP evaluates the security policy rules concerning ongoing control rules, and returns the XACML response to the CH;
13. If the response is "deny", see the step 14. Otherwise, "grant" is received and the access can be continued, thus the CH translates it and replies to the UM. Steps 9-13 are repeated until either the PDP returns "deny" or the PEP sends the "endaccess" message: in this case go to the step 15;
14. If the PDP returns "deny", the CH sends the access revocation message to the PEP. Then, the PEP terminates A;
15. The PEP also may stop the session due to the normal ending of access. The PEP notifies the CH by sending the "endaccess" message;
16. The CH constructs the XACML request to the PDP;
17. The PDP evaluates the security policy rules concerning end of access, and returns the XACML response to the CH. The response could specify some post obligations or post updates that must be executed;
18. The CH destroys the running UM instance which monitors A;
19. Finally, the CH responses to the PEP. This message includes the request for executing post obligations, if any.

```
<PolicySet PolicyCombiningAlgId="deny-override" ... >
 <!-- - Access control Policy --!><Policy ... ><Rule Effect="Permit" ... >
    <Target><AttributeValue> TRYACCESS </AttributeValue> ... AttributeId="action-id" ... </Policy>

 <!-- Usage control: authorizations and revocation --!>
 <PolicySet PolicyCombiningAlgId="permit-override" ... >
   <Target><AttributeValue> STARTACCESS </AttributeValue> ... AttributeId="action-id" ...
   <!-- permit part --!><Policy RuleCombiningAlgId="permit-override"... >
     <Rule Effect="Permit" ... <Condition> ... </Condition></Rule>
     <ObligationExpressions ... ObligationId="call-me-back" FulfillOn="permit" ... </Policy>

   <!-- deny part --!><Policy RuleCombiningAlgId="deny-override"... >
     <Rule Effect="Deny" ... > ... </Rule>
     <ObligationExpressions ... ObligationId="post-update" FulfillOn="deny" ... </Policy>
 </PolicySet>

 <!-- Usage control: ongoing obligations and updates --!>
 <Policy RuleCombiningAlgId="permit-override"... >
   <Target><AttributeValue> STARTACCESS </AttributeValue> ... AttributeId="action-id" ...
   <Rule Effect="Permit" ... > ... </Rule>
   <ObligationExpressions ... ObligationId="ongoing-update" FulfillOn="permit" ... </Policy>

 <!-- Usage control: end of access --!><Policy RuleCombiningAlgId="permit-override"... >
   <Target><AttributeValue> ENDACCESS </AttributeValue> ... AttributeId="action-id" ...
   <Rule Effect="Permit" ... ></Rule>
   <ObligationExpressions ... ObligationId="post-update" FulfillOn="permit" ... </Policy>
</PolicSet>
```

Fig. 5. Access and Usage Control Policy in XACML Syntax

4.2 Implementing U-XACML Policies Exploiting XACML

The implementation of the framework for the enforcement of the U-XACML policies exploits existing engines for the evaluation of XACML policies. Since U-XACML is based on XACML, we implemented the continuous control combining original XACML constructs. The basic idea is to insert a looping construct of the access re-evaluation inside XACML's obligations. An obligation is an action which must be executed by the PEP along with the enforcement of an access decision. The semantics of obligations is not fixed by XACML, thus it can be exploited to encode any kind of duties. Hence, we exploit obligations for implementing Usage Control. In particular, the PDP evaluates the policy and, in case of an ongoing condition, it sends the access decision along with a so-called "call-me-back" obligation which forces the PEP to call the PDP again to trigger the access right re-evaluation. This routine is repeated while the policy is satisfied and the access does not terminate. When the policy is violated, instead, no "call-me-back" obligation is returned.

We represent a U-XACML policy exploiting a tuple of 5 XACML policies. One of these policies encodes the traditional access control (i.e., pre decisions), while the other policies express Usage Control features and represent: (U-OAC) ongoing authorization and conditions, which must be satisfied during the usage; (U-OBU) ongoing obligations and attribute updates; (U-PBUR) post-obligations and updates in a case of access revocation; (U-PBUE) post-obligation and updates in a case of a normal termination. Figure 5 contains an overall UCON policy structure in XACML syntax. Notice, that non-critical elements are omitted due to space limitation. This structure should be preserved and a policy should abide the following requirements:

- Access control policy should include all predicates over static attributes since there is no need to re-evaluate these predicates when the access is ongoing;
- Usage policy for ongoing authorizations and conditions should be modeled as a policy set with two sub-policies: permitting and denying. The permitting policy, i.e., the U-OAC policy, should contain a "call-me-back" obligation, whereas the denying policy, i.e., the U-PBUR policy, includes post-updates and post-obligations that must be executed in a case of a policy revocation. Ongoing authorizations may be placed in any sub-policy. If a policy designer is more comfortable to specify conditions which must always hold during the access then these conditions are included in the permitting policy, and if it is more intuitive to express negative rules - to the denying policy;
- Usage Control policy for end of access, i.e., the U-PBUE policy, should contain no conditions in a policy rule and the rule's effect should be "permit". The policy applicability is defined by the action attribute "action-id" with the value equals to "endaccess";
- Obligations returned to the PEP should be a composition of obligations whose "FulfillOn" attribute and the effect of a policy evaluation matches with the effect returned after the evaluation of the overall policy.

We transformed policies written in U-XACML to XACML using the XSLT technology[1]. In fact, this transformation adheres to the requirements listed here and the final policy ported for the evaluation looks like one given in Figure 5. Since we implemented U-XACML policies exploiting standard XACML constructs, one might question whether U-XACML is really needed. The main reason is that the U-XACML policy allows to naturally express Usage Control features with specific constructs, hence it is more user-friendly. System administrators can transform their access control policies written in XACML in Usage Control policies with a minimal effort. They should identify which of the conditions and obligations in their access control policies must hold during the usage of the resource, and insert the clause `DecisionTime="on"` in the XACML element that declares these conditions and obligations.

Moreover, the proposed use of the original XACML constructs for implementing Usage Control has some drawbacks. Firstly, the PEP, besides being responsible for the enforcement of the PDP decisions, is also in charge of iteratively triggering the PDP for the policy re-evaluation. Secondly, a "call-me-back" obligation may contain a policy-sensitive data and its disclosure is unwanted. Therefore, we introduced the UM, a new component, which enforces the call-me-back obligation by retrieving fresh attributes. The prototype given in this paper has a simple implementation of Usage Control which is based on standard techniques and shows a relatively good performance.

---

[1] http://xml.apache.org/xalan-j

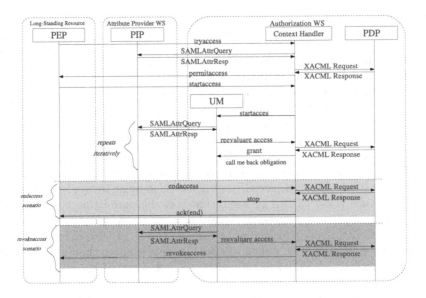

Fig. 6. A Sequence Diagram of Access and Usage Control Enforcement

4.3   Prototype Implementation

The core of our framework is the *authorization service* which implements functionality of the UM, the CH, the PDP, the PAP, and it was realized exploiting the web service technology (see Figure 6). An instance of the authorization service is created per an instance of the usage session. The service instance is destroyed when the violation of the policy happens or the usage session ends normally. This is a preliminary implementation of the framework, where all concurrent usage sessions run in parallel and their monitors do not cooperate on attributes retrieval.

We exploited the Sun's XACML engine[2] for implementing the PDP. This engine evaluates access and usage policies. At this stage, we do not provide an engine for the evaluation of the attribute retrieval policy. We leave it for the future work. Instead, in the current implementation we provide the possibility to retrieve all attributes repeatedly, waiting a time interval (e.g., every 10 seconds).

The PIP manages real attributes and provides interfaces to query their values. The PIP was realized as a web service and its clients are the authorization service and the PEP. The PIP communicates over HTTP/SOAP and accepts the *SAML attribute queries* as requests and replies with the *SAML assertions*. We used the OpenSAML2.0 Extension Library[3] to support the SAML profile of XACML[4].

The PEP is a process which runs along with the execution of the long-standing action on the resource. The PEP enhanced with Usage Control features should be

[2] http://sunxacml.sourceforge.net
[3] http://www.bccs.uib.no/~hakont/SAMLXACMLExtension
[4] http://saml.xml.org/saml-specifications

powerful to destroy the running action if the authorization service claims about a policy violation or to notify the authorization service if the execution of the action ends normally. We provided a set of Java APIs which the designer of a system should use for the Usage Control support. These APIs implement the communication between the PEP and the CH, the PEP and the PIP with the support of the HTTP/SOAP/SAML-XACML protocol stack. The PEP is the Axis2[5] client of the authorization and attribute provider services. Since the time of the usage session in unbounded, the PEP communicates with the authorization service in *asynchronous* mode which enables the processing of the "startaccess" and "revokeaccess" messages in two different threads. Also, two different transport channels are used to send these messages. The PEP starts the usage session after sending the "startaccess" and idles. Later, when the response from the authorization service about the policy violation arrives, the PEP resumes its execution by destroying the usage session.

Figure 6 presents a sequence diagram for the enforcement of the access and usage policy given in Subsection 2.1. It starts with the access control and the CH is responsible to collect attributes. When the usage sessions begins, the UM becomes in charge for the retrieval of fresh attribute values. When new attribute values violate a security policy, the authorization service informs the PEP and both terminate. In case of normal end of access, the new instance of the authorization service is created to process the "endaccess" request. Before replying to the PEP, this instance stops the primary running instance of the authorization service created on the "startaccess".

4.4   Performance Evaluation

As a Usage Control requires an extra process for each usage session, the performance should be considered. Since this process is outsourced to the authorization service, we measured its performance in the presence of a plenty of running usage sessions. We deployed the authorization and attribute provider services inside Axis2. The server was hosted on a machine with Ubuntu 10 and Java 1.6 support and which has Intel Core 2 Duo 3.16 GHz CPU and 3.4 GB memory.

First, we measured how many instances of the authorization service per second can be created. This gives a number of usage sessions which the PEP can start and be aware that the authorization service will serve them all. The creation of the authorization service instance starts when the PEP sends "startaccess" and lasts until the UM receives the result of the first access reevaluation (i.e., steps 7-13 in Figure 4). We obtained that 47 new usage sessions in average can be created by the authorization service, or approximately 21.5 ms goes for the creation of a single service instance. Although, we experimented with a faster CPU the obtained results shown that our system performs comparably to one given in [12] where the average time per access evaluation only takes 45.3 ms.

Then, we measured the *revocation response time* for a single usage session in dependence on the number of ongoing usage sessions serviced by the

---

[5] http://axis.apache.org/axis2

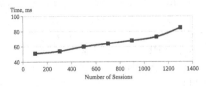
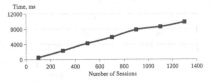

(a) Revocation of a Single Session   (b) Massive Revocation of Sessions

Fig. 7. Performance of Access Revocation

authorization service. The revocation response time defines the period of time passed from the point when the PIP replies to the UM with the attribute value which violates the security policy until the PEP receives the "revokeaccess" (i.e., steps 9-14 in Figure 4). We varied the number of the authorization service instances running concurrently with the test usage session from 100 to 1300. We assume that an execution time of a single session is quite long, thus the authorization service could maintain a large number of concurrent sessions started at different time points. Since the authorization service can create only 47 new sessions per second, the starting time between 1st and 1300th sessions and the minimum execution time of any session should be at least 26 seconds. Figure 7(a) shows the results obtained. We see that the response time of the access revocation is moderate and increases slowly with the growth of the number of concurrently running sessions.

Finally, we measured the revocation time of all sessions whose policies use the same security attribute which changes its value from good to bad and violates the policies. The revocation time of all sessions defines the period of time passed from the point when the first until the last sessions receive the "revokeaccess". We configured the retrieval policy in such a way that the UM refreshes attributes and re-evaluates the usage policy every *10* seconds. Figure 7(b) shows the results obtained. We see that the revocation time of all sessions grows linearly in the number of running sessions.

5   Related Work

Several papers stated that XACML needs extension to capture the continuous policy enforcement [12,8]. Some attempts were done to enforce UCON policies exploiting XACML [9,12,6]. These approaches introduce events reporters that trigger the policy re-evaluation when the access is in progress. Security checks are invoked by the changes of subject, object, and/or environmental attributes. Instead, we assume that the authorization framework is responsible to retrieve fresh attributes. Moreover, they consider what parts of UCON can be modelled in XACML. In contrast, our approach considers how XACML should be extended to capture the continuous control and we introduced the prototype which is capable to deal with the main UCON features. The approach given in [7] proposed to integrate together the attribute retrieval and security policies in a single XACML policy. We, instead, separate them because the attribute retrieval is usually environment-specific while security policies are not and usually encode high-level security goals.

6   Conclusions and Future Work

This paper presented an authorization framework for the enforcement of Usage Control policies expressed with the U-XACML language, along with a web-services based proof-of-concept implementation that, although very simple, showed promising results from the performance point of view. The main advantage of the proposed framework is that it supports U-XACML, thus simplifying significantly the enforcement of Usage Control. As a matter of fact, exploiting U-XACML, system administrators can transform their access control policies written in XACML in Usage Control policies in a straightforward way. In particular, they should identify which of the conditions and obligations in their access control policies must hold during the usage of the resource, and insert the clause `DecisionTime="on"` in the XACML element that declares these conditions and obligations.

Another advantage of the proposed framework is that most of the interactions between the framework components are implemented through standard protocols, thus allowing the substitution of the existing component with enhanced (e.g., more efficient) ones.

We are currently working for refining several aspects of the authorization framework. Firstly, we are working on refining the support for attributes retrieval policies, e.g., we are implementing publish/subscribe retrieval policies. Moreover, we would like move to a *state-full* version of the authorization service implementing an architecture with a single Usage Monitor component that will manage all the ongoing accesses. We believe that these changes will enhance the framework performance and robustness especially in the case of a large number of long lasting concurrent accesses.

References

1. Abadi, M.: Logic in access control. In: Proceedings of the 18th Annual IEEE Symposium on Logic in Computer Science, Washington, DC, USA, p. 228 (2003)
2. Colombo, M., Lazouski, A., Martinelli, F., Mori, P.: A proposal on enhancing XACML with continuous Usage Control features. In: Proceedings of CoreGRID ERCIM Working Group Workshop on Grids, P2P and Services Computing, pp. 133–146. Springer (2010)
3. OASIS XACML TC. eXtensible Access Control Markup Language (XACML) Version 3.0 (2010)
4. Park, J., Sandhu, R.: Towards usage control models: Beyond traditional access control. In: SACMAT 2002: Proceedings of the Seventh ACM Symposium on Access Control Models and Technologies, NY, USA, pp. 57–64 (2002)
5. Zhang, X., Parisi-Presicce, F., Sandhu, R., Park, J.: Formal model and policy specification of usage control. ACM Transactions on Information and System Security (TISSEC) 8(4), 351–387 (2005)

6. Feng, J., Wasson, G., Humphrey, M.: Resource usage policy expression and enforcement in grid computing. In: IEEE/ACM International Workshop on Grid Computing, pp. 66–73 (2007)
7. Gheorghe, G., Crispo, B., Carbone, R., Desmet, L., Joosen, W.: Deploy, Adjust and Readjust: Supporting Dynamic Reconfiguration of Policy Enforcement. In: Kon, F., Kermarrec, A.-M. (eds.) Middleware 2011. LNCS, vol. 7049, pp. 350–369. Springer, Heidelberg (2011)
8. Hafner, M., Memon, M., Alam, M.: Modeling and enforcing advanced access control policies in healthcare systems with Sectet, pp. 132–144 (2008)
9. Katt, B., Zhang, X., Breu, R., Hafner, M., Seifert, J.-P.: A general obligation model and continuity: enhanced policy enforcement engine for usage control. In: SACMAT 2008: Proceedings of the 13th ACM Symposium on Access Control Models and Technologies, New York, USA, pp. 123–132 (2008)
10. Lazouski, A., Martinelli, F., Mori, P.: Usage control in computer security: A survey. Computer Science Review 4(2), 81–99 (2010)
11. Vollbrecht, J., Calhoun, P., Farrell, S., Gommans, L., Gross, G., de Bruijn, B., de Laat, C., Holdrege, M., Spence, D.: AAA authorization framework (2000)
12. Zhang, X., Nakae, M., Covington, M.J., Sandhu, R.: Toward a usage-based security framework for collaborative computing systems. ACM Transactions on Information and System Security (TISSEC) 11(1), 1–36 (2008)

A Conceptual Framework for Trust Models*

Francisco Moyano, Carmen Fernandez-Gago, and Javier Lopez

University of Malaga, Department of Computer Science,
29071 Malaga, Spain
{moyano,mcgago,jlm}@lcc.uma.es

Abstract. During the last twenty years, a huge amount of trust and reputation models have been proposed, each of them with their own particularities and targeting different domains. While much effort has been made in defining ever-increasing complex models, little attention has been paid to abstract away the particularities of these models into a common set of easily understandable concepts. We propose a conceptual framework for computational trust models that will be used for analyzing their features and for comparing heterogeneous and relevant trust models.

1 Introduction

The concept of trust in Computer Science derives from the concept in sociological, psychological and economical environments. The definition of trust is not unique. It may vary depending on the context and the purpose where it is going to be used. Despite it is admitted of paramount importance when considering systems security, a standard definition of trust has not been provided yet. However, it is wide accepted that trust might assist decision-making processes such as those involved in access control schemes.

Reputation and trust are related concepts, although they have different meanings. Reputation is defined by the Concise Oxford Dictionary as 'what is generally said or believed about a person or the character or standing of a thing' while trust is defined as 'the firm belief in the reliability or truth or strength of an entity'. From these definitions we can infer that the concept of reputation is more objective compared to the concept of trust. Actually, both concepts are strongly related as reputation can be used as a means to determine whether an entity can trust another entity [10]. Trust and reputation services assure the trustworthiness on the entities that take part of any system, reducing the uncertainty during the interactions of such entities.

The origins of computational trust date back to the nineties, when Marsh [13] analyzed social and psychological factors that have an influence on trust and replicated this concept in a computational setting. A few years later, Blaze [3] identified trust management as a way to leverage and unify authentication and access control in distributed

---

* This work has been partially funded by the European Commission through the FP7/2007-2013 project NESSoS (www.nessos-project.eu) under grant agreement number 256980, and by the Spanish Ministry of Science and Innovation through the research project ARES (CSD2007-00004) and SPRINT (TIN2009-09237). The first author is funded by the Spanish Ministry of Education through the National F.P.U. Program.

S. Fischer-Hübner, S. Katsikas, G. Quirchmayr (Eds.): TrustBus 2012, LNCS 7449, pp. 93–104, 2012.

settings. These two early contributions show that trust can be conceived in different ways and for different purposes. From these seminal works onwards, different types of trust models have been proposed, with different purposes and targeting different settings. A trust model comprises the set of rules and languages for deriving trust among entities in an automatic or semi-automatic way.

This heterogeneity often leads to confusion as one might easily lose the most relevant concepts that underlie these trust models. This is precisely the motivation for this work. We aim to shed light on computational trust concepts and how they relate to each other. By trust concept or trust-related concept, we refer to any notion that has a high relevance, according to how frequently the notion arises in existing trust models. Our intention is to build the foundations towards the design of a development framework that supports the acommodation of heterogeneous trust and reputation models. We advocate that the identification of the main trust-related concepts can help in the design of such a framework.

Note that, due to space limitations, it is out of the scope of this paper to provide details on existing trust models. For this, the reader is advised to read the surveys considered in this work (see Table 1). We intend to provide the main concepts that are common in most trust management models. In order to achieve this, we have reviewed some of the most relevant surveys that have been written during the last years in the area of trust management. We also considered other relevant works that abstract away from the particularities of different trust models in order to elicitate their commonalities. These works have assisted us in making the following contributions: (i) identification of trust concepts and how they relate to each other; (ii) categorization of trust models into different types; (iii) and elaboration of a conceptual framework onto which it is possible to compare different types of trust models, building on the concepts and relations previously identified.

Table 1. Contributions mainly considered while the elaboration of the conceptual framework for trust

	2000	2005	2006	2007	2008	2009	2011
Surveys	[7]	[24] [19] [21]		[10] [2]	[27]		[28]
Others			[25]			[11]	[22]

The rest of the paper is organized as follows. Section 2 explores several definitions of trust provided during the last years, and it extracts the most important concepts related to it. In Section 3, we categorize trust models and raise their most relevant concepts. We elaborate on these concepts in Section 4 in order to build a conceptual framework onto which to compare some relevant trust models. Finally, Section 5 concludes the paper and provides lines of future research.

2   Trust Definitions Concepts

Many definitions of trust have been provided along the years. This is due to the complexity of this concept, which spans across several areas such as psychology, sociology, economics, law, and more recently, computer science. The vagueness of this term is well represented by the statement "trust is less confident than know, but also more confident than hope" [16]. In this section, we plan to revise the definitions that have been mostly considered in the literature when designing computational trust and reputation models. We advocate that making an effort to understand this term and its implications is crucial if we want to implement meaningful models. On the other hand, understanding trust and reputation allows for a better trust-related concepts identification as well as for building a more comprehensive conceptual framework for trust models comparison. Definitions are presented in chronological order.

Gambetta [6] defines trust as "a particular level of the subjective probability with which an agent will perform a particular action [...] in a context in which it affects our own action". McKnight and Chervany [15] explain that trust is "the extent to which one party is willing to depend on the other party in a given situation with a feeling of relative security, even though negative consequences are possible". For Olmedilla et al. [18], "trust of a party A to a party B for a service X is the measurable belief of A in that B behaves dependably for a specified period within a specified context (in relation to service X)". Ruohomaa and Kutvonen [21] state that trust is "the extent to which one party is willing to participate in a given action with a given partner, considering the risks and incentives involved". Finally, Har Yew [8] defines trust as "a particular level of subjective assessment of whether a trustee will exhibit characteristics consistent with the role of the trustee, both before the trustor can monitor such characteristics (or independently of the trustor's capacity ever to be able to monitor it) and in a context in which it affects the trustor's own behavior".

These definitions are used as an input to build the concepts cloud depicted in Figure 1. There are other relevant definitions, apart from those written above, which contributed to this cloud, although they have not been included due to space limitations. Yet Table 2 summarizes all the definitions considered, which were processed following several rules. A word that appears several times in the same definition is counted just once. We only take into consideration words that mean something by themselves and do not require surrounding words to mean something (e.g. *particular level* does not make sense separately). If two words with the same meaning appear either in plural and singular, it is expressed in singular. Dependability is splitted into security and reliability. Party, agent, entity, trustor and trustee are named as entity. Most words are adjectives and nouns, since they are more meaningful without a context than verbs, but some relevant verbs are considered as well. Assessment is used in place of *quantifiable*, *measurable*, *describable* and alike terms. The resulting concepts were introduced in Wordle[1].

In a glimpse, the figure reveals that entity is the main concept, and this is obvious, given that trust has no sense if there are neither entities that trust nor entities in which to trust. Context appears as the other big concept since trust is very context-dependent. Other important concepts include imprecise concepts such as subjective, belief, willingness or expectation. They show that trust is strongly related to *uncertainty* about an entity's behaviour. Finally, it is important to note that even though the concept of risk is not explicitly present in all the definitions, a careful reading reveals that it is indeed

---

[1] http://www.wordle.net/ is a free online tool to generate words clouds.

Table 2. Trust Definitions

1988	1991	1995	1996	2000	2002	2005	2011
[6]	[4]	[14]	[15]	[7]	[17]	[19] [18] [21]	[28] [8]

Fig. 1. Concepts Cloud for Trust Definitions

implicitly considered in almost all of them. As a wrap-up, trust is beneficial in the presence of uncertainty and risk during the interaction of two entities, which are willing to collaborate and to depend on each other.

3   Trust Models Concepts

Trust models are very hetereogeneous. This heterogeneity depends on many factors such as the trust definition they use or their application domain. In order to provide a conceptual framework for trust models we first establish a classification of them. However, this task is not straightforward and there are many ways to tackle it. We propose the following classification:

- *Decision Models.* Trust management has its origins in these models [3]. They aim to make more flexible access control decisions, simplifying the two-step authentication and authorization process into a one-step trust decision. *Policy models* and *negotiation models* fall into this category. They build on the notions of policies and credentials, restricting the access to resources by means of policies that specify which credentials are required to access them.
- *Evaluation Models.* These models are often referred to as *computational trust*, which has its origin in the work of Marsh [13]. Their intent is to evaluate the reliability (or other similar attribute) of an entity by measuring certain factors that have an influence on trust in the case of *behaviour models*, or by disseminating trust information along trust chains, as it is the case in *propagation models*. An important sub-type of the former are *reputation models*, in which entities use other entities' opinions about a given entity to evaluate their trust on the latter.

Making a classification is important as it eases the extraction of common features between different classes of models. It is not possible (or better said, it is not useful) to compare policy models such as PolicyMaker [3] with a behaviour model such as eBay's reputation system [20], because their nature and workings are very different. However, it makes sense to extract some common features for all types of models. Each type of model exhibits its own features which allow us to identify the most meaningful ones. This leads in turn to a more consistent comparison framework. For the sake of simplicity, we divide our conceptual framework into three concepts blocks. The first block contains concepts that are applicable to any trust model, independently from its type. The next two blocks gather concepts specific to the types of models identified above.

3.1 Common Features

A trust model aims to capture how trust is perceived, computed and transmitted in a computational setting. This setting must have, at least, two entities which have to interact in some way. In any trust setting, an entity plays a role, or even several ones. In the simplest case, these roles are trustor, the entity which places trust, and trustee, the entity on which trust is placed. However, depending on the context and complexity of the model, other roles are possible. For example, an entity can be a witness that informs about its opinion of an entity based on observations or its own experience. Some specializations of trustors and trustees include a requester of a service or resource, the provider of a service or resource, or a trusted third party that issues credentials or gathers feedbacks to compute a centralized reputation score. Once there exist a trustor and a trustee, we say that a trust relationship has been established. In the case of evaluation models, this relationship is tagged by a trust value. This is further discussed in Sections 3.3.

In any trust model, establishing a trust relationship has a purpose. According to Jøsang et al. [10], a trust purpose is an instantiation of any of the following trust classes identified by Grandison and Sloman [7]: access trust, provision trust, identity trust, and infrastructure trust (considering delegation a sub-class of provision trust). The instantiation is due to the fact that trust is context-dependent, one of the most important properties of trust, since it influences all the other concepts, such as the purpose, the type of entities and the role that they can play. Other factors, in addition to the context, that have an influence on trust are the trustee's subjective and objective properties, and the trustor's subjective and objective properties. The reader is advised to read [27] for examples on these properties.

Note that trust can be also conceived as a strong belief about a given property of the trustee. From a theoretical perspective, there would be no purpose under this trust conception. Yet we are interested in trust models from a more pragmatic perspective. Thus, trust in a given property would eventually assist in making a decision for some purpose. For instance, if an entity believes that another entity is competent to encrypt files, it would select the latter among other candidates less qualified (according to the entity's belief). In this example, the purpose will therefore be the provision of an encryption service (i.e. provision trust).

A trust model also makes some assumptions, such as "entities will provide only fair ratings" or "initial trust values are assumed to exist", and might follow different modeling methods, including mathematic, linguistic and graphic. The resulting conceptual model that gathers these concepts is depicted in Figure 2.

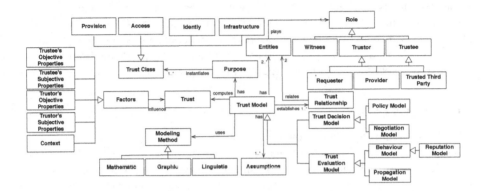

Fig. 2. Common Concepts for Trust Models

3.2   Concepts for Trust Decision Models

As their name suggests, policy models (e.g. PolicyMaker [3]) use policies, which specify the conditions under which access to a resource is granted. These conditions are usually expressed in terms of credentials, signed logical statements that assert that an entity is which it claims to be, or that it is member of a group. Credentials might have different formats, including X.509 certificates and XML. Another concept of policy models is the compliance checker, in charge of checking whether the credentials satisfy the policies. Policies are written in a policy language. Policy languages used by these models might consider policy conflicts resolution. Likewise, the model might also support the search for a credential through credential chains. Some models also include the required components to verify that a credential is valid.

The other type of trust decision models are negotiation models, being TrustBuilder [26] the first representative implementation of them. Trust negotiation models add a protocol, called *negotiation strategy*, during which two entities perform a step-by-step, negotiation-driven exchange of credentials and policies until they decide whether to trust each other or not. This strategy allows protecting the privacy of the entities as policies and credentials are only revealed when required. A later work [11] supports the implementation of different trust negotiation models. Here the authors state that trust negotiation can use evidence types, which represent information about the negotiation process (e.g. certain steps of the negotiation were already accomplished) and have a purpose (e.g. optimization of the negotiation).

The conceptual model for decision models is depicted in Figure 3.

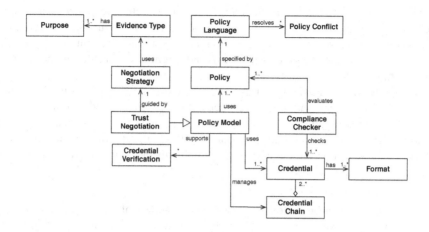

Fig. 3. Concepts for Decision Models

3.3   Concepts for Trust Evaluation Models

Concepts for Behaviour Models. Behaviour models often follow a trust lifecycle with three phases. First, a bootstrapping phase might be required to assign initial trust values to the entities of the system; some other times initial values are assigned. Trust propensity is a concept related to the bootstrapping phase and it refers to the propensity of the model towards high or low trust values in the beginning. Second, monitoring is performed to observe an attribute or set of attributes. Finally, an assessment process is done in order to assign values to the monitored qualities and to aggregate them into a final trust or reputation score.

In behaviour trust, each trust relationship is tagged with a trust value that indicates to what extent the trustor trusts the trustee. This value can be uni-dimensional or multi-dimensional, and according to Jøsang [10], might have different degrees of objectivity and scope. The former refers to whether the measure comes from an entity's subjective judgement or from assessing the trusted party against some formal criteria. The latter specifies whether the measure is done against one factor or against an average of factors.

Trust values are assigned to relations using a trust assessment process, where trust metrics are used to compute them. Trust metrics use variables, such as risk or utility, and combine them in order to yield a final score for the measured attribute(s). Basic examples of attributes are trust and reputation. Attributes can be more specific, such as "quality of service provider" or "reliability of a seller". Trust metrics use computation engines, which may include simple summation or average engines, continous engines, discrete engines, belief engines, bayesian engines, fuzzy engines or flow engines. Jøsang [10] provides a summary of their features.

The source of information that feeds the metric might come from direct experience (either direct interaction or direct observation), sociological and psychological factors. Reputation models use public trust information from other entities to compose a trust evaluation. Reputation models can be centralized, where there is an entity in charge of collecting and distributing reputation information; or distributed, when there is no such an entity and each one has to maintain a record of trust values for other entities, and send this information to the rest of entities. Regardless of which information source is used to compute the trust value, the model might consider how certain or reliable this information is (e.g. credibility of witnesses), and might also consider the concept of time (e.g. how fresh the trust information is).

Finally, a behaviour model might use a game-theoretic approach (as most existing trust models do), where relationships between entities is emphasized in terms of direct experience, feedbacks, utility, risk, and so forth; or it might be socio-cognitive, where mental models of entities are built to consider beliefs in properties. All the concepts discussed in this section are depicted in Figure 4, together with propagation models concepts, which are described next.

Concepts for Propagation Models. Propagation models often assume that several trust relationships have already been established and quantified, although this is not always the case. They aim to create new trust relationships by disseminating the trust values information to other entities. Some models assume that trust is transitive and exploit this property, although transitivity is not, in general, considered as a property that holds for trust [5].

Some behaviour models implement propagation mechanisms. For example, Advocato [12] is a reputation model that allows users of the community to provide a ranking for other users. However, it is also a propagation model, since it allows computing a reputation flow through a network where members are nodes and edges are referrals between nodes.

New trust values are often computed by means of operators, and in several models, we find two of them: a concatenator and an aggregator. The former is used to compute trust along a trust path or chain, whereas the latter aggregates the trust values computed for each path into a final trust value. For example, in [1] the authors use a sequential and a parallel operator in order to compute trust along a path. Subjective logic [9] uses a discounting operator to compute opinions along different trust paths, and a consensus operator to combine them into a final opinion. All the concepts discussed are shown in Figure 4.

4   Conceptual Framework

The concepts identified in the previous section constitute a conceptual framework for the comparison of trust models. As a way to validate our framework, we have chosen a set of relevant trust models that represent the types discussed earlier, namely Policy-Maker [3], TrustBuilder [26], Marsh's model [13], Jøsang's belief model [9], Agudo et al. [1], eBay reputation model [20] and REGRET [23]. Table 3 shows the comparison among these models under the lens of their common features. In Table 4 we compare the trust decision models, whereas trust evaluation models are compared in Table 5. Note that the classification has been made according to the features explicitly presented by the corresponding authors, and that due to the diversity of the models, in some circumstances the classification for some concepts is subjective according to our own intepretation.

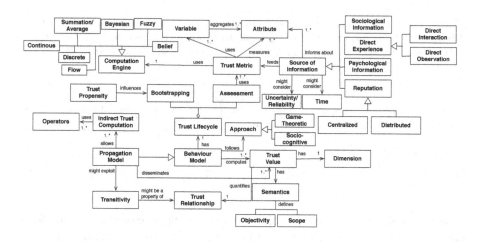

Fig. 4. Concepts for Evaluation Models

Table 3. Common Features Comparison. (*T=trustor/trustee, R/P=requester/provider, W=Witness, TTP = Trusted Third Party, AT=Access Trust, IT=Identity Trust, PT=Provision Trust, PM=Policy Model, NM=Negotiation Model, BM=Behaviour Model, PrM=Propagation Model, RM=Reputation Model*)

Model	Role	Purpose	Type	Method
PolicyMaker	R, P	AT, IT	PM	Linguistic
TrustBuilder	R, P	AT, IT	NM	Linguistic
Marsh's	T, W	AT, PT	BM, PrM	Mathematic
Jøsang's	T, W	AT, PT	RM, PrM	Mathematic
Agudo et al.	T, W	AT, PT	PrM	Graphic, Mathematic
eBay	R, P, W, TTP	PT	RM	Mathematic
REGRET	R, P, W	PT	RM	Mathematic

Table 4. Decision Models Comparison. (*PC=Policy Conflict detection, CC=Credential Chaining support, CV=Credential Verification support, ET=Evidence Type, -=undefined or not explicitly mentioned*)

Model	P. Language	C. Format	PC	CC	CV	Trust Negotiation Strategy	ET
PolicyMaker	PolicyMaker	PGP's sig, X.509 cert	-	-	-	-	-
TrustBuilder	XML, IBM's TPL	X.509 cert	-	✓	✓	✓	-

4.1 Discussion

By observing Table 3, the reader can see that decision models follow a linguistic modeling method, embodied in the policy and credential languages. The purpose of decision models is often either access trust (a provider wants to protect a resource from malicious requesters) or identity trust (trust in a requester is based on its identity).

Table 5. Evaluation Models Comparison. (*DI=Direct Interaction, DO=Direct Observation, SI=Sociological Information, PI=Psychological Information, R=Reputation, C=Centralized, D=Distributed, GT=Game-Theoretic, I.Trust=Indirect Trust, -=undefined or not explicitly mentioned*)

Model	Approach	Dimension	C.Engine	Source of Information					I. Trust	Uncertainty	Time
				DI	DO	SI	PI	R			
Marsh's	GT	1	Continuous	✓	-	-	-	-	✓	-	✓
Jøsang's	GT	3	Belief	✓	-	-	-	D	✓	✓	-
Agudo et al.	-	1	Flow	-	-	-	-	D	✓	-	-
eBay	GT	1	Summation	-	-	-	-	C	-	-	-
REGRET	GT	1	Fuzzy	✓	-	✓	✓	D	-	✓	✓

Regarding evaluation models, their purpose might be either to protect a requester from malicious providers (provision trust), or protect providers from malicious requesters (access trust). The only pure propagation model is Agudo et al. Since it is based on graph theory, it uses a graphic and mathematic modeling method. The rest of models are based on reputation, except for Marsh's, which does not consider this concept.

As the reader might notice from the inspection of Table 5, most existing evaluation models follow a game-theoretic approach, except for Agudo et al., the only pure propagation model. Also, most models provide a single-dimension value, except for Jøsang's, which provides a vector of values that represent belief, disbelief and uncertainty. Semantics have been omitted as all trust models consider trust under some sort of *subjective* judgement (and not as formal measurements) and take into account *general* properties (and not specific ones). Indirect trust indicates whether the model proposes ways to create indirect trust relationships from direct ones by disseminating trust information. Uncertainty specifies whether the model considers uncertainty or reliability in the trust information, whereas time refers to whether the model takes into account this parameter when computing trust values. Note that there is not any model that accommodates all these factors. Also, few models consider sociological factors, such as the role played by the entities in the system or their location. In terms of sources of information, REGRET is one of the most complete models. However, as far as we know, no current models exploit direct observation as a source of information.

5 Conclusion and Future Work

In this paper, we propose a conceptual framework for trust. The purpose of this framework is twofold: (i) the identification of trust concepts that are often present in very heterogeneous types of models, as well as the relationships among these concepts; and (ii) the provision of a foundation onto which to compare different types of trust models.

Given the high heterogeneity of trust models, it is challenging to provide a general framework. We first identify and relate concepts that are general enough to be common to every trust model. After classifying trust models into different types, we then identify and relate a set of concepts that are more closely related to each type of model. Thus, we suggest a two-dimensional framework in which we make a explicit differentiation between common and specific concepts.

As future work, we are interested in exploiting the conceptual framework in order to build a development framework that supports the flexible acommodation of different trust models. We think that the conceptual framework presented in this work can simplify the design of this development framework, by mapping the trust concepts into classes and components. Finding this mapping, in turn, might also assist in refining our conceptual framework.

The development framework will allow designers and developers to implement applications on top of a huge heterogeneity of trust models, according to the application needs. This provides support for the natural inclusion of trust requirements at design time, instead of adding trust as an after-the-fact property, which is the standard nowadays.

References

1. Agudo, I., Fernandez-Gago, C., Lopez, J.: A Model for Trust Metrics Analysis. In: Furnell, S.M., Katsikas, S.K., Lioy, A. (eds.) TrustBus 2008. LNCS, vol. 5185, pp. 28–37. Springer, Heidelberg (2008)
2. Artz, D., Gil, Y.: A survey of trust in computer science and the Semantic Web. Web Semantics: Science, Services and Agents on the World Wide Web 5, 58–71 (2007)
3. Blaze, M., Feigenbaum, J., Lacy, J.: Decentralized trust management. In: IEEE Symposium on Security and Privacy, pp. 164–173 (1996)
4. Boon, S., Holmes, J.: The dynamics of interpersonal trust: Resolving uncertainty in the face of risk, pp. 190–211 (1991)
5. Christianson, B., Harbison, W.S.: Why Isn't Trust Transitive? In: Lomas, M. (ed.) Security Protocols 1996. LNCS, vol. 1189, pp. 171–176. Springer, Heidelberg (1997)
6. Gambetta, D.: Can we trust trust? In: Trust: Making and Breaking Cooperative Relations, pp. 213–237. Basil Blackwell (1988)
7. Grandison, T., Sloman, M.: A survey of trust in internet applications. IEEE Communications Surveys & Tutorials 3(4), 2–16 (2000)
8. Yew, C.H.: Architecture Supporting Computational Trust Formation. PhD thesis, University of Western Ontario, London, Ontario (2011)
9. Jøsang, A.: A logic for uncertain probabilities. International Journal of Uncertainty, Fuzziness and Knowledge-Based Systems 9(3), 279–311 (2001)
10. Jøsang, A., Ismail, R., Boyd, C.: A survey of trust and reputation systems for online service provision. Decision Support Systems 43(2), 618–644 (2007)
11. Lee, A.J., Winslett, M., Perano, K.J.: TrustBuilder2: A Reconfigurable Framework for Trust Negotiation. In: Ferrari, E., Li, N., Bertino, E., Karabulut, Y. (eds.) IFIPTM 2009. IFIP AICT, vol. 300, pp. 176–195. Springer, Heidelberg (2009)
12. Levien, R.: Attack Resistant Trust Metrics. PhD thesis, University of California at Berkeley (2004)
13. Marsh, S.: Formalising Trust as a Computational Concept. PhD thesis, University of Stirling (April 1994)
14. Mayer, R.C., Davis, J.H., David Schoorman, F.: An integrative model of organizational trust. Academy of Management Review 20(3), 709–734 (1995)
15. Harrison McKnight, D., Chervany, N.L.: The meanings of trust. Technical report, University of Minnesota, Management Information Systems Research Center (1996)
16. Miller, K.W., Voas, J., Laplante, P.: In Trust We Trust. Computer 43, 85–87 (2010)
17. Mui, L., Mohtashemi, M., Halberstadt, A.: A computational model of trust and reputation, pp. 280–287 (2002)

18. Olmedilla, D., Rana, O.F., Matthews, B., Nejdl, W.: Security and trust issues in semantic grids. In: Proceedings of the Dagsthul Seminar, Semantic Grid: The Convergence of Technologies, vol. 5271 (2005)
19. Ramchurn, S.D., Huynh, D., Jennings, N.R.: Trust in multi-agent systems. The Knowledge Engineering Review 19(01), 1–25 (2005)
20. Resnick, P., Zeckhauser, R.: Trust among strangers in Internet transactions: Empirical analysis of eBay's reputation system. In: Baye, M.R. (ed.) The Economics of the Internet and E-Commerce. Advances in Applied Microeconomics, vol. 11, pp. 127–157. Elsevier Science (2002)
21. Ruohomaa, S., Kutvonen, L.: Trust Management Survey. In: Herrmann, P., Issarny, V., Shiu, S.C.K. (eds.) iTrust 2005. LNCS, vol. 3477, pp. 77–92. Springer, Heidelberg (2005)
22. Saadi, R., Rahaman, M.A., Issarny, V., Toninelli, A.: Composing Trust Models towards Interoperable Trust Management. In: Wakeman, I., Gudes, E., Jensen, C.D., Crampton, J. (eds.) IFIPTM 2011. IFIP AICT, vol. 358, pp. 51–66. Springer, Heidelberg (2011)
23. Sabater, J., Sierra, C.: Regret: reputation in gregarious societies. In: Proceedings of the Fifth International Conference on Autonomous Agents, AGENTS 2001, pp. 194–195. ACM, New York (2001)
24. Sabater, J., Sierra, C.: Review on Computational Trust and Reputation Models. Artificial Intelligence Review 24, 33–60 (2005)
25. Suryanarayana, G., Diallo, M.H., Erenkrantz, J.R., Taylor, R.N.: Architectural Support for Trust Models in Decentralized Applications. In: Proceeding of the 28th International Conference, pp. 52–61. ACM Press, New York (2006)
26. Winslett, M., Yu, T., Seamons, K.E., Hess, A., Jacobson, J., Jarvis, R., Smith, B., Yu, L.: Negotiating trust in the Web. IEEE Internet Computing 6(6), 30–37 (2002)
27. Yan, Z., Holtmanns, S.: Trust Modeling and Management: from Social Trust to Digital Trust. Computer Security, Privacy and Politics: Current Issues, Challenges and Solutions (January 2008)
28. Zhang, P., Durresi, A., Barolli, L.: Survey of Trust Management on Various Networks. In: 2011 International Conference on Complex, Intelligent and Software Intensive Systems (CISIS), pp. 219–226 (2011)

Advances and Challenges in Standalone Host-Based Intrusion Detection Systems

Vit Bukac[1], Pavel Tucek[1], and Martin Deutsch[2]

[1] Faculty of Informatics
[2] Institute of Computer Science
Masaryk University
Brno, Czech Republic
{bukac,deutsch}@mail.muni.cz, pavel.tucek@hotmail.com

Abstract. Lately a significant research effort was given to the development of network-based, hybrid and collaborative intrusion detection systems. Standalone host-based intrusion detection systems (HIDSs) were out of the main focus of security researchers. However, the importance of standalone HIDSs is still considerable. They are a suitable alternative when we need to secure notebooks traversing between networks, computers connected to untrusted networks or mobile devices communicating through wireless networks. This survey presents recent advances in standalone HIDSs, along with current research trends. We discuss the detection of intrusions from a host network traffic analysis, process behavior monitoring and file integrity checking. A separate chapter is devoted to the protection of HIDS against tampering.

Keywords: host-based IDS, intrusion detection, survey, HIDS.

1 Introduction

Intrusion detection systems are one of the key parts of the layered computer security. An intrusion detection system (IDS) is defined as a device or a software application that *monitors network and/or system activities for malicious activities or policy violations* and produces reports to a management station. We recognize four categories of IDS: network-based IDS (NIDS), host-based IDS (HIDS), wireless IDS and a network behavior analysis system [21]. Sometimes we can also encounter the term hybrid IDS which denotes a combination of one or more IDS categories.

The *host-based IDS* is defined as an IDS which *monitors the characteristics of a single host* and events occurring within that host for suspicious activities. In practice HIDSs usually monitor the behavior of running processes, enforce the integrity of critical system files and registry keys, perform complex log analyses and monitor the host network traffic.

In the last years much effort was put into a research of network-based intrusion detection systems at an expense of host-based IDS. According to J. Hu there are two main reasons [4]: *Networking factor*, and *real time and computing resource*

S. Fischer-Hübner, S. Katsikas, G. Quirchmayr (Eds.): TrustBus 2012, LNCS 7449, pp. 105–117, 2012.

restraint. We add another three reasons: the *ground truth problem, deployment issues* and *single machine attack class limitation*. The final list is then as follows:

- **Real-time and computing resource restraint**: An intrusion should be detected during or immediately after it happened. However, traditional HIDS techniques (e.g., log analysis, offline integrity checking) bring undesirable delays. NIDS usually detects intrusions in real-time.
- **Networking factor**: Nowadays, most applications are network-based. Over the years these applications became a primary attack vector against end hosts. Therefore, there is a strong tendency to protect network applications in a well-arranged centralized manner.
- **Ground truth problem**: Information supplied to and from HIDS could be forged or altered by an attacker who took control of an underlying operating system. Existing common privilege control mechanisms allow the administrator to modify every aspect of the system, including the kernel configuration and the code stored in programmable hardware. Also, an attacker with root privileges can alter logs to hide any traces of her actions.
- **Deployment issues**: Current networks are heterogenous, comprising of hosts with different capabilities and different operating systems. Devising a tool which could be applied generally is a difficult process.
- **Single machine attack class limitation**: Attacks that are manifested over multiple computers (e.g., horizontal port scans) might not be detected when we are limited to a single host. Network-based IDS can correlate events from the entire network and detect such attacks accordingly. An alternative approach is to employ a collaborative HIDS that can benefit from exchanging messages with other hosts in the network.

We believe that the importance of the first reason will decrease, because current fast hardware allows security researchers to develop new complex detection techniques with required properties. The *ground truth problem* is also well understood and *steadily researched* both by the academic community and the private sector. Some example solutions are presented in chapter 5.

Moreover, there are strong arguments supporting the development of HIDSs:

- **Semantic information**: HIDS is close to protected resources, in the best position to observe the behavior of the operating system or applications. Alert reports can be very *precise*, including a name of a malicious process or an identity of a user under whose context the process was run.
- **Network traffic interpretation**: If we can solve the ground truth problem, the network traffic data is more precise than in case of NIDS. Host-based IDS interprets packets in the same way as applications. The majority of *IDS evasion techniques* (e.g., obfuscation, data encryption, different interpretation by different operating systems [19]) is *not useable* against HIDS.
- **Best effort**: We often encounter situations in which *other IDS categories are not usable* (e.g., notebooks connecting through untrusted WiFi, GSM mobile devices). In some cases even if malicious activity was detected, network administrators may not be willing to share information about the problem. Then we must rely on HIDS to provide at least a minimal level of protection.

A distinct trend in the modern host-based intrusion detection is to pursue a *conjunction with existing virtualization technologies*. Virtualization allows to separate an analysis engine from a protected operating system, therefore, increase the *resistancy* of HIDS against tampering. Also, input data can be collected from the outside of virtual machines (VM) through a virtual machine manager, making HIDS *easier to deploy* on multiple heterogenous operating systems. With virtualization a single HIDS analysis engine can process separate inputs from multiple virtual machines, yet still maintain a close view on events which are happening inside. Such centralization leads to an *easier management* and a *better overview* of VM security states.

Our survey focuses on development of standalone HIDSs. An extensive survey of collaborative intrusion detection systems is presented by Zhou, Leckie and Karunasekera [28].

The rest of the paper is organized as follows: In chapter 2 we present advances in the area of a behavioral monitoring of running processes. Chapter 3 is concerned with techniques for ensuring the integrity of critical files. Chapter 4 focuses on the analysis of a host network traffic. Chapter 5 presents existing mechanisms which can support the HIDS tamper resistance. Results and courses of future research are discussed in chapter 6. Chapter 7 summarizes the paper.

2   Process Monitoring

Traditionally, the process monitoring was mainly concerned whether a particular process is running, suspended or killed. Therefore, it could be noticed if important system processes, usually security-related (e.g., logging processes, an antivirus software), were not tampered with.

Subsequently, an interest in monitoring the process behavior shifted to discovering whether the *process itself is exhibiting a malicious behavior*. Observation techniques can range from rather simple (e.g., CPU and memory consumption measurements, file access monitoring) to quite complex (e.g., system calls monitoring). A careful balance between the *method complexity* and *CPU and memory costs* is required. Often, a *whitelisting principle* for already examined applications is used to lower resource demands. Process monitoring can be *online or offline*. Offline processing is usually performed in a sandbox environment, which allows running a potentially malicious application without risking harm to the computer. On the other hand, online monitoring can adapt to changes in the process behavior in real-time.

Baliga et al. proposed a solution for a *real-time automated detection and containment of rootkit attacks* using the virtual machine technology [1]. They developed a prototype using VMware Workstation to illustrate the solution. Their analysis and experimental results indicate that this approach can successfully detect and contain effects of a large percentage of known Linux rootkits. They also demonstrate effectiveness of this approach, particularly against the malware that uses rootkits to hide.

An effective and efficient malware detector is presented by Kolbitsch et al. [8]. The detector is behavior-based. First, each program is executed in a *controlled environment* and its interactions (i.e., system calls) with the operating system are observed. If the program exhibits a malicious behavior then a model of this behavior is created. The model is generated automatically. It is represented as a behavior graph with nodes as system calls which could be used for malicious activities. During subsequent executions, the model is compared with an actual program behavior in real-time. The described technique has an advantage that it detects whole *malware families*, not just a single instance of a malicious code. Also, it cannot be easily evaded by the obfuscation or polymorphic techniques.

A new platform-independent HIDS based on an *analysis of system calls* is presented by Sujatha et al. [24]. The HIDS monitors system calls for both user and host activity. A set of relevant parameters, the *behavior set*, is established to distinguish between normal and anomaly events. These parameters are: cpu-usage, disk-usage, login-time, I/O activities, frequency of applications launched and network speed. Values are processed with a neural network, specifically the *self-organizing map*. The self-organizing map is trained with the Simple Competitive Learning algorithm. The learning phase is unsupervised and spans over multiple training cycles. With more learning cycles the false positives rate and the true negatives rate are decreasing.

Ozyer et al. proposed a method based on an iterative rule learning using a *fuzzy rule-based genetic classifier* [15]. Their approach is mainly composed of two phases. First, a large number of candidate rules is generated for each class using a fuzzy association rules mining. Rules are pre-screened using a two-rule evaluation criteria in order to reduce the fuzzy rule search space. Candidate rules obtained after pre-screening are used in a genetic fuzzy classifier to generate rules for the classes specified in IDS: normal, probe, denial of service, user to root and remote to local. During the next stage, a boosting genetic algorithm is employed for each class to find its fuzzy rules required to classify data each time a fuzzy rule is extracted and included in the system. A boosting mechanism evaluates the weight of each data item to help the rule extraction mechanism focus on data having relatively more weight.

PROBE by Kwon et al. is a HIDS based on an analysis of *relationships between processes* [10]. The system consists of three components: tree builder, path checker and process controller. The tree builder constructs a tree with processes as nodes and child-parent relationships as edges. The path checker subsequently analyzes the tree to discover anomalous spawning of child processes. For each edge three weights identifying the child (application, shell, clone) are calculated. If all three weights exceed predefined thresholds, the process is considered abnormal. The process controller either blocks or allows the new process. The graph analysis is *lightweight*, with memory and processing time requirements lower than common detection techniques based on system calls, while maintaining a reasonable precision.

3   Integrity Checking

The integrity checking is aimed to protect critical system files from *unsolicited changes*. Changes can be a result of hardware and software errors, intentional attacks or inadvertent harmful user actions. Control *checksums* are calculated with cryptographic hash functions both in keyed and unkeyed variants and stored in a secured database. During every subsequent check the stored value is compared with the newly calculated value. If values differ, the file was tampered with [22]. Some integrity checkers also provide means to block file operations before they are finished or to restore files to their original states.

File changes can be detected *periodically or in the real time*. Real-time integrity checkers require hooks in the kernel so as HIDS could intercept system calls. Periodical integrity checkers are simpler and can be implemented in the user space. However, they can provide only the attack detection, not the attack prevention. Once in a time period the integrity of all files is verified. With short time periods, attacks are detected sooner, however, overall *system performance* can be affected, because the stored value must be accessed from a slow persistent storage. The similar problem is encountered when we require to verify integrity of many files. Therefore, usually it is necessary to identify critical system files whose integrity would most likely be compromised during the attack. Another approach is to use *caching*. Hash values for files which are accessed repeatedly are stored in a fast dynamic memory and can be recovered quickly.

A *trusted persistent storage* becomes a performance weak point. It usually has a limited capacity and read/write rates. Therefore, a careful design of integrity checking algorithms is required. Oprea and Reiter designed integrity constructions which require only a *constant amount* of trusted storage per file [14]. The integrity checking is intended for use in cryptographic file systems and works on a memory block level. Hashes are stored only for blocks which are indistinguishable from blocks with random data. Requirements for the trusted storage are further decreased by exploiting the sequentiality of memory block writes.

Patil et al. proposed a *real-time integrity checker* called I3FS [17]. The integrity of each file is verified before the file is made available to a requesting application. The proposed solution utilizes a layer of a virtual file system between user processes and an arbitrary real file system. I3FS is configurable by security policies which can be modified by host system administrators. It is implemented as a loadable kernel module for file systems.

The ICAR (Integrity Checking and Restoring) system was developed by Kaczmarek and Wrobel [6]. ICAR enables a *real-time restoration* of compromised system files from a read-only external memory. A kernel module monitors the application behavior. When a file is requested, an integrity check is performed. If the file was compromised and the backup is present on the external memory, the file is restored real-time and the event is logged. Access to the file is allowed only if the integrity checksum was correct or if the file was restored from the backup.

Jin et al. propose a *real time integrity checking method* for virtual machines [5]. The method does not require installation of kernel hooks or any other modifications of existing virtual machines, therefore ensuring a low dependency on a chosen operating system and a high attack resistance. A system call sensor module is inserted in the virtual machine manager. All file operations of protected virtual machines are intercepted by the module and rerouted to the integrity checker which runs in a secured privileged virtual machine. Files are monitored with regard to three policies. *Significant files* cannot be modified, modifications of *sensitive files* are always logged and *remaining files* are not monitored. Initially, the list of significant and sensitive files is provided by an administrator. Subsequently, a sensitivity weight is computed for each other file. If the weight of a file reaches a predefined threshold, the file is included in the significant set or the sensitive set. The weight is computed from the frequency of usage of the file and the significance of its parent directory.

4   Network Traffic Monitoring

A network traffic HIDS monitors incoming and outgoing packets for signs of unwanted data flows. *Data encryption* on network layer or transport layer *does not affect HIDS* capability, because it can obtain an access to the decrypted payload at application layers. Gathered traffic is interpreted by HIDS similarly as by client applications, opposite to ambiguities which are typical for network intrusion detection systems.

When a host is incorporated in a botnet it can be misused for a variety of illegal activities (i.e., denial-of-service attacks, spamming, online fraud). Many of these activities cause *changes in the host's behavior on the network*. Even when the bot does not exhibit malicious activity it still communicates with its command and control servers on the Internet. Upon discovering, that the host participates in any of these specific data flows, we can assume the host was compromised and should be quarantined and examined.

HIDS often perform the *deep packet analysis* of all data traffic. At a typical end host connection speed (i.e., 100 Mb/s Fast Ethernet, 1 Gb/s Gigabit Ethernet) it is often possible without dedicated HW modules. A random *packet sampling* technique can be used to keep an acceptable CPU load even during traffic peaks.

4.1   Malware Detection

A generic *collaborative framework for bot detection* is presented by Takemori et al. in [25]. Victims of attacks report their IP addresses and timestamps of attacks to a central authority. Other nodes periodically download a list of victims and compare it with own outgoing packets. If there is a match, a compromised node knows it has been compromised. Further inspection of compromised hosts allows discovering command and control servers even if the attack traffic itself has spoofed source IP addresses.

Host compromise by a bot can be discovered from an outgoing traffic. Kwon and Lee describe two properties which differentiate bot and human processes in a host machine [9]. First, whether the *behavior was initiated by a user*, which can be decided from I/O events (i.e., interaction with input devices) and types of Windows GUI reports. Second, whether the *behavior is malicious*. Two types of malicious behavior are classified and used for detection: distributed denial-of-service attacks and spamming. DDoS attacks are recognized by an incoming/outgoing packet asymmetry and spamming hosts are identified by the quantity and the periodicity of the mail traffic. If both properties hold for a packet, the responsible process is reliably identified even if its port-binding information is hidden from HIDS.

Bot infected hosts often request commands and updates from botnet command and control servers. Takemori et al. suggested to *compare a host outgoing traffic with whitelists* in order to discover computer-originated malicious data flows [26]. Initially, whitelists are populated whith IP addresses of well-known services (DNS servers, patch servers, antivirus servers etc.) and of computers in a local network. After the first installation of the operating system a few days *learning period* takes place, during which users can not work with the computer and intrusions must not take place. During this period computer-originated outgoing packets are monitored and destination domain names are added to whitelists. After the learning period, packets which do not match any whitelist entry are dropped. To ensure the user-originated traffic is not affected, traffic is allowed through during a short time after each interaction between the user and the computer (i.e., a keyboard operation).

Modern malware often exploits HTTP traffic over TCP port 80 for its communication, because this port is usually open at firewalls on the path. Xiong et al. present a HIDS which *parses the outgoing HTTP traffic for signs of intrusion* and permits or denies the traffic according to a *whitelist* [27]. Each HTTP request is processed *independently on the requesting browser* in case the browser was compromised. A source domain is identified for each HTTP object in the response. If the domain is already on the whitelist, the object is allowed. Otherwise the user is queried whether he explicitly requested the object and if so, the domain is added to the whitelist. An experiment has shown that users tend to visit a limited set of IP addresses, but regularly. Such result supports the usability of the presented HIDS.

4.2 Network Attack Recognition

Active probing mechanism to detect the ARP spoofing, malformed ARP packets and the ARP denial-of-service attack in a local network without the need for a central entity is suggested by Barbhuiya et al. [2]. Each received *ARP request and response are verified* by broadcasted confirmation requests. If IP and MAC addresses were already considered trustworthy, ARP packets are accepted. Otherwise a simple verification process is performed during which all hosts are queried. If the attacker is present in the network and attempts the ARP spoofing, query responses from hosts are not uniform and the spoofing is detected.

DDoSniffer from Laurens et al. is a tool for the *detection of outgoing TCP SYN denial-of-service attacks* [12]. The tool parses outgoing TCP packets. If a packet begins a new TCP connection a new record is created in the Newconn table and in the Conn table. When a packet counter of a particular connection exceeds four (i.e., The TCP handshake was finished and the connection was fully established.), the record is removed from the Newconn table. An alarm is reported when the number of records in the Newconn table exceeds predefined threshold or when any of connections in the Conn table has incoming to outgoing packet ratio higher than four (i.e., The host sends outgoing packets at a high rate without receiving TCP acknowledgements.). Alarms are also raised if the *IP spoofing* is taking place.

5   HIDS Security

Host-based intrusion detection systems are *vulnerable when an attacker took control of the underlying operating system.* HIDS can be shut down, analysis engine could be influenced, critical files changed or deleted, input data altered or output alerts dropped. Ensuring a reliable input and output in a potentially *hostile environment* is a challenging task.

Molina and Cukier define the *HIDS resiliency* as a probability that HIDS will be subverted in the event of an attack against the system under supervision [13]. They argue that the resiliency is closely linked with the *independency*. HIDS should be most independent of the supervised system, because shared system elements can serve as attack vectors. The HIDS resiliency is defined as a quantitative, attack-dependent metric, whereas the HIDS independency is defined as a qualitative attack-independent metric. A sample independence analysis of Semhain HIDS over Gentoo Linux is provided.

Laureano et al. suggested that HIDS could be protected in a *virtual environment* [11]. Processes and events are monitored inside a virtual machine, but the analysis is performed by HIDS which is placed on an underlying physical machine. HIDS is separated from attacker but it still possess all knowledge about the system.

XenFIT by Quynh and Takefuji is a new *file integrity checker with a high tamper resistance* [20]. It is intended for virtual machines hosted on the Xen hypervisor. The HIDS is running in the user space in a separate highly secured privileged virtual machine. From there it has access to file systems of protected virtual machines. Access to the protected virtual machine data is via *breakpoints in specific system calls* in the kernel memory of the protected VM. Therefore, no program code is running inside the protected VM. An attacker who obtained root privileges to the protected VM can disable breakpoints, but cannot tamper with the HIDS itself. Also, minimal changes to protected VM make XenFIT hardly detectable for the attacker.

Srivastava and Giffin presented VMwall, an *application-level firewall* for Xen virtual environments with a *high tamper resistance* [23]. VMwall function is not affected even if the attacker takes control of the protected virtual machine. VMwall utilizes the *virtual machine isolation* and the *virtual machine introspection* for a secured monitoring of the network traffic of protected virtual machines. A kernel module intercepts packets destined to and coming from the protected VM and decides if they are forwarded. A user agent correlates packets with processes running in the VM. Both the kernel module and the user agent are placed in a secured VM. Data structures which are necessary for VMwall are secured with existing kernel integrity protection mechanisms. VMwall can successfully block backdoor, bot and worm traffic emanating from the protected system.

Payne et al. present Lares, an architecture for a *secured active monitoring* in the virtualized environment [18]. Lares allows that *system hooks* can be placed in untrusted virtual machines, therefore enabling the active monitoring, opposite from the more common VM interspection technique. The protected VM contains system hooks and a "trampoline" code which mediates the communication with an analysis engine in a secured VM. The trampoline functionality is *self-contained* (i.e., does not depend on kernel functions), *non-persistent* (i.e., does not require data which was generated during previous hook activations) and *atomical*. Hooks are secured with a memory protection mechanism. When a guest VM requires a write change in a certain memory page, the hypervisor verifies whether the requested memory address is not designated as write-protected. If so, the change is not allowed and the required change from the guest VM is not propagated into the actual physical memory. A list of protected memory regions is stored and maintained by a Lares component.

Parno et al. argue that network devices devote a lot of their precious resources to reconstructing the state information which is already known to end hosts [16]. Proliferation of TPM-equipped computers and secure smartphones encourages us to use trusted elements of end hosts to support host trustfulness. They designed an architecture where information from trusted *clients* is collected by trusted *verifiers* and verifiers make recommendations how to react on the traffic to network *filters*. Clients have a minimal-size hypervisor incorporated. The hypervisor ensures a secure boot of the client and that the agent application was not modified. Once clients authorize verifiers, clients can cryptographically prove their traffic by a *hardware-based cryptographic attestation*. Any change to the protective hypervisor layer makes the authentication token inaccessible, forbidding the client to further authenticate its traffic. Filters allow, block or inspect the network traffic based on recommendations from verifiers.

Another approach to protect HIDS process is presented by Khurana et al. [7]. A new *monitoring process* MonitorIDS is implemented. Whenever it detects the HIDS process was killed it starts it again. Whenever a file is modified, a timestamp is appended and the last modification time is encrypted. If the encrypted value does not match during any subsequent accesses to the file, the file is automatically restored from backup.

Not-a-bot (NAB) system by Gummadi et al. mitigates network attacks by an *automatic validation of the user-originated traffic* [3]. For each request, the originator is automatically determined. If the originator is the user or an application running on user behalf, the request is allowed, otherwise the request is blocked. Decision on whether the request comes from the user is based on *user's interactions with a computer*. After each keystroke or mouse movement there is a period during which requests are allowed through. Allowed requests are *attested* with a digital signature. Attesting module cannot be altered because its integrity is protected by a TPM. The attestation is responder-specific, content-specific and challenger-specific. Attested requests are analyzed by verifiers who may take appropriate actions. NAB can be used for existing network protocols, however, client applications require modifications for NAB to be supported.

6   Research Challenges

We have identified two main research trends: the utilization of *virtualization technologies* and the shift towards a *real-time detection*. Achieving the real-time detection is a necessary step towards functional host-based intrusion prevention systems. Virtualization can affect virtually every aspect of HIDS, with attack detection, management simplification and tamper resistance being the most notable. However, in most cases changes must be made to the virtualization layer or a custom-based hypervisor must be created. This may limit the usability and flexibility of virtualization-based solutions. Virtualization-based approaches are indeed functional; however, usually they can be used only for VMs hosted in datacenters.

In our view, the future of HIDSs lies mainly in smartphones, tablets and other general-purpose devices. These devices regularly connect to untrusted networks, communicate with possibly infected peers in range and often contain both valuable personal and enterprise data.

We are convinced that host-based intrusion detection systems should always be considered an important part of overall intrusion detection architecture. In this architecture, their tasks will be to *confirm and stop the intrusion, identify attack vectors and help to restore the secured state*. On the other hand, HIDS may also work separately, without the support, and still provide a decent level of protection.

We are currenly investigating option for the design of an anomaly-based HIDS capable of detecting outgoing denial-of-service attacks, types of these attacks, intended targets and originator processes. Therefore, when an ongoing attack is detected, we can inform the administrator of the computer that the computer was either infected with malware or the operator is deliberately misusing computer resources. The detection will be based on an analysis of host data traffic, combined with the knowledge of basic system properties (e.g., host IP address, logged user name). We believe that such a self-contained detection module can function independently, providing a best effort service, but can also be incorporated in a large intrusion detection architecture, where it can serve as a complementary source of information.

Interesting findings are linked with the *user-friendliness*. Although performance measures are common and researchers struggle to maintain low computational and memory requirements, many solutions have a very high false positives rate (i.e., several percent). We are convinced that the system which disturbs users from their ordinary work is unacceptable and cannot be deployed in real environment. The same situation is with HIDSs which require a human input (i.e., solve a puzzle, confirm change) unless they are carefully balanced.

Another fruitful area of research that we have identified concerns the ways how trusted platform modules or cryptographic smartcards could be used in connection with an HIDS to (partially) solve the ground truth problem. For a collaborative HIDS the ground truth problem can be solved with reputation systems, which are slow to discover misbehaving hosts. For a standalone HIDS the ability to reason about the validity of provided information would be invaluable.

7 Conclusion

In this survey the state of the art in a standalone host-based intrusion detection systems research is presented. HIDSs are divided by their detection approach into three categories: network traffic analysis, process monitoring and integrity checking. A separate chapter is devoted to the protection against tampering. In the sixth chapter, we have highlighted current research trends towards the use of virtualization, trusted platform modules and real-time detection. We encourage further research of standalone HIDS for mobile devices.

Acknowledgements. Authors would like to thank to Vashek Matyas and Marek Kumpost for their comments and valuable suggestions. The first two authors also wish to acknowledge support and discussions of the Czech research project VG20102014031, programme BV II/2 - VS.

References

1. Baliga, A., Iftode, L., Chen, X.: Automated containment of rootkits attacks. Computers & Security 27(7-8), 323–334 (2008)
2. Barbhuiya, F.A., Roopa, S., Ratti, R., Hubballi, N., Biswas, S., Sur, A., Nandi, S., Ramachandran, V.: An Active Host-Based Detection Mechanism for ARP-Related Attacks. Advances in Networks and Communications 132, 432–443 (2011)
3. Gummadi, R., Balakrishnan, H., Maniatis, P., Ratnasamy, S.: Not-a-Bot (NAB): Improving Service Availability in the Face of Botnet Attacks. In: NSDI 2009 Proceedings of the 6th USENIX Symposium on Networked Systems Design and Implementation. USENIX Association, Berkeley (2009)
4. Hu, J.: Host-Based Anomaly Intrusion Detection. In: Handbook of Information and Communication Security, pp. 235–255. Springer, Heidelberg (2010)
5. Jin, H., Xiang, G., Zou, D., Zhao, F., Li, M., Yu, C.: A guest-transparent file integrity monitoring method in virtualization environment. Computers & Mathematics with Applications 60(2), 256–266 (2010)
6. Kaczmarek, J., Wróbel, M.: Modern Approaches to File System Integrity Checking. In: 1st International Conference on Information Technology, pp. 1–4 (May 2008)
7. Khurana, S.S., Bansal, D., Sofat, S.: Recovery Based Architecture to Protect Hids Log Files using Time Stamps. Journal of Emerging Technologies in Web Intelligence 2(2), 110–114 (2010)
8. Kolbitsch, C., Comparetti, P.M., Kruegel, C., Kirda, E., Zhou, X., Wang, X.: Effective and Efficient Malware Detection at the End Host. In: SSYM 2009 Proceedings of the 18th Conference on USENIX Security Symposium. USENIX Association, Berkeley (2009)

9. Kwon, J., Lee, J., Lee, H.: Hidden Bot Detection by Tracing Non-human Generated Traffic at the Zombie Host. In: Bao, F., Weng, J. (eds.) ISPEC 2011. LNCS, vol. 6672, pp. 343–361. Springer, Heidelberg (2011)
10. Kwon, M., Jeong, K., Lee, H.: PROBE: A Process Behavior-Based Host Intrusion Prevention System. In: Chen, L., Mu, Y., Susilo, W. (eds.) ISPEC 2008. LNCS, vol. 4991, pp. 203–217. Springer, Heidelberg (2008)
11. Laureano, M., Maziero, C., Jamhour, E.: Protecting host-based intrusion detectors through virtual machines. Computer Networks: The International Journal of Computer and Telecommunications Networking 51(5), 1275–1283 (2007)
12. Laurens, V., El Saddik, A., Dhar, P.: DDoSniffer: Detecting DDOS Attack at the Source Agents. International Journal of Advanced Media and Communication 3(3) (2009)
13. Molina, J., Cukier, M.: Evaluating Attack Resiliency for Host Intrusion Detection Systems. Journal of Information Assurance and Security 4, 1–9 (2009)
14. Oprea, A., Reiter, M.K.: Integrity Checking in Cryptographic File Systems with Constant Trusted Storage. In: SS 2007 Proceedings of 16th USENIX Security Symposium on USENIX Security Symposium, pp. 183–198. USENIX Association, Berkeley (2007)
15. Ozyer, T., Alhajj, R., Barker, K.: Intrusion detection by integrating boosting genetic fuzzy classifier and data mining criteria for rule pre-screening. Journal of Network and Computer Applications - Special Issue: Network and Information Security: A Computational Intelligence Approach 30(1), 99–113 (2007)
16. Parno, B., Zhou, Z., Perrig, A.: Help Me Help You: Using Trustworthy Host-Based Information in the Network. Technical report (2009)
17. Patil, S., Kashyap, A., Sivathanu, G., Zadok, E.: I3FS: An In-Kernel Integrity Checker and Intrusion Detection File System. In: LISA 2004 Proceedings of the 18th USENIX Conference on System Administration, pp. 67–78. USENIX Association, Berkeley (2004)
18. Payne, B.D., Carbone, M., Sharif, M., Lee, W.: Lares: An Architecture for Secure Active Monitoring Using Virtualization. In: SP 2008 Proceedings of the 2008 IEEE Symposium on Security and Privacy, pp. 233–247 (May 2008)
19. Ptacek, T.H., Newsham, T.N.: Insertion, Evasion, and Denial of Service: Eluding Network Intrusion Detection. Technical report (1998)
20. Quynh, N.A., Takefuji, Y.: A Novel Approach for a File-system Integrity Monitor Tool of Xen Virtual Machine. In: ASIACCS 2007 Proceedings of the 2nd ACM Symposium on Information, Computer and Communications Security. ACM, New York (2007)
21. Scarfone, K., Mell, P.: Guide to Intrusion Detection and Prevention Systems (IDPS). Technical report (2007)
22. Sivathanu, G., Wright, C.P., Zadok, E.: Ensuring Data Integrity in Storage: Techniques and Applications. In: StorageSS 2005 Proceedings of the 2005 ACM Workshop on Storage Security and Survivability, pp. 26–36. ACM, New York (2005)
23. Srivastava, A., Giffin, J.: Tamper-Resistant, Application-Aware Blocking of Malicious Network Connections. In: Lippmann, R., Kirda, E., Trachtenberg, A. (eds.) RAID 2008. LNCS, vol. 5230, pp. 39–58. Springer, Heidelberg (2008)
24. Kola Sujatha, P., Kannan, A., Ragunath, S., Sindhu Bargavi, K., Githanjali, S.: A Behavior Based Approach to Host-Level Intrusion Detection Using Self-Organizing Maps. In: ICETET 2008 Proceedings of the 2008 First International Conference on Emerging Trends in Engineering and Technology, pp. 1267–1271. IEEE Computer Society, Washington, DC (2008)

25. Takemori, K., Fujinaga, M., Sayama, T., Nishigaki, M.: Host-based traceback; tracking bot and C&C server. In: ICUIMC 2009 Proceedings of the 3rd International Conference on Ubiquitous Information Management and Communication. ACM, New York (2009)
26. Takemori, K., Nishigaki, M., Tomohiro, T., Yutaka, M.: Detection of Bot Infected PCs Using Destination-based IP and Domain Whitelists during a Non-operating Term. In: GLOBECOM 2008 Proceedings of the Global Communications Conference, pp. 2072–2077. IEEE Computer Society, Washington, DC (2008)
27. Xiong, H., Malhotra, P., Stefan, D., Wu, C., Yao, D.: User-Assisted Host-Based Detection of Outbound Malware Traffic. In: Qing, S., Mitchell, C.J., Wang, G. (eds.) ICICS 2009. LNCS, vol. 5927, pp. 293–307. Springer, Heidelberg (2009)
28. Zhou, C.V., Leckie, C., Karunasekera, S.: A survey of coordinated attacks and collaborative intrusion detection. Computers & Security 29(1), 124–140 (2010)

Encrypted Adaptive Storage Model – Analysis and Performance Tests

Marcin Gorawski[1,2], Michal Lorek[3], and Michal Gorawski[2]

[1] Wroclaw University of Technology, Institute of Computer Science,
Wybrzeze Wyspianskiego 27, 50-370 Wroclaw, Poland
Marcin.Gorawski@pwr.wroc.pl
[2] Silesian University of Technology, Institute of Computer Science,
Akademicka 16, 44-100 Gliwice, Poland
{Marcin.Gorawski,Michal.Gorawski}@polsl.pl
[3] Gala Coral Group, Castle Boulevard, Nottingham, NG7 1FT, United Kingdom
Michal.Lorek@galacoral.com

Abstract. The presented paper describes an efficient method of storing crypto-grams in a relational database management system. We focus solely on the encryption of tables with columns defined using fixed size data types. Next, we propose a new storage model called EASM that improves page utilization and minimizes encryption related padding overhead and reduces encryption computational overhead. This model is compared to PPC since they both originate from NSM and are designed to protect data confidentiality. Both of these models utilize symmetric key encryption. Finally we present and analyze the results of the conducted tests.

Keywords: Symmetric Key Encryption, N-ary Storage Model, Data Privacy.

1   Introduction

Data security plays an evermore important role both in business management and successful business development strategies. With the increasing popularity of Internet applications and mobile phone services, there is a legal requirement to monitor and store information describing end-user actions [1-3]. In addition, rising end-user awareness of data confidentiality through security breaches from household brands forces companies to take the problem of secure data storage seriously.

It is common practice in modern business to collect and analyse information describing customers' activity for commercial gain and statistical purposes. The need to process large volumes of sensitive data raises a significant question, how to store data securely and efficiently.

Since data is an valuable asset for organized crime and the number of attempts of unauthorized access to confidential information is on the rise [4-6]. Any potential data leaks can discredit individuals [7-8] and damage business reputation and profits, therefore, it is crucial to develop means both to protect data and efficiently manage an access to it.

S. Fischer-Hübner, S. Katsikas, G. Quirchmayr (Eds.): TrustBus 2012, LNCS 7449, pp. 118–128, 2012.

2   Data Encryption

Modern cryptography is distinguished between two main encryption algorithm classes such as public key and symmetric key encryption. For the purpose of data confidentiality protection both classes provide sufficient level of encryption strength. However, there are number of advantages and disadvantages associated with each of them. For instance, while providing excellent performance when securing large quantities of data, symmetric encryption requires additional encryption mechanisms to protect its keys, whereas the public key encryption is characterized by significantly larger performance overhead while providing secure key exchange protocol for participating parties [9].

Our research focuses mainly on secure and efficient way of storing large volumes of information in RDBS. Therefore, we decided to choose symmetric key encryption to support our approach.

From many different symmetric encryption algorithms, that are widely available, we consider AES[1]. Since its introduction [10] the AES has been highly recommended and eventually broadly adopted by many government institutions [11] or financial organization [12]. It has also superseded DES[2] [13-14] and become a new cryptographic standard to protect top secret information in US government [11].

To prove AES popularity, Intel designed a new family of processors that include a set of instructions supporting AES cryptographic operations known as AES-NI [15]. According to Intel [16] AES-NI can be up to 10 times faster than software implementation of the algorithm. Intel performance tests [17] show that AES operating in CBC mode can complete decryption 3 times faster than encryption.

AES is a block cipher with a fixed block size of 128 bits (16 bytes) which supports key size of 128, 192 and 256 bits respectively [18]. Hence, during the encryption process the input plaintext is organized into 16 bytes blocks sequence. Naturally, in some cases the last block of the plaintext message can be shorter than AES's block size. In this situation padding string is appended to the message's last block so that its length can match cipher's block size. However, if the length of the last plaintext block is equal to the block size, an additional 16 bytes of padding string is also attached to the input message. This concept is illustrated in Figure 1. In it, encryption of 29 bytes long plaintext message results in 32 bytes long ciphertext. Comparably, the second 16 bytes long plaintext when encrypted also gives 32 bytes long ciphertext. Depending on selected padding scheme [19], different values are used to generate padding string. The grayed area in block1 represents PKCS7 padding string [20].

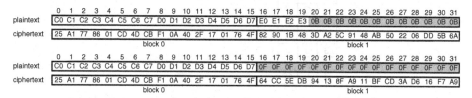

Fig. 1. An example of PKCS7 padding

The fact that the padding string has to be attached to short messages can result in undesired data size growth. This can be especially intolerable when encryption is performed in RDBMS environment on sub-blocksize data types such as *integer*, *numeric* or *datetime*. On top of that, knowing that table attributes which length is a multiple of 16 bytes are extended by an additional full length of blocksize, one can wonder if there is any way to optimize usage and storage of cryptogram in order to minimize the overall padding overhead. The proposed solution that mitigates this problem will be described in details in the following section.

3   Encrypted Adaptive Storage Model

Previous researches in the field of database storage models describe various methods that improve the process of storing and accessing data by RDBMS. The majority of them however, such as NSM [21], DSM [23] and PAX [22] do not the address data encryption problem.

Generally, the N-ary Storage Model (NSM) describes the way data records are stored in a database [22]. According to its definition, rows are placed sequentially on data pages with the first row in the table inserted at the beginning of the page just after page's header. Every other newly inserted record is placed behind the previous one, creating a list of rows adjacent to each other filling up page space. In addition, each page has an offset table located at the end, which stores pointers to each record's position on the page. This model has been widely adopted and currently used in practically all major RDBMS[3].

From a data encryption point of view the NSM was modified to balance data encryption and cryptogram storage efficiency by introducing PPC[4] model which divides the data page into two mini-pages, storing unencrypted and encrypted data respectively [21].

R	U	C1	C2
	1	A	1
	1	B	2
	1	C	3
	1	D	4
	2	E	5
	2	F	6
	2	G	7
	2	H	8
	3	I	9
	3	J	10
	4	K	11
	4	L	12

A	U	CT {C1C2,(...)}
	1	{A1,B2,C3,D4}
	2	{E5,F6,G7,H8}
	3	{I9,J10}
	4	{K11,L12}

Fig. 2. An example of conceptual schema relation and its transposed form

---

[3]   RDBMS - Relational Database Management System.
[4]   PPC - Partition Plaintext and Ciphertext Model.

The proposed Encrypted Adaptive Storage Model is another approach to optimize the storage of the cryptograms on data page. In this instance, we focus solely on using symmetric key encryption to encode logically co-dependent attributes. We deliberately choose this particular level of encryption granularity to demonstrate the strengths of our method. We also assume that columns storing both plaintext and sensitive information are defined using fixed size primitive data types. This fact allows better planning of the cryptogram size in order to maximize page usage. Figure 2 illustrates how example schema relation *R* can be stored using EASM, where *U* attribute represents user identifier and *C1* and *C2* attributes determine their transaction. *C1* and *C2* attributes represent part of the relation *R* that contains sensitive information.

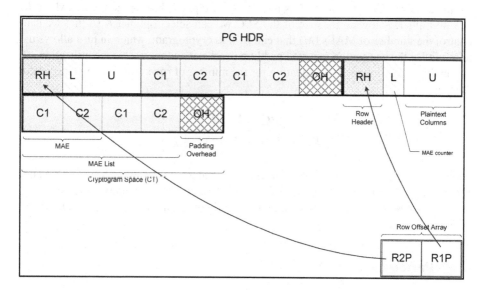

Fig. 3. Sample EASM page

The presented method, similarly to PPC [21], also differentiates between plain text data area and cryptogram data space, however, all logically co-dependent attributes (*C1* and *C2*) are grouped together and form new item - multi-attribute element (MAE). Next, these items are arranged into a set which is subsequently encrypted. This set comprises only the rows associated with a particular entity's instance (*U*). Figure 3 illustrates an example of the EASM page.

Furthermore, depending on size of the group of columns that need to be securely stored, it is possible to calculate and select an appropriate cryptogram size (expressed as a multiple of symmetric encryption algorithm block size), which when used to define crypt-text data space, guarantees optimal fill of the page. For instance, total length of attributes (*SEC*) that need to be encrypted can be expressed by equation

$$SEC = C_1 + C_2 + \ldots + C_n \, , \tag{1}$$

where $C_1,...,C_n$ are the sizes of particular attributes storing confidential data. The following equations allow to determine EASM's crypt-text size, number of MAEs in cryptogram, relation between page size, number of rows stored on page and parameters describing a row structure.

$$CT = K \cdot BLK, K \in (1,2,...,) \qquad (2)$$

$$M = \left\lfloor \frac{CT - 1}{SEC} \right\rfloor \qquad (3)$$

Crypt-text size (CT) is expressed as a multiple of cipher's block-size (BLK), where K is a multiplier. Knowing the size of the SEC we can select optimal K so that we can control the number of MAEs (M) that can fit into cryptogram, which in turn allows us to minimize the encryption incurred padding overhead and increase page utilization.

Finally, the following is an equation for the number of rows that can be placed onto the page

$$N = \left\lfloor \frac{PG - HDR}{RH + PT + CT + OT + L} \right\rfloor, \qquad (4)$$

where PG is the size of the page, HDR is page header size. RH (row header size) and OT (offset table entry size) are size of row overhead and PT (plaintext columns size) and CT express length of the actual data respectively. In addition, L represents MAE counter.

4   Performance Tests

This section presents a comparison between PPC and EASM and the way they utilize the page. We demonstrate that it is possible to select value of the K parameter in order to maximize the amount of data stored securely while keeping the padding overhead to a minimum.

The purpose of the conducted tests is to compare the amount of information stored on page in both storage models and to measure page utilization. We deliberately do not focus on speed.

4.1   Test Parameters

To evaluate EASM performance, firstly we assume sample relation that comprises of three attributes: *UserID*, *IPAddress*, *DateTimeVisited*, which can all be stored using fixed size data types, i.e. *bigint*, *int*, *datetime* respectively. IPAddress and DateTime-Visited attributes values are regarded as sensitive information, therefore their content is encrypted.

Secondly, the following inequations (representing EASM and PPC respectively)

$$PG - HDR \geq N \cdot (RH + PT + CT + OT + L) \tag{5}$$

$$PG - HDR \geq N \cdot (RH_1 + PT + OT_1) + \left\lceil \frac{N \cdot (RH_2 + SEC + OT_2) + 1}{BLK} \right\rceil \cdot BLK \tag{6}$$

are used to exemplify the relation between plaintext and ciphertext sizes in both storage models. In addition, they also illustrate the relation among number of rows stored on the page and row overhead incurred by each model.

Based on Microsoft SQLServer 2008 engine's internal structure [24], we select the following values for EASM parameters that remain constant throughout the tests: RH - 7 bytes, OT - 2 bytes, PG - 8000 bytes, HDR - 0 bytes. Moreover, the L parameter associated with EASM is set to 2 bytes and remains unchanged during the tests. It represents number of MAEs currently stored in CT. Subsequently, we assume that PPC related parameters are set to: RH_1, RH_2 - 2 bytes, OT_1, OT_2 - 2 bytes.

In the conducted test the parameters PT, CT and K take the values from the following ranges: PT - 4 ÷ 16 bytes, SEC - 4 ÷ 128 bytes and K - 1 ÷ 128. The tests were run for 100,000 sample users, each with 100,000 randomly generated transactions.

4.2   Test Results

The graphs below present the results of the conducted tests. As expected, in terms of storage usage, EASM outperforms PPC.

We compared the amount of encrypted data stored on the page for both models. We observed that while the number of rows decreases inversely proportional to the K parameter value, the number of MAEs stored on the page increases and resembles a saw wave form with a widening wave period. This is illustrated in Figures 4 and 6. Similarly, EASM page utilization follows the same pattern, which is clearly shown in Figures 5 and 7.

Tests revealed that by adjusting the K parameter value we were able to achieve over 95% page utilization for relatively small values of SEC, compared to approximately 70% in PPC. However, it was noted that with the increase of the SEC length, the EASM efficiency deteriorated and exhibited performance almost identical to that of PPC, as shown in Figures 8 and 9. Nevertheless, it was still possible to select such K parameter values to achieve better results than PPC. It should be pointed out that for SEC values larger than multiple of blocksize EASM utilization cannot be defined since SEC cannot fit into CT for K parameter lower than K_T, where K_T is defined as follows

$$K_T = \left\lceil \frac{SEC + 1}{BLK} \right\rceil . \tag{7}$$

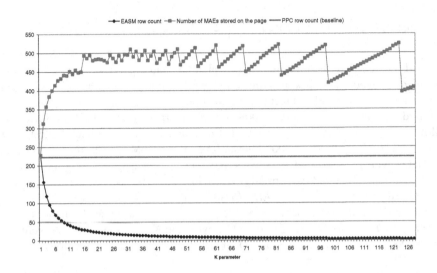

Fig. 4. Comparison of EASM and PPC. Total number of rows (N) and MAEs ($N \cdot L$) stored on page versus K parameter value, compared to PPC row count. The *PT* and *SEC* parameters were set to 8 and 15 bytes respectively.

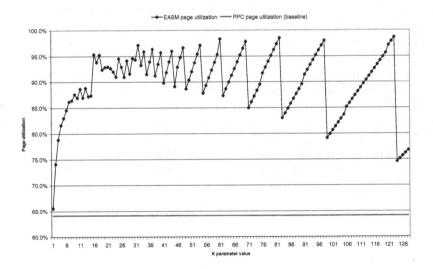

Fig. 5. Comparison of EASM and PPC. Page utilization against K parameter value. The *PT* and *SEC* parameters were set to 8 and 15 bytes respectively.

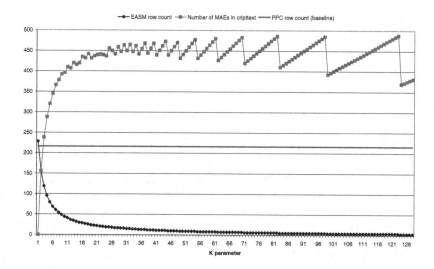

Fig. 6. Comparison of EASM and PPC. Total number of rows (*N*) and MAEs (*N · L*) stored on page versus *K* parameter value, compared to PPC row count. The *PT* and *SEC* parameters were set to 8 and 16 bytes respectively.

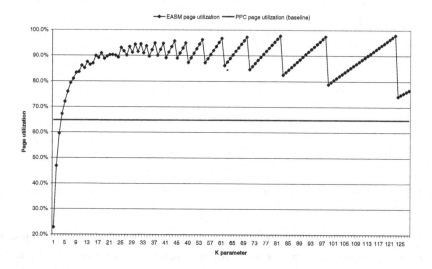

Fig. 7. Comparison of EASM and PPC. Page utilization versus K parameter value. The *PT* and *SEC* parameters were set to 8 and 16 bytes respectively.

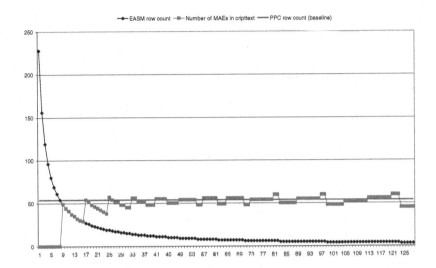

Fig. 8. Comparison of EASM and PPC. Total number of rows (N) and MAEs ($N \cdot L$) stored on page versus K parameter value, compared to PPC row count. The *PT* and *SEC* parameters were set to 8 and 128 bytes respectively.

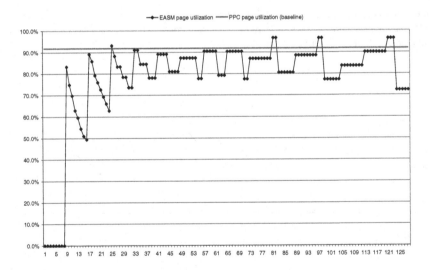

Fig. 9. Comparison of EASM and PPC. Page utilization versus K parameter value. The *PT* and *SEC* parameters were set to 8 and 128 bytes respectively.

Figure 10 summarizes all previous observations. It demonstrates that for small SEC parameters page usage is notably more efficient than PPC with minimal detrimental affect by the K parameter. For mid-range SEC parameters performance degrades yet still outperforms PPC. For longer SEC parameters, only some of the K parameter degrade performance compared to PPC, others remain more efficient.

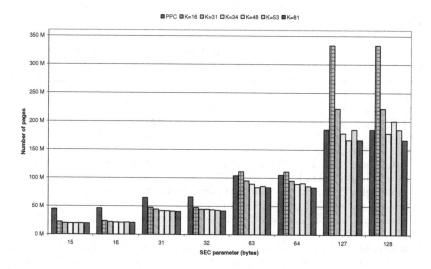

Fig. 10. Comparison of EASM and PPC. Number of pages against *SEC* parameter demonstrated for various values of *K* parameter.

5   Conclusion

The proposed solution has shown that it is possible to efficiently apply symmetric key encryption while maximizing data page utilisation and minimizing the padding overhead required by the chosen encryption algorithm, which consequently leads to reduced storage cost.

Although EASM introduces a hierarchical paradigm, which denormalises the relational model, its impact is minimal since the method is mainly optimised for storing infrequently accessed data. Therefore, drawbacks such as increased storage complexity and reduced data independence can be disregarded to some extent.

In addition, the row reconstruction overhead during the retrieval phase is compensated by reduced cryptogram data print on the page. As opposed to PPC, where row inserts require ciphertext mini-page to be decrypted entirely, adding a new row to an EASM page is less exhaustive operation and requires only a single cryptogram decryption. In EASM, the cryptogram size associated with particular table depends on the chosen *K* and in most cases can be significantly smaller than a PPC ciphertext mini-page. Therefore, decryption and encryption process requires less computational resources.

Currently, the biggest disadvantage of the presented solution is an inability to predict size of cryptograms for variable size data types and to construct relevant structure that can hold them efficiently. At present, EASM only supports symmetric key encryption, however, we plan to modify the current model so that it can also exploit Elliptic Curve Cryptography [9]. This functionality can be especially useful in environments where data relevant to a specific user is encrypted using a key pertaining to that user.

References

1. EUR-Lex - Access to European Union Law, `http://eur-lex.europa.eu/LexUriServ/LexUriServ.do?uri=OJ:L:2006:105:0054:0063:EN:PDF`
2. Electronic Frontier Foundation, `https://www.eff.org/issues/mandatory-data-retention`
3. Legislation.gov.uk, `http://www.legislation.gov.uk/ukdsi/2009/9780111473894/pdfs/ukdsi_9780111473894_en.pdf`
4. ITPro, `http://www.itpro.co.uk/609662/millions-of-jobseeker-details-stolen-in-monster-hack`
5. ZDNet, `http://www.zdnet.com/blog/security/chinese-hacker-arrested-for-leaking-6-million-logins/11064`
6. The Huffington Post, `http://www.huffingtonpost.com/2011/09/30/cyber attacks-rise-2011_n_988573.html`
7. The Telegraph, `http://www.telegraph.co.uk/news/majornews/2191680/Child-benefit-data-loss-timeline-of-scandal.html`
8. News.com.au, `http://www.news.com.au/business/clients-identified-from-stolen-hsbc-data-prosecutor/story-e6frfm1i-1225853492208`
9. Menezes, A., van Oorshot, P., Vanstone, S.: Handbook of Applied Cryptography. CRC Press, New York (1997)
10. National Institute of Standards and Technology, `http://csrc.nist.gov/publications/fips/fips197/fips-197.pdf`
11. National Institute of Standards and Technology, `http://csrc.nist.gov/groups/ST/toolkit/documents/aes/CNSS15FS.pdf`
12. `http://www.europeanpaymentscouncil.eu/documents/EPC342-08%20Guidelines%20on%20algorithms%20usage%20and%20key%20management%20v1.1%20approved.pdf`
13. National Institute of Standards and Technology, `http://csrc.nist.gov/publications/fips/fips46-3/fips46-3.pdf`
14. National Institute of Standards and Technology, `http://csrc.nist.gov/publications/fips/05-9945-DES-Withdrawl.pdf`
15. Intel, `http://software.intel.com/en-us/articles/intel-advanced-encryption-standard-instructions-aes-ni/`
16. Intel, `http://software.intel.com/en-us/articles/intel-advanced-encryption-standard-aes-instructions-set/`
17. Intel, `http://software.intel.com/file/27067/`
18. Daemen, J., Rijmen, V.: The Design of Rijndael: AES - The Advanced Encryption Standard. Springer, Berlin (2002)
19. Schneier, B.: Applied Cryptography. John Wiley and Sons, New York (1996)
20. Internet Engineering Task Force, `http://tools.ietf.org/html/rfc5652#section-6.3`
21. Iyer, B., Mehrotra, S., Mykletun, E., Tsudik, G., Wu, Y.: A Framework for Efficient Storage Security in RDBMS. In: Bertino, E., Christodoulakis, S., Plexousakis, D., Christophides, V., Koubarakis, M., Böhm, K. (eds.) EDBT 2004. LNCS, vol. 2992, pp. 147–164. Springer, Heidelberg (2004)
22. Ailamaki, A., et al.: Weaving Relations for Cache Performance, `http://www.vldb.org/conf/2001/P169.pdf`
23. Copeland, G., Khoshafian, S.: A Decomposition Storage Model, `http://db.inf.uni-tuebingen.de/files/teaching/ws1011/relsystems/p268-copeland.pdf`
24. Delaney, K., et al.: Microsoft SQL Server 2008 Internals. Microsoft Press, Redmond (2009)

Efficient Comparison of Encrypted Biometric Templates

Michael Dorn, Peter Wackersreuther, and Christian Böhm

Ludwig-Maximilians-Universität, Munich, Germany
dornm@cip.ifi.lmu.de, {wackersr,boehm}@dbs.ifi.lmu.de

Abstract. Recently, a large amount of security relevant systems assure the permitted access to sensible data by biometric approaches. As also the biometric data itself deserve a high degree of protection, these data are stored encrypted by so-called template protection techniques in the database. But, such an encryption impedes the comparison of two biometric data instances significantly, and therefore we need advanced approaches to apply template protection techniques for identification purposes. In this paper, we present an efficient identification solution that is based on encryped minutiae data of fingerprints, called ECEBT. We evaluate our algorithm on synthetic data concerning multiple noise effects, and on the real world biometric database FVC-2002 DB1 concerning efficiency and effectiveness.

1 Introduction

Biometric features are omnipresent in identification systems. The systems verify the identity on the basis of a person's anatomical and behavioral traits. An advantage over password-based authentication is that biometric data are ubiquitous, unique, persistent and personal. However, these systems require the storage of biometric reference data, which poses high privacy risks itself, as extremely sensitive information can be derived from the biometric data, like ethnic background or health status.

Template protection approaches play an important role in secure storage of the sensitive data. Among these approaches, the Fuzzy-Vault scheme [1] is the most widespread technique. Its ability to deal with unordered sets, which are commonly encountered in biometrics, and its error-tolerance, which is necessary because even two samples of the same biometric trait can differ substantially, qualifys it for biometric crypto systems. Basically, the transformation of a biometric template is realized through a generation of random artificial attributes, which are interspersed to mask the actual template. Finally, only the transformed template is stored. Figure 1 shows the generation of the database template by means of fingerprint data.

A remaining challenge is the matching procedure of a pair of corresponding templates. Several existing approaches already proposed the application of the Fuzzy-Vault scheme to fingerprint minutiae [2–4]. However, these approaches are only dedicated to the authentication processes, where the subject's identity is known apriori. This concept can not be extended in a straightforward way for the identification process, as in addition to an efficient verification process the number of potentially matching templates needs to be reduced significantly.

Recent techniques make use of index structures and filter architectures to reduce the time amount of identification systems [5, 6]. However, these approaches suffer from the

S. Fischer-Hübner, S. Katsikas, G. Quirchmayr (Eds.): TrustBus 2012, LNCS 7449, pp. 129–142, 2012.
© Springer-Verlag Berlin Heidelberg 2012

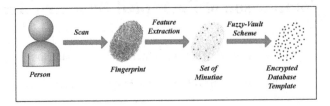

Fig. 1. Generation of a encrypted biometric template

drawback of providing unsatisfactory results on many noise effects of biometric data. In this paper, we present ECEBT, an **E**fficient **C**omparison algorithm of **E**ncrypted **B**iometric **T**emplates. ECEBT makes use of the prominent string matching algorithm by Needleman and Wunsch [7]. Our approach outperforms BioSimJoin [5], a recent approach for efficient filtering of encryped biometric fingerprint data, in terms of robustness against multiple noise effects. Furthermore, we demonstrate the practical feasibility of ECEBT by means of the fingerprint database FVC-2002 DB1 [8].

The rest of the paper is organized as follows. In Section 2, we summarize the encoding of biometric data by the Fuzzy-Vault scheme and survey recent approaches for an efficient biometric identification process. Section 3.1 formalizes the theoretic background and presents some concepts and algorithms that build the basis for ECEBT. Afterwards, our new technique is described in detail in Section 3.2. The experimental evaluation of ECEBT follows in Section 4. Finally, the paper is concluded in Section 5.

2 Biometric Template Protection and Prior Work

Biometric databases exemplarily store a fingerprint image for each user. Each fingerprint is represented by the set of its features, namely the 2-dimensional minutiae positions $m = (m_x, m_y)$. The biometric identification procedure then mathches a query template Q against a database $\mathcal{R} = \{R_1, R_2, \cdots, R_n\}$ of n reference templates. Each reference template R_k is stored encrypted by the Fuzzy-Vault scheme [1].

Fuzzy-Vault. Imagine a player, called Alice, who places a secret value κ in a fuzzy vault and *locks* it using a set A of elements from some public universe U. If another player, lets say Bob, tries to *unlock* the vault using a set B of similar size, he obtains the secret value κ only if B is close to A, i.e., only if both sets overlap substantially. In contrast to previous approaches, Fuzzy-Vault provides order invariance, meaning that the ordering of A and B is immaterial to the functioning of the vault. Hence, it is well applicable for the template protection of unordered biometric features of fingerprint images. In detail, Alice locks κ under A by a polynomial p such that p has an embedding of the secret value in its coefficients. Each element of A is then projected onto points lying on p. Alice additionally generates a number of random values, called chaff points that do not lie on the polynomial, but conceal it from an attacker. The entire point set, covering the genuine points and the chaff points, constitutes a commitment of the polynomial, which refers to κ. Suppose now that Bob tries to unlock κ by means of B. If B and A overlap substantially, then B identifies many points that lie on the polynomial. In this case,

Bob is able to recover a point set that is largely correct, but perhaps is contaminated by a small amount of noise. Using error correction, he is able to reconstruct p exactly, and thereby the secret value κ. If B does not overlap substantially with A, then it is infeasible for Bob to learn the secret, because of the presence of many chaff points.

The so-called verification is then the comparison of the query minutiae $m_Q \in Q$ with a reference template $R_k \in \mathcal{R}$. Hence, this procedure determines the degree of overlap between A and B.

Verification. The verification of biometric templates is based on a match of corresponding points in due consideration of global translations and rotations of the query template Q, and a tolerance parameter concerning position deviations. The matching points are used, together with the associated values, for the reconstruction of the polynomial p by means of the Reed-Solomon-Decoder [9].

In the following, we survey the application of the Fuzzy-Vault approach for the encrypted biometric identification process.

Biometric Identification Process. A naive way to perform the identification of a person on the basis of biometric features, is to use authentication systems (e.g. the approach by Korte *et al.* [10]) for a sequential scan of the complete database until a match is found. But, such approaches are not practicable for large databases. Rather, we have to determine the relevant reference templates, so that the exact verification is only performed on a reduced set of persons. The work by [5] proposes two techniques, called GeoMatch and BioSimJoin. Both algorithms provide a ranked list of candidates in order to reduce the time for the identification procedure.

GeoMatch. The GeoMatch approach decomposes the general matching problem of query template Q and reference template R_k into small units, on which individual matchings are performed, and afterwards, these local solutions are checked for global consistency. GeoMatch calculates a set of triangles for both templates, which are defined by those coordinate triplets, whose pairwise Euclidean distances (cf. Section 3.1) are outside of a given range. To balance the influence of local misplacements of minutiae caused by inaccuracies during the capture procedure of the data, the similarity check of two edges considers a given tolerance value. The comparison of these local patterns is independent of the global positioning or rotation, and hence translation invariant. For each pair of similar triangles, GeoMatch determines their relative rotation to each other, and finally, it checks for global consistency. The larger the number of similar rotated matchings, the higher is the probability for the similarity of both templates. Subsequently, all reference objects R_k are prioritized for the verification process.

BioSimJoin. GeoMatch suffers from the drawback, that the comparison is very time-consuming. Hence, BioSimJoin, stores the coded fingerprint information, including minutiae and chaff points in an index structure, i.e. the R-tree [11]. First, a range query is performed for each minutia $m_i \in Q$ for the query template with radius r. In this manner, BioSimJoin aims for answering questions like "Find all minutiae/chaff points in the database that are located within a range r around the query minutia". This procedure is

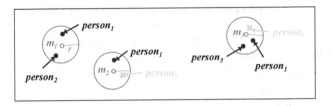

Fig. 2. Identification during the BioSimJoin approach

illustrated in Figure 2. In this example, the query fingerprint consists of three different minutiae m_1, m_2 and m_3. Genuine minutiae that are located within the requested range are illustrated as black points, whereas grey crosses indicate chaff points. BioSimJoin determines a list of relevant minutiae/chaff points for each query minutia m_i. In addition, for each of these points, an ID of the corresponding individual is stored. In our example, for the query minutia m_3 two genuine minutiae and one chaff point within the range r are identified. The grey chaff point, as well as the minutia on the right belong to the individual $person_1$. The minutia on the left refers to $person_3$. In the end, BioSimJoin provides the following list of candidates (w.r.t. all three minutiae of the query person): Four hits for $person_1$, two hits for $person_2$, and one hit for $person_3$. Supported by an index structure, this list can be determined very efficiently. However, rotations and translations are not handled explicitly by BioSimJoin.

3   Efficient Comparison of Encrypted Biometric Templates

In this Section, we introduce the theoretic background and present some concepts and algorithms, ECEBT is based on. Afterwards, we describe our new technique for efficient comparison of encrypted biometric templates in detail.

3.1   Theoretical Background

Distance Matrix. A distance matrix D is a 2-dimensional array containing the pairwise distances of a point set. D has a size of $n \times n$, where n is the number of points. The pairwise distances are defined by a distance function. For ECEBT, we use the Euclidian distance between pairs of minutiae.

Euclidian Distance. The Euclidian distance $d_{euclidian}$ is the *ordinary* distance between two points p and q, and is given by the Pythagorean formula.

$$d_{euclidian}(p,q) = \sqrt{\sum_{i=1}^{dim}(p_i - q_i)^2},$$

where dim is the dimensionality of the points p and q.

Each distance function d satisfies the following three conditions:

1. $d(p, q) \geq 0$, and $d(p, q) = 0$ if and only if $p = q$. (Distance is positive between two different points, and is zero precisely from a point to itself.)
2. d is symmetric: $d(p, q) = d(q, p)$. (The distance between two points is the same in either direction.)
3. d satisfies the triangle inequality: $d(p, z) \leq d(p, q) + d(q, z)$. (The distance between two points is the shortest distance along any path).

For ECEBT, we also need to calculate the distance beetween pairs of strings. Typically, this is done by the Needleman-Wunsch algorithm, which originates from the field of Bioinformatics to align protein or nucleotide sequences. In contrast to distance measures, Needleman-Wunsch consideres the *similarity* score of two sequences, which is only a orthogonal perception.

Needleman-Wunsch Algorithm. The basic idea behind the Needleman-Wunsch algorithm [7] is the following question: How can we transform the string S_1 into another string S_2 with a minimal number of edit operations (match, insertion, deletion)?

Given the strings S_1 and S_2 of lengths $|S_1| = m$ and $|S_2| = n$, and an initialization value iv, where iv stands for the penalty of a deletion, insertion or substitution. To find the alignment of S_1 and S_2 with the highest score, a matrix D is allocated, where $D_{i,j}$ denotes the entry in row i and column j. There is one column for each character in string S_1, and one row for each character in string S_2.

D is initialized as follows. $D_{0j} = iv \times j$ and $D_{i0} = iv \times i$. As the algorithm progresses, each entry $D_{i,j}$ is determined based on the principle of optimality:

$$D_{i,j} = \max(D_{i-1,j-1}, \ D_{i,j-1} + iv, \ D_{i-1,j} + iv).$$

Hence, $D_{i,j}$ is assigned to be the optimal score for the alignment of the first $i = 0, \cdots, m$ characters in S_1 and the first $j = 0, \cdots, n$ characters in S_2. Once the matrix D is computed, the entry $D_{n,m}$ gives the maximum score among all possible alignments. To determine an alignment that actually gives this score, you start from the bottom right cell, and compare the value with the three possible sources match (i-th character in S_1 and j-th character in S_2 are aligned), deletion (i-th character in S_1 is aligned with a gap), and insertion (j-th character in S_2 is aligned with a gap). In general, more than one choices may have the same value, leading to alternative optimal alignments.

Convex Hull. ECEBT approximates the set of minutiae by its convex hull. The convex hull for a point set P is the minimal convex set containing P. Figure 3(b) illustrates the convex hull for a set of minutiae. There are many algorithms that compute the convex hull of a finite point set in the plane. For ECEBT, we use Graham's Scan.

Graham's Scan. The Graham-Scan algorithm computes the convex hull for a given set of 2-dimenional points with time complexity $O(n \log n)$, where n is the number of points, published by Ronald Graham [12]. The algorithm works in three phases:

(a) False positive minutiae.   (b) Convex hull of the set of minutiae.

Fig. 3. Preprocessing steps for the generation of the query matrix

1. Choose the point with largest coordinate value in one dimension as extreme point, the so-called pivot. This point is guaranteed to be on the hull.
2. Sort the points in order of increasing angle about the pivot, resulting in a star-shaped polygon.
3. Create the hull, by marching around the star-shaped polygon, adding edges for each left turn, and back-tracking for each right turn.

3.2   ECEBT

Our new approach is based on a match of a set of points (the minutiae of the query fingerprint) with a encrypted fingerprint database, where each entry again is represented by a set of minutiae and chaff points. ECEBT stores the query fingerprint Q, as well as an database entry R_k in a matrix – the query matrix D_Q and the reference matrix D_{R_k}. The matching process of these two matrices is performed by a double-stage Needleman-Wunsch algorithm (cf. Section 3.1). The resulting distance measure stands for the matching score of Q and R_k. Finally, ECEBT provides an list of reference fingerprints ordered according the matching score.

Query Matrix. The query matrix D_Q stores the pairwise distances of the minutiae of the query fingerprint Q, where the 2-dimensional minutiae coordinates are ordered by their second dimension values. ECEBT only consideres reliable minutiae, i.e. minutiae that are misleadingly identified by the scanner (often at the border of the fingerprint image) are discarded. Figure 3(a) shows an example. The detected minutiae are marked by black dots. The highlighted region describes false positive features.

ECEBT discards these minutiae by an approximation of the set of features. For this purpose, we use the corresponding convex hull, determined by the Graham-Scan algorithm (cf. Section 3.1). This approximation is robust against rotated or imperfectly scanned fingerprints. Finally, we scale down the convex hull by the parameter ϵ, to accept only genuine minutiae. This procedure is depicted in Figure 3(b).

By using the pairwise distances, rather than the concrete minutiae positions, ECEBT is robust against shift effects of the fingerprint images. However, an open challenge

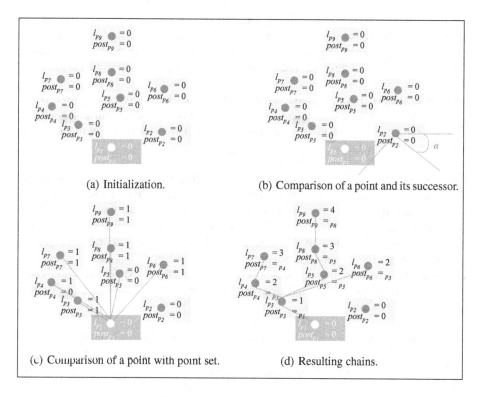

(a) Initialization.

(b) Comparison of a point and its successor.

(c) Comparison of a point with point set.

(d) Resulting chains.

Fig. 4. Detecting the longest chain

are rotated fingerprint images, as a rotation impacts the order of the points within the distance matrices. We address this problem by choosing a selected set of minutiae for the generation of D_Q. The selection acts in accordance to a maximum allowed rotation angle α and a concept, called *longest chain*.

The longest chain is a list of points, where the successive point (according the specified order) must be located within the region defined by α. In thiscase, the order of the points is invariant, as long as the rotation degree of the fingerprint image does not exceed α.

Detecting the Longest Chain. In order to find the longest chain of points within the approximated set of points, we allocate the parameters l and $post$ to each point p of the point set. l stores the length of the chain including p, and $post$ describes the successive point. Both parameters are initialized by zero (cf. Figure 4(a)). Then, we check for each point p_i if p_i is located within the α-region of its successive point p_{i+1}, where α is a user-defined threshold, i.e. $\alpha = 20$ for typical biometric datasets. This procedure is illustrated in Figure 4(b). For each positive check, we update the parameters as follows. If $l_{p_i} + 1 > l_{p_{i+1}}$, i.e. the length of the chain via p_i exceeds the length of the previous chain: (1) $l_{p_{i+1}} = l_{p_i} + 1$ and (2) $post_{p_{i+1}} = p_i$. This procedure is also done for each point above p_i (cf. Figure 4(c)). Finally, we end up in a network of multiple chains across the point set, as shown in Figure 4(d). In our example, this network consists of three different chains, where the path $p_1 \rightarrow p_3 \rightarrow p_5 \rightarrow p_8 \rightarrow p_9$ refers to the longest chain. Its length is determined by the value of the parameter l ($l_{p_9} = 4$). The corresponding path is backtraced by following the links given by each *post* value. The members of the longest chain build the point set of the query matrix D_Q.

Reference Matrix. Each database entry is represented by a reference matrix D_{R_k}, where each D_{R_k} is a distance matrix according the minutiae and chaff points of the reference template R_k. The order of the points is analogous with the order of the corresponding query template.

Matching-Process. After generating the query matrix D_Q and each database entry D_{R_k}, ECEBT performs the actual matching-process, i.e. we try to embed D_Q into each D_{R_k} and determine the corresponding matching score. This procedure is done by a double-stage approach. An outer Needleman-Wunsch (cf. Section 3.1) procedure NW_{outer} aligns each row i of D_Q and each column j of D_{R_k}. For each entry of NW_{outer}, we perform an inner procedure NW_{inner}, where NW_{inner} calculates the distances between concrete pairs of points (minutiae/chaff points). The result of each NW_{inner} procedure serves as matching-value for NW_{outer}. In detail, we describe this procedure by an example.

Given a query template $Q = \{(1,2),(5,5),(3,7)\}$ and a reference template $R_k = \{(1,2),(8,2),(5,4),(8,4),(3,6),(10,8)\}$. Following an Euclidian distance function (cf. Section 3.1), we achieve the query matrix D_Q and the reference matrix D_{R_k} defined as follows.

$$D_Q = \begin{pmatrix} 0.00 & 5.00 & 5.39 \\ 5.00 & 0.00 & 2.83 \\ 5.39 & 2.83 & 0.00 \end{pmatrix} \quad D_{R_k} = \begin{pmatrix} 0.00 & 7.00 & 4.47 & 7.28 & 4.47 & 10.82 \\ 7.00 & 0.00 & 3.61 & 2.00 & 6.40 & 6.32 \\ 4.47 & 3.61 & 0.00 & 3.00 & 2.83 & 6.40 \\ 7.28 & 2.00 & 3.00 & 0.00 & 5.39 & 4.47 \\ 4.47 & 6.40 & 2.83 & 5.39 & 0.00 & 7.28 \\ 10.82 & 6.32 & 6.40 & 4.47 & 7.28 & 0.00 \end{pmatrix}$$

Furthermore, we are given $iv_{inner} = -2$, $|D_Q| = m = 3$ and $|D_{R_k}| = n = 6$. Then we calculate the initialization value of the outer procedure iv_{outer} by the following formula, which guarantees a reliable comparison of matrices of different sizes.

$$iv_{outer} = \frac{(m + n - |m - n|) * iv_{inner}}{4} = \frac{(3 + 6 - |3 - 6|) * -2}{4} = -3$$

Hence, NW_{outer} is initialized as depicted in Figure 5(a). The score for a match of entry $NW_{outer_{1,1}}$ (marked in grey) is determined by the corresponding alignment of the strings belonging to row $i = 1$ and column $j = 1$. This alignment is performed by the inner procedure NW_{inner} (cf. Figure 5(b)). In our example, the strings

$$(0.00 \ 7.00 \ 4.47 \ 7.28 \ 4.47 \ 10.82) \text{ and } (0.00 \ 5.00 \ 5.39)$$

are aligned with a matching score of -7.44. Also in this case, we have to consider the different lengths of the strings.

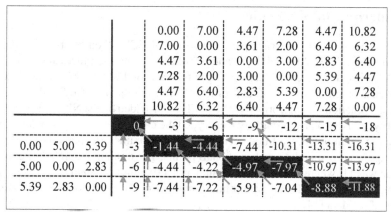

(a) Initialization of NW_{outer}.

(b) Alignment of $NW_{outer_{1,1}}$.

(c) Resulting alignment.

Fig. 5. Example of ECEBT

$$score_{normalized} = score - (|m - n| * iv_{inner}) = -7.44 - (|6 - 3| * -2) = -1.44$$

After defining $score_{normalized}$ as matching score for NW_{outer}, we are now in the position to fill the entry $NW_{outer_{1,1}}$ as follows.

$$NW_{outer_{1,1}} = \max($$
$$NW_{outer_{0,0}} + NW_{inner}(NW_{outer_{0,0}}) = 0 - 1.44 = -1.44,$$
$$NW_{outer_{1,0}} + iv_{outer} = -3 - 3 = -6,$$
$$NW_{outer_{0,1}} + iv_{outer} = -3 - 3 = -6)$$
$$= \mathbf{-1.44}.$$

Analogously, we compute the complete matrix of NW_{outer}. For each entry, we also store the used edit operation to trace back the optimal alignment, shown in black color in Figure 5(c). Finally, ECEBT provides a list of reference templates ordered by the normalized matching scores. For our example, ECEBT would insert D_{R_k} with a normalized score of $-11, 88 - (|6 - 3| * -3) = -2, 88$.

Runtime Analysis. Generating all reference-matrices D_{R_k} demand one complete scan of the database. As this is a singular preprocesing step only, we do not consider it for the runtime analysis. Also the amount for generating D_Q can be neglected as it is comparatively small.

For the actual comparison, ECEBT computes a matrix of size $(m + 1) \times (n + 1)$, where $m = |D_Q|$ and $n = |D_{R_k}|$ in a procedure NW_{outer}. Each entry of the matrix is derived from three possible sources resulting from different edit operations. Whereas insertions and deletions can be calculated in constant time, a match again requires the comutation of a $(m + 1) \times (n + 1)$ matrix, the result of NW_{inner}. Hence, the runtime of one entry of NW_{outer} is $O(mn)$, and the complete runtime is $O(m^2 n^2)$.

4   Experimental Evaluation

First, we estimate an appropriate parametrization of ECEBT on the basis of the biometric database FVC-2002 DB1 [8] and thus demonstrate the practical feasibility of ECEBT. This database covers eight records for each of 110 finger print images. The evaluation is based on a trade-off concerning the robustness of ECEBT and its runtime. Minutiae extraction was performed by MINDTCT, provided by the NIST Biometric Image Software (NBIS) [13]. Finally, we encryped the data using the Fuzzy-Vault scheme (cf. Section 2). In detail, we filled each point set of genuine minutiae up to 200 points by adding the correspondig number of chaff points. The minimum number of extracted minutiae was 11, whereas a maximum number of 119 minutiae could be extracted from one single finger print. Hence, a minimum number of 81 chaff points guarantees the security of the data [14].

All experiments are performed on workstations, equipped with an Intel Dual Core 7120 M processor with 3,0 GHz and 32 GByte main memory ($WS1$), and an Intel Core2 Duo E6750 processor with 2,66 GHz and 4 GByte main memory ($WS2$), respectively.

4.1   Parameter Evaluation

Here, we evaluate the initialization parameter iv, the maximum rotation angle α and ϵ, the parameter that eliminates minutiae that are located at the borders of the fingerprint (cf. Section 3.2). In each run, we check each fingerprint against the complete database, and return the resulting list of relevant candidates ordered by three different criteria (score, distance, α). Score refers to the matching score of the compared templates. Distance and α are evaluation measures w.r.t. the minutiae positions of the aligned templates.

The initialization by iv mostly affects the result of ECEBT. Small values tolerate larger distances between corresponding pairs of minutiae. We evaluated iv on workstation $WS2$ in a range of -1 to -20 in combination with commonly accepted values for the remaining parameters ($\alpha = 45°$, $\epsilon = 10$ px). Figure 6(a) shows the average position of the query fingerprint Q ordered by α (marked by a triangle), distance (marked by a square), and the score (marked by a diamond). All curves indicate their minimum at $iv = -4$. Figure 6(b) illustrates the runtime of ECEBT during these experiments. It remains relatively constant, because it only depends on the constant number of minutiae. The average runtime for one search against the complete database took about 38 sec, where one single comparison took about 43 ms in average.

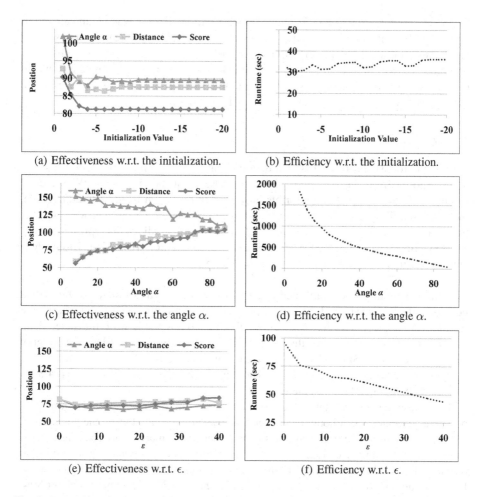

Fig. 6. Evaluation of the parameters of ECEBT concerning effectiveness (w.r.t. three different ordering criteria) and efficiency

We evaluated the maximum rotation angle α by the use of workstation $WS1$, with a parametrization from 8° to 88°. ECEBT was initialized by $iv = -4$ and $\epsilon = 10$ px. Two different observations result from Figure 6(c). First, the effectivity of ECEBT increases w.r.t. the ordering criteria score and distance for larger α values. Our results argue for a parametrization of $\alpha = 8$, which means an average position of $Q = 56$ and $Q = 58$, respectively. Second, the effectivity decreases concerning an ordering by α, but underlies the remaining results in all cases. Hence, we chose a small value that still tollerates typical rotations (e.g. $\alpha = 20$). Figure 6(d) shows that the runtime strongly decreases for higher α values, which results from a lower number of necessary comparisons of minutiae of Q and minutiae/chaff points of the reference template, which also confirms our parametrization for α.

The experiments for ϵ were executed on workstation $WS2$. ϵ was parameterized in a range of 0 to 40, $iv = -4$ and $\alpha = 20$, respectively. Figure 6(e) illustrates that ϵ has a minor influence on the effectivity of ECEBT. However, $\epsilon = 8$ px results in an optimum w.r.t. all ordering criteria. Note that an $\epsilon = 0$ px averaged involves a worse result, as outer points (that are not genuine minutiae) are wrongly part of Q. The runtime consequently decreases for higher ϵ vales (cf. Figure 6(f)).

4.2 Robustness

We test the robustness of ECEBT on datasets that cover 50 fingerprint templates randomly chosen from the FVC-2002 DB1 database as query objects Q. We searched against a database of 1000 fingerprints (also randomly chosen from FVC-2002 DB1), including the 50 query objects. We analyzed four different effects: (1) Rotating, (2) translating, (3) adding and (4) deleting single minutiae of Q. All results represent the average position of Q within the list of candidates. As competitor, we used the BioSimJoin approach with the parameterization suggested in [5].

We evaluate the impact of translated fingerprints on translated 2-dimensional minutiae positions of Q in a range of 10 to 100 px. Translated minutiae that desert the image region, were neglected. Figure 7(a) shows, that ECEBT is stable w.r.t. translated data, as it is only based on relative distances w.r.t. all ordering criteria (depicted by grey curves), whereas BioSimJoin fails for fingerprints that are translated more than 38 px, as can be seen by the black dotted line. The runtime of ECEBT amountet to 5474.8 ms (standard deviation: 248.6 ms) on average.

The consequences of rotations are evaluated in a range of 2° to 68°. For this purpose, we generated a synthetic dataset that consists of the rotated minutiae positions of Q, where only minutiae which are part of the image region are cosidered. Figure 7(b) shows the practicability of ECEBT, as typical enrolement systems accept a maximum rotation of $\alpha = 20°$. Q is always ranked first, independent of the ordering criterion. Higher rotations effect less robust results. Nevertheless, ECEBT excludes about 80% of the fingerprints succesfully, if Q is rotated by $\alpha = 60°$ (concerning the score). BioSimJoin underlies ECEBT in almost all cases. The runtime decreases, as strong rotations produce many minutiae that are not part of the image region. An average identification took 4730.5 ms.

Deleting up to 40 random minutiae from Q simulates the problem that some minutiae are not identified succesfully during the verification process. Figure 7(c) shows that ECEBT is totally stable until a deletion of 28 minutiae, and also for higher values, ECEBT exceeds BioSimJoin in all cases. The runtime of ECEBT decreases, as less minutiae have to be processed. The average runtime took 2351.8 ms.

We added up to 40 random minutiae to Q to simulate the inverse case. Figure 7(d) demonstrates that the adding up to 20 minutiae has just a minor effect on the robustness of ECEBT concerning the score. Nevertheless, insertions affect ECEBT stronger than the competitor BioSimJoin. The runtime of ECEBT increases, as more features have to be considered. In average, one search took 8133.8 ms.

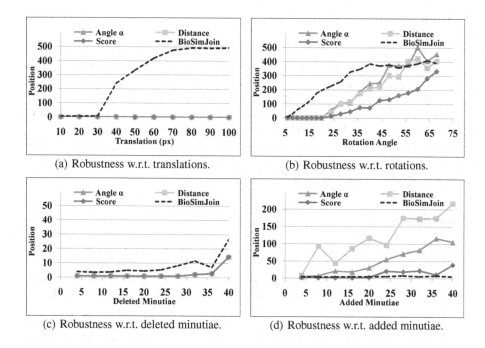

(a) Robustness w.r.t. translations.

(b) Robustness w.r.t. rotations.

(c) Robustness w.r.t. deleted minutiae.

(d) Robustness w.r.t. added minutiae.

Fig. 7. Evaluation of the robustness (w.r.t. three different ordering criteria) of ECEBT in contrast to the approach BioSimJoin

4.3   Efficiency

The runtime of ECEBT was evaluated on workstation $WS2$ using one query fingerprint against a database consisting of different numbers of minutiae, ranging from 50000 to 350000. Figure 8 shows the runtime of ECEBT and the competitor BioSimJoin contingent on the database size in logarithmic scale. The runtime of ECEBT turned out to be linear, whereas BioSimJoin possesses a stronger increase. Nevertheless, BioSimJoin outperforms ECEBT by one order of magnitude in terms of efficiency.

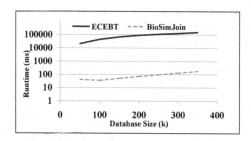

Fig. 8. Runtime evaluation w.r.t. the database size

5   Conclusion

We presented ECEBT – an efficient approach for comparing encrypted biometric templates. ECEBT provides a prioritized list of candidates for the complex verification process, based on the concept of string alignments. ECEBT is robust against rotation and translation effects, as it is based on pairwise distances rather than concrete minutiae positions. We demonstrated the practical feasibility of ECEBT on the real world database for fingerprints FVC-2002 DB1. However, ECEBT suffers from the drawback of relatively high runtimes which result from the nested procedure for calculating the string alignments. In a further step, we will parallelize some of these calculation steps in order to accelerate the overall runtime of ECEBT.

References

1. Juels, A., Sudan, M.: A Fuzzy Vault Scheme. Des. Codes Cryptography 38(2), 237–257 (2006)
2. Uludag, U., Pankanti, S., Jain, A.K.: Fuzzy Vault for Fingerprints. In: Kanade, T., Jain, A., Ratha, N.K. (eds.) AVBPA 2005. LNCS, vol. 3546, pp. 310–319. Springer, Heidelberg (2005)
3. Nandakumar, K., Jain, A.K., Pankanti, S.: Fingerprint-Based Fuzzy Vault: Implementation and Performance. Transactions on Information Forensics and Security 2(4), 744–757 (2007)
4. Merkle, J., Niesing, M., Schwaiger, M., Ihmor, H., Korte, U.: Performance of the Fuzzy Vault for Multiple Fingerprints. In: BIOSIG, pp. 57–72 (2010)
5. Böhm, C., Färber, I., Fries, S., Korte, U., Merkle, J., Oswald, A., Seidl, T., Wackersreuther, B., Wackersreuther, P.: Filtertechniken für geschützte biometrische Datenbanken. In: BTW, pp. 379–389 (2011)
6. Böhm, C., Färber, I., Fries, S., Korte, U., Merkle, J., Oswald, A., Seidl, T., Wackersreuther, B., Wackersreuther, P.: Efficient Database Techniques for Identification with Fuzzy Vault Templates. In: BIOSIG, pp. 115–126 (2011)
7. Needleman, S.B., Wunsch, C.D.: A General Method Applicable to the Search for Similarities in the Amino Acid Sequence of Two Proteins. JMB 48(3), 443–453 (1970)
8. Maltoni, D., Maio, D., Jain, A.K., Prabhakar, S.: Handbook of Fingerprint Recognition (2009)
9. Reed, I.S., Solomon, G.: Polynomial Codes over Certain Finite Fields. In: SIAM, pp. 300–304 (1960)
10. Korte, U., Merkle, J., Niesing, M.: Datenschutzfreundliche Authentisierung mit Fingerabdrücken. Datenschutz und Datensicherheit - DuD 33(5), 289–294 (2009)
11. Guttman, A.: R-Trees: A Dynamic Index Structure for Spatial Searching. In: SIGMOD, pp. 47–57 (1984)
12. Graham, R.L.: An Efficient Algorithm for Determining the Convex Hull of a Finite Planar Set. Inf. Process. Lett. 1(4), 132–133 (1972)
13. Watson, C.I., Garris, M.D., Tabassi, E., Wilson, C.L., McCabe, R.M., Janet, S., Ko, K.: User's Guide to NIST Biometric Image Software (NBIS), National Institute of Standards and Technology (2007)
14. Mihailescu, P., Munk, A., Tams, B.: The Fuzzy Vault for Fingerprints is Vulnerable to Brute Force Attack. In: BIOSIG, pp. 43–54 (2009)

Short and Efficient Identity-Based Undeniable Signature Scheme

Rouzbeh Behnia[1], Swee-Huay Heng[1], and Che-Sheng Gan[2]

[1] Faculty of Information Science and Technology, Multimedia University, Malaysia
[2] Faculty of Engineering and Technology, Multimedia University, Malaysia
{rouzbeh.behnia,shheng,csgan}@mmu.edu.my

Abstract. The first provably secure identity-based undeniable signature schemes was proposed by Libert and Quisquater, where they formulated the security model of undeniable signature schemes in an identity-based setting for the first time. Later, Wu et al. proposed a convertible identity-based undeniable signature scheme. Both of the proposed schemes require pairing evaluations in their signing algorithm. In this paper, we propose an efficient identity-based undeniable signature scheme and prove its security in the random oracle model. Due to its efficient signing algorithm and short signature length, our scheme can be applied to systems with low-computation power which are operating in low-bandwidth communication channels (e.g. mobile phones, PDAs, etc.).

Keywords: Identity-based, undeniable signature, random oracle model, short signature.

1 Introduction

Identity-based cryptography was put forth by Shamir [7] to overcome the well-documented issues inherited in traditional public key cryptography. In such systems, the public key of the user is derived from her public information (e.g. IP address, passport number, etc.). The user's private key on the other hand, is computed by a trusted third party called the Private Key Generator (PKG).

In 1989, Chaum and van Antwerpen [3] proposed the notion of undeniable signature schemes to limit the self-authenticating property of ordinary digital signatures. In undeniable signature schemes, signature verification can only take place upon direct interaction with the signer (i.e. via the confirmation or disavowal protocol). Undeniable signatures provide the signer with a special ability to decide who can be convinced from the validity of the signatures. From the main applications of undeniable signature schemes, we can name software licensing [3] and e-vote [2].

The first provably secure identity-based undeniable signature scheme was due to the work of Libert and Quisquater [6]. The authors formulated the security model of undeniable signature schemes in an identity-based setting for the first time and proved the security of the proposed scheme based on some pairing-based related assumptions. In 2008, Wu et al. [8] proposed the first convertible

S. Fischer-Hübner, S. Katsikas, G. Quirchmayr (Eds.): TrustBus 2012, LNCS 7449, pp. 143–148, 2012.

identity-based undeniable signature scheme which enables the signer to convert one or all of her undeniable signatures to ordinary digital signatures. However, both of the proposed schemes require at least one pairing evaluation in their signing algorithm.

In this paper, we propose a provably secure short and efficient identity-based undeniable signature scheme. The signature generation in our scheme does not need any pairing evaluation, and the signature size of our scheme is significantly smaller than the ones in [6,8]. Moreover, we rely the security of our scheme based on the hardness of some well-known assumptions in the random oracle model.

In Section 2, we first recall the properties of pairing over elliptic curves and introduce some definitions which are going to be used throughout this paper. In Section 3, we formally define the security notions related to identity-based undeniable signature schemes. In Section 4, we propose our concrete scheme in detail and discuss about its efficiency. We provide a formal security analysis of our scheme in Section 5. Finally, we conclude our paper in Section 6.

2   Preliminaries

2.1   Bilinear Pairing and Computational Problems

We let $\mathbb{G}_1$ be an additive cyclic group of prime order q with P as its generator, and $\mathbb{G}_2$ be a multiplicative cyclic group of the same order. An admissible bilinear pairing $e : \mathbb{G}_1 \times \mathbb{G}_1 \to \mathbb{G}_2$ is given which is to satisfy the properties of bilinearity, non-degeneracy and computability. The modified Weil pairing [1] is a well accepted instance of admissible bilinear maps which is considered and employed throughout this paper.

Computational Diffie–Hellman (CDH) Problem: Given $aP, bP \in \mathbb{G}_1$, for P as a generator of $\mathbb{G}_1$ and the random choice of $a, b \in \mathbb{Z}_q$, the CDH problem is to compute abP.

xyz-Decisional Diffie-Hellman (xyz-DDH) Problem: Given $aP, bP, cP, Z \in \mathbb{G}_1$, for P as a generator of $\mathbb{G}_1$, and the random choice of $a, b, c \in \mathbb{Z}_q$, the xyz-DDH problem is to decide whether $Z = abcP$.

2.2   Identity-Based Undeniable Signature Scheme

Setup: By inputting the security parameter k, the PKG computes its key pair (s, P_{Pub}) and generates and publishes the system public parameters *params*.

Extract: Given the user's identity ID, the PKG uses its secret key s to compute the user's private key D_{ID} and sends it to the user via a secure channel.

Sign: Provided a message m and the private key of the signer D_{ID}, the signer generates an undeniable signature σ on m.

Confirmation: Given a valid message-signature pair (m, σ), the alleged signer uses her private key to generate a non-transferable confirmation proof transcript on the validity of σ.

Disavowal: Similar to the confirmation protocol, except that an invalid signature is provided and the output is a proof on the invalidity of σ.

3 Security Notions of Identity-Based Undeniable Signature Schemes

The two important security notions of identity-based undeniable signature schemes are depicted as follows:

3.1 Existential Unforgeability

Definition 1. *An identity-based undeniable signature scheme is said to be existentially unforgeable under adaptive chosen message and identity attack if no probabilistic polynomial time (PPT) adversary $\mathcal{A}$ has a non-negligible advantage in the following game:*

The challenger $\mathcal{B}$ initiates the Setup algorithm and sends the system public parameters $params$ to $\mathcal{A}$. The adversary $\mathcal{A}$ is able to perform polynomially bounded number of adaptive queries which are either an extract query, a signature query, or a confirmation/disavowal query. At the end of the game, $\mathcal{A}$ outputs a tuple (ID^*, m^*, σ^*). $\mathcal{A}$ wins the game if the identity ID^* was never queried to the Extract oracle, and the pair (ID^*, m^*) was never queried to the Sign oracle. $\mathcal{A}$'s advantage in this game is defined to be $Adv(\mathcal{A}) = Pr[\mathcal{A}\ wins]$.

3.2 Invisibility

Definition 2. *An identity-based undeniable signature scheme is said to have the property of invisibility under adaptive chosen message and identity attack if no PPT distinguisher $\mathcal{D}$ has a non-negligible advantage in the following game:*

The challenger $\mathcal{B}$ initiates the Setup algorithm and sends the system public parameters $params$ to $\mathcal{D}$. The distinguisher $\mathcal{D}$ is able to perform polynomially bounded number of adaptive queries as in the game of Definition 1. After the first round of queries, $\mathcal{D}$ outputs a message-identity pair (m^*, ID^*), wherein ID^* was never queried to the Extract oracle and requests a challenge signature on (m^*, ID^*). The challenge signature σ^* is generated by the challenger $\mathcal{B}$ based on the outcome of a hidden and random coin toss $b \in \{0, 1\}$. If $b = 1$, σ^* is generated by initiating the Sign oracle. Otherwise, σ^* is chosen randomly from the signature space S. $\mathcal{D}$ performs the second round of queries, however, he is prevented to query the Sign oracle on (m^*, ID^*), the Extract oracle on identity ID^*, or the Confirmation/Disavowal oracle on (m^*, σ^*, ID^*). After the second round of queries, $\mathcal{D}$ outputs his guess b'. The distinguisher wins the game if $b' = b$. $\mathcal{D}$'s advantage in this game is defined to be $Adv(\mathcal{D}) = |Pr[b' = b] - \frac{1}{2}|$.

4 Short and Efficient Identity-Based Undeniable Signature Scheme

In this section, we first propose our short and efficient identity-based undeniable scheme and then, compare its efficiency with the existing identity-based undeniable signature schemes in the literature [6,8].

4.1   The Proposed Scheme

Setup: By taking as input a security parameter k, the PKG generates groups $\mathbb{G}_1$ and $\mathbb{G}_2$ of prime order $q > 2^k$, and an admissible pairing $e : \mathbb{G}_1 \times \mathbb{G}_1 \to \mathbb{G}_2$. Next, it picks an arbitrary generator $P \in \mathbb{G}_1$, a random secret $s \in \mathbb{Z}_q$, and sets the system public key as $P_{Pub} = sP$. Finally, the PKG chooses four cryptographic hash functions where $H_1 : \{0,1\}^* \to \mathbb{G}_1$, $H_2 : \mathbb{G}_1 \times \{0,1\}^* \to \mathbb{Z}_q$, and $H_3, H_4 : \mathbb{G}_1 \times \ldots \times \{0,1\}^* \to \mathbb{Z}_q$, and publishes the system public parameters as $params = (q, \mathbb{G}_1, \mathbb{G}_2, P, P_{Pub}, H_1, H_2, H_3, H_4)$.

Extract: Provided the user's identity ID, the PKG computes $Q_{ID} = H_1(ID)$, and uses the master secret key s to compute and output the user's partial private key as $D_{ID} = sQ_{ID}$.

Sign: Given a message $m \in \{0,1\}^*$ to be signed, the signer with identity ID_S, picks $r \in \mathbb{Z}_q$ at random to compute $\mathcal{S}_1 = rP$, $\mu = H_2(\mathcal{S}_1, m)$ and $\mathcal{S}_2 = (\mu r + r)D_S$ and forms the signature as $\sigma = (\mathcal{S}_1, \mathcal{S}_2)$.

Confirmation: Given a valid message-signature pair $(m, \sigma = (\mathcal{S}_1, \mathcal{S}_2))$, the alleged signer (with identity ID_S) takes the following steps in order to create a non-transferable proof for the designated verifier with identity ID_V. She first sets $Q_V = H_1(ID_V)$ and chooses $v \in \mathbb{Z}_q$ and $U, R \in \mathbb{G}_1$ at random to compute $W = e(P, U)e(P_{Pub}, Q_V)^v$, $Z_1 = e(P, R)$, and $Z_2 = e(\mu \mathcal{S}_1 + \mathcal{S}_1, R)$. Next, she sets $h_C = H_3(W, Z_1, Z_2, \mathcal{S}_1, \mathcal{S}_2, m)$ and $T = R + (h_C + v)D_S$ and forms the proof as (U, v, h_C, T).

   After receiving the proof (U, v, h_C, T), the designated verifier computes $\mu = H_2(\mathcal{S}_1, m)$ and $Q_S = H_1(ID_S)$ to form $W' = e(P, U)e(P_{Pub}, Q_V)^v$, $Z_1' = e(P, T)e(P_{Pub}, Q_S)^{(h_C+v)}$, and $Z_2' = e(\mu \mathcal{S}_1 + \mathcal{S}_1, T)e(P, \mathcal{S}_2)^{(h_C+v)}$. The verifier accepts the proof only if $h_C = H_3(W', Z_1', Z_2', \mathcal{S}_1, \mathcal{S}_2, m)$.

Disavowal: Given an invalid message-signature pair $(m, \sigma = (\mathcal{S}_1, \mathcal{S}_2))$, the alleged signer (with identity ID_S) takes the following steps in order to generate a non-transferable proof for the designated verifier with identity ID_V. She first sets $Q_V = H_1(ID_V)$ and $\mu = H(\mathcal{S}_1, m)$ and chooses $v, \tau \in \mathbb{Z}_q$ and $U \in \mathbb{G}_1$ at random to compute $W = e(P, U)e(P_{Pub}, Q_V)^v$ and $C = (\frac{e(\mu \mathcal{S}_1 + \mathcal{S}_1, D_S)}{e(P, \mathcal{S}_2)})^\tau$. Next, she has to prove her knowledge of a tuple $(\omega, X) \in \mathbb{Z}_q \times \mathbb{G}_1$, where, $C = \frac{e(\mu \mathcal{S}_1 + \mathcal{S}_1, X)}{e(P, \mathcal{S}_2)^\omega}$ and $\frac{e(P, X)}{e(P_{Pub}, Q_S)^\omega} = 1$. In order to do so, she picks $j \in \mathbb{Z}_q$ and $Y \in \mathbb{G}_1$ at random to compute $N_1 = \frac{e(P, Y)}{e(P_{Pub}, Q_S)^j}$, $N_2 = \frac{e(\mu \mathcal{S}_1 + \mathcal{S}_1, Y)}{e(P, \mathcal{S}_2)^j}$, $h_D = H_4(C, W, N_1, N_2, \mathcal{S}_1, \mathcal{S}_2, m)$, $K = Y - (h_D + v)X$, and $a = j - (h_D + v)\omega$ and forms the proof as (C, U, v, h_D, K, a).

   After receiving the proof (C, U, v, h_D, K, a), the designated verifier rejects the proof if $C = 1$, and otherwise computes $W' = e(P, U)e(P_{Pub}, Q_V)^v$, $N_1' = \frac{e(P, K)}{e(P_{Pub}, Q_S)^a}$, and $N_2 = \frac{e(\mu \mathcal{S}_1 + \mathcal{S}_1, K)}{e(P, \mathcal{S}_2)^a}C^{(h_D+v)}$ and accepts the proof only if $h_D = H_4(C, W', N_1', N_2', \mathcal{S}_1, \mathcal{S}_2, m)$.

4.2   Efficiency

Comparing to the existing identity-based undeniable signature schemes [8,6], our scheme does not need any pairing evaluations in its signing step and its signature size is considerably smaller. Table 1 below provides a quick efficiency and size comparison between our scheme and the existing ones [8,6].

Table 1. Efficiency Comparison

	Signing	Signature Length
Libert and Quisquater [6]	pe	$|\mathbb{G}_2| + |r|$
Wu et al. [8]	$pe + pm + pa$	$2|\mathbb{G}_2| + |r|$
Proposed Scheme	$2pm$	$2|\mathbb{G}_1|$

In the above table, pe denotes pairing evaluation and pm and pa denote point multiplication and point addition (in group $\mathbb{G}_1$), respectively. As aforementioned, the cost of point addition and multiplication is insignificant comparing to the cost of pairing evaluation. As depicted in the table above, our signature size is cogently smaller than the ones in [6,8]. Libert and Quisquater's and Wu et al.'s signature length are 1124 and 1284 bits (for $|r| = 100$), respectively, while our signature length is only 320 bits.

We note that we can use the same method as in [6] in order to enable the signer in our scheme to selectively convert her undeniable signatures to the universally verifiable ones.

5   Security Analysis

The method used in the confirmation and disavowal protocols of our scheme is the pairing-based version of the non-interactive designated verifier proofs proposed by Jakobsson, Sako and Impagliazzo [5] which was also employed in [6,8]. Therefore, using the same method as in [6], we can prove that both the confirmation and disavowal protocols of our scheme are sound, complete and non-transferable.

Theorem 1. *If there exists an adversary $\mathcal{A}$ that can submit q_E extract queries, q_S signature queries, and q_{H_i} queries to the random oracle H_i for $i \in \{1, 2, 3, 4\}$ and win the game defined in Section 3.1 with non-negligible success probability $\epsilon_{\mathcal{A}}$, then there exists a PPT algorithm $\mathcal{B}$ which can use $\mathcal{A}$ to solve a random instance (P, aP, bP) of the Computational Diffie-Hellman problem with probability $\epsilon_{\mathcal{B}} \geq (1 - \frac{1}{q_{H_2}})^{q_E}(1 - \frac{1}{q_{H_2}})^{q_S} \frac{1}{q_{H_2}} \epsilon_{\mathcal{A}}$.*

Proof. Please refer to the full version of the paper.

Theorem 2. *If there exists a distinguisher $\mathcal{D}$ that can submit q_E extract queries, q_S signature queries, and q_{H_i} queries to the random oracle H_i for $i \in \{1, 2, 3, 4\}$ and win the game defined in Section 3.2 with non-negligible success probability $\epsilon_{\mathcal{D}}$, then there exists a PPT algorithm $\mathcal{B}$ which can use $\mathcal{D}$ to solve a random instance (P, aP, bP, cP, Z) of the xyz-Decisional Diffie-Hellman problem with probability $\epsilon_{\mathcal{B}} \geq (1 - \frac{1}{q_{H_2}})^{q_E}(1 - \frac{1}{q_{H_2}})^{q_S} \frac{1}{q_{H_2}} \epsilon_{\mathcal{D}}$.*

Proof. Please refer to the full version of the paper.

We can use the same technique as in [4] to rely the anonymity of our scheme to the hardness of the xyz-DDH problem.

6   Conclusion

In this paper, we proposed an efficient identity-based undeniable signature scheme. Our scheme does not need any pairing evaluation in its signing algorithm which makes it considerably efficient comparing to the existing schemes in the literature [6,8]. The signature size of our scheme is also significantly smaller than the ones in the existing schemes.

Acknowledgement. This research was supported by the FRGS grant (FRGS/2/2010/TK/MMU/02/03) and Multimedia University Graduate Research Assistant (GRA) scheme.

References

1. Boneh, D., Franklin, M.: Identity-Based Encryption from the Weil Pairing. In: Kilian, J. (ed.) CRYPTO 2001. LNCS, vol. 2139, pp. 213–229. Springer, Heidelberg (2001)
2. Boyd, C., Foo, E.: Off-Line Fair Payment Protocols Using Convertible Signatures. In: Ohta, K., Pei, D. (eds.) ASIACRYPT 1998. LNCS, vol. 1514, pp. 271–285. Springer, Heidelberg (1998)
3. Chaum, D., van Antwerpen, H.: Undeniable Signatures. In: Brassard, G. (ed.) CRYPTO 1989. LNCS, vol. 435, pp. 212–216. Springer, Heidelberg (1990)
4. Galbraith, S.D., Mao, W.: Invisibility and Anonymity of Undeniable and Confirmer Signatures. In: Joye, M. (ed.) CT-RSA 2003. LNCS, vol. 2612, pp. 80–97. Springer, Heidelberg (2003)
5. Jakobsson, M., Sako, K., Impagliazzo, R.: Designated Verifier Proofs and Their Applications. In: Maurer, U. (ed.) EUROCRYPT 1996. LNCS, vol. 1070, pp. 143–154. Springer, Heidelberg (1996)
6. Libert, B., Quisquater, J.-J.: Identity Based Undeniable Signatures. In: Okamoto, T. (ed.) CT-RSA 2004. LNCS, vol. 2964, pp. 112–125. Springer, Heidelberg (2004)
7. Shamir, A.: Identity-Based Cryptosystems and Signature Schemes. In: Blakely, G.R., Chaum, D. (eds.) CRYPTO 1984. LNCS, vol. 196, pp. 47–53. Springer, Heidelberg (1985)
8. Wu, W., Mu, Y., Susilo, W., Huang, X.: Provably Secure Identity-Based Undeniable Signatures with Selective and Universal Convertibility. In: Pei, D., Yung, M., Lin, D., Wu, C. (eds.) Inscrypt 2007. LNCS, vol. 4990, pp. 25–39. Springer, Heidelberg (2008)

Damage Sharing May Not Be Enough: An Analysis of an Ex-ante Regulation Policy for Data Breaches*

Giuseppe D'Acquisto[1], Marta Flamini[2], and Maurizio Naldi[3]

[1] Garante per la protezione dei dati personali, Roma, Italy
g.dacquisto@garanteprivacy.it
[2] Università telematica internazionale UNINETTUNO, Roma, Italy
m.flamini@uninettunouniversity.net
[3] Università di Roma Tor Vergata, Roma, Italy
naldi@disp.uniroma2.it

Abstract. Data breaches, occurring either on the customer's PCs or on the service provider's equipment, expose customers to significant economic losses. An ex-ante regulation policy that apportions a fraction of the losses to the service provider (a damage-sharing policy) may reduce the burden for the customer and lead the service provider to invest more in security. We analyse this regulation policy through a game-theoretic approach, where the customer acts on the amount of personal information it reveals, and the service provider acts on the amount of security investments. We show that the game exhibits a single Nash equilibrium in a realistic scenario. In order to optimize the social welfare, the regulator has to choose the fraction of damage apportioned to the service provider. We show that the policy is relatively ineffective unless the fraction of damage charged to the service provider is quite large, beyond 60%. On the other hand, if the policy is applied with a large damage-sharing factor, the overall social welfare falls heavily.

Keywords: Privacy, Data breach, Game theory, Security economics, Security investments.

1 Introduction

Data breaches, the malicious access to personal (often sensitive) information, are rising. After an apparent decrease in the number of compromised records (from 361 million in 2008 to 144 million in 2009 [1]), the number of incidents has increased again in 2011 [2].

The information obtained through a data breach is often employed for criminal actions, and may cause significant economic losses for the person, or company, to

---

* The support of the Euro-NF Network of Excellence is gratefully acknowledged by the third author. The paper reflects the personal opinion of the authors and cannot be regarded as an official position of the Garante on the subject.

S. Fischer-Hübner, S. Katsikas, G. Quirchmayr (Eds.): TrustBus 2012, LNCS 7449, pp. 149–160, 2012.
© Springer-Verlag Berlin Heidelberg 2012

which those information refer. The persistence of attacks calls for enhancing security measures, which in turn require investments. Service providers have to assess how much to invest. This is particularly relevant in cloud storage, where customer's data may be distributed or replicated among several physical locations. In the absence of external constraints, Gordon and Loeb have devised a well-known model to evaluate where security investments have to be concentrated, given the wide range of vulnerable devices with different levels of vulnerability [3].

However, the playing field is not level, since service providers have the investment leverage that may help reduce the losses, but most of the losses are suffered by customers. A regulatory action has therefore been advocated to achieve a wider front against security attacks [4]. Since the regulatory intervention may lead to larger costs for the service provider, a balance has to be achieved between government-dictated investments in security and the aim of companies to maximize their profits [5].

An ex-ante regulation policy, based on the damage-sharing principle, has been proposed in [6], where the service provider is charged a fraction of the expected losses due to data breaches. Such fraction is set by the regulatory body, though the customer and the service provider play a strategic game (see [7] for a general introduction to games), based respectively on the amount of personal information released and the amount of security investments. As stated in [5], the choice of the level of the regulatory intervention is delicate: how is the data breach related damage to be shared between customers and service providers ?

Here we consider a game-theoretic framework to assess the optimal level of regulatory intervention in a damage-sharing policy. Optimality is defined as maximizing the social welfare, made of the sum of the customer's and service provider's surpluses. For a realistic scenario, we solve the game numerically, and show that the damage-sharing policy is relatively ineffective, unless the fraction of damage apportioned to the service provider is quite large, beyond 60%.

The paper is organized as follows. The relationship between security investments, personal information, and service demand is modelled in Section 2. In Section 3, we define the damage-sharing regulation policy, which determines the surplus functions reported in Section 4. We formulate the strategic decision framework for the regulator in Section 5. Finally, we define a realistic scenario and evaluate the effectiveness of the damage-sharing policy in Section 6.

2   Demand and Security Investments

When the customer releases personal data to get a service, it does so with the perspective of getting a benefit. Its demand is influenced by the relationship with the service provider, but what it releases impacts on the probability that a data breach occurs and the economic loss it may suffer. In this section, we explore that relation, and provide both the demand model and a model for the link between security investment and data breach probability. We largely draw on the model put forward in [8] and already employed in [6].

We consider first a linear demand function. If the unit price set by the service provider is p, the customer buys a quantity q of services, described by the following equations

$$q = \begin{cases} q^* \left(1 - \frac{p}{p^*}\right) & \text{if } p < p^* \\ 0 & \text{if } p \geq p^* \end{cases} \tag{1}$$

where p^* is the maximum price the customer can tolerate (its willingness-to-pay), and q^* is the maximum amount of service the customer is capable to consume, even if the service is free.

After the release of personal data, the customer can both access more services and enjoy an easier access. Since both these improvements leave to an increased consumption, the demand curve changes. If we indicate the consumption increase factor by α, the useful portion of the curve becomes

$$q = q^*(1 + \alpha)\left(1 - \frac{p}{p^*}\right). \tag{2}$$

But the release of personal information exposes the customer to the risk of data theft and the ensuing economic loss. We can envisage that the degree α of consumption increase favoured by the service provider represents a sort of reward for the personal information, and has to increase with the associated economic loss. In order to describe the relation between α and the economic loss (we indicate by L the potential money loss, and by $L_{\max}$ its upper bound), we employ the following power law:

$$\alpha = \alpha_{\max} \left(\frac{L}{L_{\max}}\right)^{\nu} \qquad 0 < \nu < 1. \tag{3}$$

After considering the relation between money loss and the amount of information released, we have to introduce the probability that the data breach (and the associated money loss) occurs. We recognize that a data breach can take place on either side of the two parties involved in the transaction: the customer and the service provider. We assume that neither party will fake failure data to take advantage of the regulatory policy. Since breaches on the two sides occur independently of each other, the overall data breach probability is

$$P_{\text{db}} = P_{\text{db}}^{(s)} + P_{\text{db}}^{(c)} - P_{\text{db}}^{(s)} \cdot P_{\text{db}}^{(c)}, \tag{4}$$

where $P_{\text{db}}^{(s)}$ is the probability of a data breach occurring on the service provider' side, and $P_{\text{db}}^{(c)}$ is the analogous for the customer.

The service provider has the possibility to mitigate its vulnerability by investing in security. Again, we assume a power law to hold:

$$P_{\text{db}}^{(s)} = P_{\max}^{(s)} \left[1 - A\left(\frac{I}{I_{\max}}\right)^k\right], \tag{5}$$

where I and $I_{\max}$ are respectively the actual investment and that corresponding to the maximum achievable security, both expressed per customer. On the service provider's side, A measures the full impact of investments, so that the probability of data breach ranges between $P_{\max}^{(s)}(1 - A)$ and $P_{\max}^{(s)}$.

The customer is more exposed to the risk of having its data stolen as it releases more data. We assume a simple power law to hold, by exploiting again the money loss as a proxy for the amount of information released:

$$P_{\mathrm{db}}^{(c)} = P_{\max}^{(c)} \left(\frac{L}{L_{\max}} \right)^{\theta} \qquad 0 < \theta < 1, \tag{6}$$

where $P_{\max}^{(c)}$ is the probability of breach corresponding to the maximum release of information.

3   Regulation Policies

The demand model provided in Section 2 tells us how the customer's demand shifts when the customer releases its personal data. However, we have seen that, by releasing personal data, the customer increases its exposure to economical losses due to identity thefts. Since data breaches may occur on the service provider's side, the latter should be held somewhat responsible for the losses incurred by the customer. If that's not the case, the service provider has few, if any, incentives to invest in security. In this section, we describe a regulation policy that may lead the service provider to improve the security of its customers' data.

When a data breach occurs, that's often the result of a malicious activity. The breacher may exploit those data to perform an identity theft, providing a damage to the customer. Some data are available on the losses suffered by victims of identity fraud. We report the data contained in the annual report by Javelin (obtained through phone interviews with 5000 U.S. adults, including 703 fraud victims) [9], on which Romanoski et alii draw [10]. In Fig. 1, we show the average loss per victim for each fraud event over 7 years. Though a slight decreasing trend is present, the average loss is anyway larger than 5000 US dollars (approximately 3800 euros).

In the absence of any regulation, such losses hit the customer only, though the latter may seek compensation through a judicial action. The service provider, who is expected to have much larger means at its disposal, could significantly reduce the probability of a data breach by investing in security. If a regulator can drive the service provider to invest more in security, it may relieve the damage to customers and achieve a better balance in the relationship between the service provider and the (weaker) customer.

We envisage two categories of regulatory actions, which we call respectively *ex-post* and *ex-ante*.

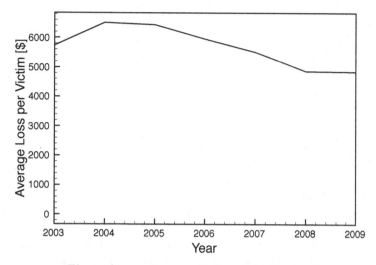

Fig. 1. Average loss per victim of identity fraud

In ex-post regulation, the regulatory body does not normally intervene in the operations of the service provider. However, if a data breach happens, and the customer suffers a damage, the regulator takes actions against the service provider, e.g., by forcing it to introduce tighter security policies. The extent of the regulatory action is not determined beforehand, but is decided case by case.

Instead, in ex-ante regulation, the regulator mitigates the damage for the customer by setting its rules in advance of the data breach event. Many regulatory policies may be envisaged. Here we consider the damage sharing policy put forward in [6]. According to this policy the overall expected damage to be suffered by the customer is apportioned to both the customer and the service provider. The service provider is charged a fraction η of the expected damage LP_{db}, with $0 < \eta < 1$. The service provider is led to invest in security, since by doing so it reduces the probability of a data breach and consequently the amount of money it is charged through the damage sharing policy.

4 The Surplus Functions

The actions of the two stakeholders (the customer and the service provider) are driven by the aim of maximizing their surplus functions, i.e., the difference between their gains and their costs. In this section, we describe the respective surplus functions.

4.1 The Customer

What the customer gains by obtaining the services it requires at the price p is the saving with respect to its willingness-to-pay. When integrated over the range of purchased quantity, the gain is given by the shaded area in Fig. 2.

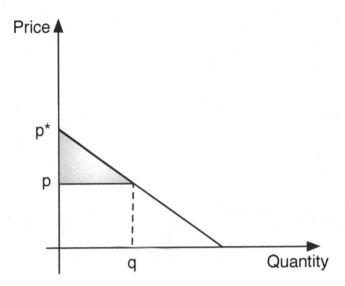

Fig. 2. Customer's gain

But the customer also suffers the loss due to the data breach, which is partly covered by the service provider through the damage sharing policy enforced by the regulator. The net surplus is then given by the difference between the above gain and the average loss

$$S_c = \frac{(p - p^*)^2}{2p^*} q^* \left[1 + \alpha_{\max} \left(\frac{L}{L_{\max}} \right)^{\nu} \right] - (1 - \eta) L P_{\mathrm{db}}. \tag{7}$$

4.2 The Service Provider

The service provider gain on each unit of service is the difference between the unit price p and its unit cost c. If we express the unit cost as a fraction of the unit price $c = \gamma p$ ($0 < \gamma < 1$), the difference $1 - \gamma$ provides the profit margin, in the absence of cash outflows related to security issues. For a wide range of companies, we can envisage γ to lie between 0.8 and 0.95 (corresponding respectively to profit margins of 20% and 5%). The net gain is further diminished by the investments I in security and the quota of data breach-caused damage apportioned to the service provider. In the end, the service provider's surplus is

$$S_{\mathrm{sp}} = qp(1 - \gamma) - I - \eta L P_{\mathrm{db}}. \tag{8}$$

5   Optimization of the Regulatory Intervention

In Section 4, we have described the surplus functions of both the customer and the service provider. Since both aim at maximizing their surplus, their interests conflict. A rational solution of their conflict can be found through a game theoretic approach, considering also the intervention of the regulatory body, which sets the damage sharing coefficient. In this section, we formulate the game between the two stakeholders and define the optimality criterion that drives the regulatory intervention.

The customer's behaviour, when maximizing its surplus given by Equation (7), is driven by two opposite requirements. If it increases the amount of information it releases, it shifts its demand curve so as to be able to gain a larger surplus. At the same time, releasing more information brings along a larger risk, so that both the data breach probability and the average money lost increase, reducing the overall surplus. The leverage the customer can maneuver is anyway the amount of information released, for which we can adopt the money loss L as a proxy.

On the other hand, the service provider can act on the amount of money it invests in security. Increasing the investment I is an expense in itself, reducing the provider's surplus, but it helps reduce the data breach probability and the amount of money transferred under the damage-sharing policy.

This situation can be modelled as a game, where the customer uses the leverage L and the service provider uses the leverage I. Since both aim at maximizing their respective surplus, their best response functions can be obtained by zeroing the derivative of the surplus with respect to the leverage employed. We can adopt normalized leverages, precisely $X = L/L_{\max}$ for the customer and $Y = I/I_{\max}$ for the service provider. In [6] the following best response functions have been derived (both expressed with Y as a function of X)

$$
Y_{\mathrm{c}} = \left[\frac{1}{A} - \frac{\Delta X_{\mathrm{opt}}^{\nu-1} - L_{\max}(1-\eta)\Lambda X_{\mathrm{opt}}^{\theta}}{\Upsilon(1 - \Lambda X_{\mathrm{opt}}^{\theta})} \right]^{1/k},
\tag{9}
$$

where we have used the following positions

$$
\begin{aligned}
\Delta &= \frac{(p^* - \hat{p})^2}{2p^*} q^* \alpha_{\max} \nu, \\
\Lambda &= P_{\max}^{(\mathrm{c})}(1+\theta), \\
\Upsilon &= P_{\max}^{(\mathrm{s})} A L_{\max}(1-\eta),
\end{aligned}
\tag{10}
$$

for the customer, and

$$
Y_{\mathrm{sp}} = \left[\frac{\Phi X \left(1 - P_{\max}^{(\mathrm{c})} X^{\theta}\right)}{I_{\max}} \right]^{\frac{1}{1-k}},
\tag{11}
$$

for the service provider, with $\Phi = \eta P_{\max}^{(\mathrm{s})} A k L_{\max}$.

By using the two best response functions above, we can obtain the Nash equilibrium at the crosspoint of the two curves, where $Y_c = Y_{sp}$. We identify the Nash equilibrium point through its coordinate (X^*, Y^*), and compute the surplus functions of both stakeholders at the Nash equilibrium point. The resulting social welfare is the sum of the two surplus values.

What we obtain depends on the damage sharing coefficient η, i.e., the level of regulatory intervention. Given its neutral stance, the natural aim for the regulatory body is to maximize the social welfare. The optimal level of intervention is therefore that maximizing the social welfare.

6   Effectiveness of the Damage-Sharing Policy

In Section 5, we have set the game and described how the regulatory body intervenes to maximize the social welfare. In this section, we define a realistic scenario for the parameters intervening in the model, and analyse the possibility for the regulator to impact significantly on both stakeholders through the damage-sharing policy.

In order to set realistic values for the parameters employed in our game model, we have gathered data from a variety of sources, including [9], [11], [12], and [13]. On the basis of all the data we have collected, concerning mainly e-commerce applications, we have set the values reported in Table 1. We have also considered several different scenarios, built by perturbing one parameter at a time with respect to the reference scenario.

Table 1. Parameters' values for the reference scenario

Parameter	Value
L_{max}	25000 €
I_{max}	20 €
p^*	350 €
p	200 €
q^*	7
α_{max}	0.15
$P_{max}^{(s)}$	$5 \cdot 10^{-3}$
$P_{max}^{(c)}$	$5 \cdot 10^{-3}$
k	0.5
A	0.9
ν	0.139
θ	0.139

We use this scenario to investigate the following issues:

1. the existence and uniqueness of a single Nash equilibrium point;
2. the impact of the regulatory intervention on the economic results of the customer and the service provider;
3. the optimization of social welfare through regulatory intervention.

We start by considering the existence of a Nash equilibrium point, i.e., of a unique solution of the game, which identifies a rational strategic decision for both players. In several scenarios considered in [6] (which was focussed on the mobile telephony case), a single Nash equilibrium had been shown to exist. Here we have observed that the two best response curves cross each other once in all the cases examined. In Fig. 3 we report a sample pair of best response functions (in the I/I_{max} vs L/L_{max} form), when the profit margin is 10% ($\gamma = 0.9$), and the damage sharing factor is $\eta = 0.5$. In that picture the general trend of the curves is clear, but the crosspoint is not visible. For that reason, we report a zoomed version of the same best response curves in Fig. 4, where we see that the two curves actually cross each other, though for very small values of the security investment per customer.

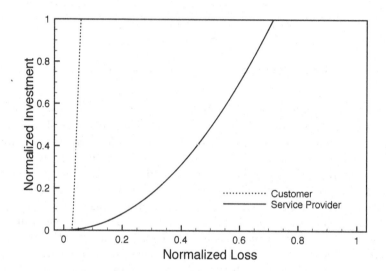

Fig. 3. Best response functions

Though the players in the game are the customer and the service provider, a key role is played by the regulator, which sets the damage sharing factor. Actually, the whole damage-sharing policy, which sets the game and determines the strategic moves by the two players, is managed by the regulator. The level of regulatory intervention is embodied by the damage sharing factor η: the larger it is, the heavier the haircut on the service provider and the incentive to invest in security. Though the regulator acts on the service provider, its aim is however to maximize the social welfare, i.e., the overall sum of the surplus of the two players. As recalled above, the leverage it can use is the damage-sharing factor: it should use the value of η maximizing the social welfare. In Fig. 5, we report both the surpluses and the social welfare obtained as η varies over the $[0.1, 0.9]$

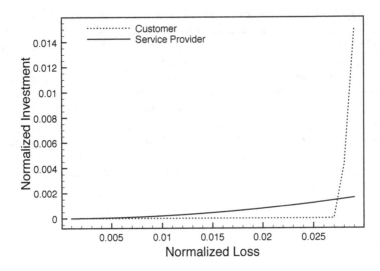

Fig. 4. Best response functions (zoomed version)

range, again for a profit margin of 10%. We recall that the values reported for the service provider are per customer. The service provider's surplus is anyway marginally affected by the regulatory intervention, as long as its participation to the customer's losses is lower than 60% roughly. If the damage sharing factor exceeds this threshold, the service provider's surplus falls quite fast. Instead, the customer is practically unaffected by the regulatory intervention. Its surplus grows by a meager 3.1% as the damage sharing factor spans its entire range. The overall result is that the welfare decreases by 10.4% over the whole range of η, but is really flat for most of that range. The regulatory intervention looks quite ineffective, unless it is very heavy, with the service provider taking on most of the losses (say, more than 60%). If the regulator applies a damage-sharing factor larger than 60%, its behaviour looks too punitive against the service provider, with the social welfare falling down as well.

Assuming, however, that the regulator threatens the service provider with reducing its profit by assigning it a large fractino of the data breach losses, we can investigate if the danger posed by that threat is more significant when the profit margin (prior to damage sharing) is lower. We would expect that a larger prior profit margin makes the service provider more robust to the regulatory action. In order to analyse such hypothesis, we have computed the social welfare resulting from the game's outcome over the range of the damage sharing factor for different values of the profit margin, i.e., of γ. In Fig. 6, we have plotted the social welfare for a profit margin ranging from 8% to 15%. Actually, the social welfare decreases as the prior profit margin shrinks, but the curve shape is nearly identical for the three values of γ, i.e., insensitive to the prior profit margin.

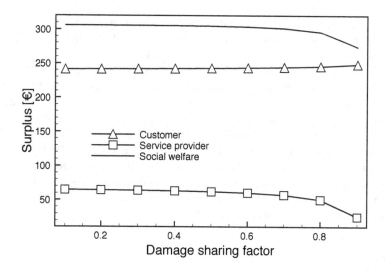

Fig. 5. Surplus and social welfare

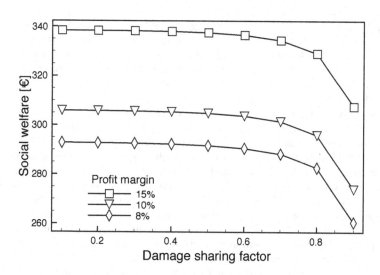

Fig. 6. Impact of profit margin on social welfare

7   Conclusions

We have examined an ex-ante regulation policy, which charges the service provider a portion of the money loss due to data breaches suffered by customers. This damage sharing policy aims at having the service provider invest more in security. The analysis, conducted through a game-theoretic approach, shows that the game between two parties (the customer and the service provider) exhibits a single Nash equilibrium in a realistic scenario. However, as an incentive to invest more in security, the damage sharing policy may be effective just if the damage apportionment rule is heavily unbalanced against the service provider: if the fraction of losses charged to the service provider is less than 60%, the service provider is relatively unaffected by the policy. On the other hand, when applied with a damage-sharing factor larger than 60%, the policy looks punitive towards the service provider and leads to an overall fall of social welfare. A more effective regulation policy may therefore be needed.

References

1. Verizon Risk Team: 2011 Data Breach Investigations Report. Technical report, Verizon (2011)
2. Hoffmann, L.: Risky business. Commun. ACM 54(11), 20–22 (2011)
3. Gordon, L.A., Loeb, M.P.: The economics of information security investment. ACM Trans. Inf. Syst. Secur. 5(4), 438–457 (2002)
4. European Network and Information Security Agency (ENISA): Economics of Security: Facing the Challenge (2011)
5. Lee, Y.J., Kauffman, R.J., Sougstad, R.: Profit-maximizing firm investments in customer information security. Decision Support Systems 51(4), 904–920 (2011)
6. D'Acquisto, G., Flamini, M., Naldi, M.: A Game-Theoretic Formulation of Security Investment Decisions under Ex-ante Regulation. In: Gritzalis, D., Furnell, S., Theoharidou, M. (eds.) SEC 2012. IFIP AICT, vol. 376, pp. 412–423. Springer, Heidelberg (2012)
7. Gibbons, R.: A Primer in Game Theory. Prentice-Hall (1992)
8. D'Acquisto, G., Naldi, M., Italiano, G.F.: Personal data disclosure and data breaches: the customer's viewpoint. ArXiv e-prints (2012)
9. Javelin: 2011 identity fraud survey report. Technical report, Javelin Strategy (2011)
10. Romanosky, S., Sharp, R., Acquisti, A.: Data breaches and identity theft: When is mandatory disclosure optimal? In: The Ninth Workshop on the Economics of Information Security (WEIS), June 7-8. Harvard University, USA (2010)
11. Osservatorio eCommerce B2c: B2c eCommerce in Italy. Technical report, Netcomm-School of Management of Politecnico di Milano (2011) (in Italian)
12. Casaleggio Associati: E-commerce in Italy 2011. Technical report (April 2011) (in Italian), http://www.casaleggio.it/e-commerce/
13. AGCOM (Italian Communications Regulatory Authority): Annual report (2011), http://www.agcom.it

Flexible Regulation with Privacy Points

Hanno Langweg and Lisa Rajbhandari

NISlab Norwegian Information Security Laboratory
Høgskolen i Gjøvik, Postboks 191, 2802 Gjøvik, Norway
{hanno.langweg,lisa.rajbhandari}@hig.no
http://www.nislab.no

Abstract. We propose a utilitarian approach to a uniform regulatory framework to assess privacy impact and to establish compensatory actions. "Privacy points" gauge the effect of measures on people's privacy. Privacy points are exchangeable and, hence, give companies room for innovation in how they improve people's privacy. Regulators lose control on details while getting the opportunity to extend their power to a larger portion of the market.

1 Introduction

The current approach to privacy regulation does not scale. It struggles with underfunded regulatory bodies, is perceived as a hindrance to innovation [1], and exhibits a low risk of audit and fines for noncompliance. Innovation and value creation is impeded by a focus on identical privacy requirements for everybody (as opposed to raising privacy for a large group). We propose a utilitarian approach to improve privacy to a level above minimum requirements.

Privacy impact can be handled in the same way as impact of building projects on ecological quality or the impact of emissions on the environment. Building codes in some jurisdictions allow property developers to compensate for ecological deterioration ("biotope-value procedure" [3]) at different places and in different form with the effect of keeping environmental quality high in the overall jurisdiction of the building code. We lack a similar mechanism of compensation for privacy-reducing measures. Regulation requires upholding minimum standards and attends to individual fairness. This does not scale well. Regulation bodies are therefore structurally unable to reach large portions of their supervised market. At the same time, global service providers need to follow different requirements in different jurisdictions.

Work has earlier been done on privacy metrics. We use these metrics to develop the concept of "privacy points" to gauge the effect of measures affecting people's privacy and to quantify compensatory actions on a collective level. We use a social networking site as an example of how privacy points could be used in regulation.

S. Fischer-Hübner, S. Katsikas, G. Quirchmayr (Eds.): TrustBus 2012, LNCS 7449, pp. 161–166, 2012.
© Springer-Verlag Berlin Heidelberg 2012

2   Previous and Related Work

Privacy metrics have been developed by various researchers. They include metrics on anonymity (an aspect of privacy by data minimization [11]), for release of anonymized dataset such as [14,2] and for anonymized communication such as [12,6]. Besides, there exist metrics for compliance with privacy regulations such as [8] and for location privacy [13]. Dayarathna [5] has put forward a taxonomy to aid in developing a "comprehensive framework and metrics for information privacy domain". In addition, surveys are conducted using metrics with Likert scales and ordinal scales to assess people's privacy concerns [4].

Privacy impact assessments determine the effect of measures on people's privacy [7,9]. Wright [15] states the importance of audits and metrics apart from making PIA obligatory.

Biotope value procedures are used in building codes, cf. [3,10]. The impact of a construction project on land use and degradation of the ecological value of an area is evaluated before and after a project. Compensatory measures need to be applied within the area of the project or in an attached project so that the sum of ecological assets is not reduced by the construction project.

Emission trading allows regulators to set a cap on all emissions to be obeyed by all regulated companies. Individual companies can decide themselves how they want to organize their business as long as they meet their emission target. In case a company desires higher emissions, it can buy emission entitlements from other companies, increasing flexibility in business while still meeting emission targets set for a whole industrial sector or geographical area.

3   Privacy Points

We propose to quantify the impact of privacy-affecting measures and to express the impact in "privacy points". The idea is similar to "eco-points" that quantify the amount of compensation for the use of natural resources in some in building codes. [3] The approach also exists in caps on fuel consumption for car fleets and in emission trading. We believe that having a simple and exchangeable expression of privacy impact will make regulation and enforcement more efficient than today.

All privacy regulators see themselves as underfunded. As an example, the Norwegian Data Inspectorate who is responsible for five million citizens employs ten people overseeing compliance of companies with privacy laws. In 2011, they managed to conduct less than 100 inspections. Individual reviews of high risk environments will continue to be a focus of regulators. We give lawmakers an additional tool to address privacy that is inexpensive in enforcement. Raising the level of privacy will be as easy for lawmakers as increasing a tax rate.[1]

---

[1] Please note that we do not claim that tax codes are easy to understand. We also do not claim that lobbying for special interest groups will disappear with privacy points. Repairing political processes is outside the scope of this article.

3.1   Common Resource

Individuals can enforce protection of their individual minimum privacy rights in court. Lawmakers need to address the overall state of privacy in an industry sector (like social networking) or in a jurisdiction (like the kingdom of Norway). It is – from a utilitarian perspective – not that important that a specific individual gets compensated for an invasion of privacy. It is more important to improve privacy for a large number of citizens/consumers. As an example, a social networking site that implements a new feature that reduces users' privacy, should be obliged to compensate for the loss of privacy within its user base, but not necessarily on an individual basis. This might happen by enabling more privacy-preserving options for other features, by limiting the number of users who can enable the new privacy-reducing feature or by contracting with a market participant to buy improvements in a comparable application. As long as the overall level of privacy is not decreased, regulators reach their goals.

3.2   Innovation

Privacy should not be a hindrance to innovation. At present, the same requirements apply to all software solutions, so that raising requirements to improve privacy affect all systems, raising the entry barrier for new services and market participants. We do not want to lower minimum requirements (although it might be debatable to do so). We intend to increase overall privacy on top of minimum requirements, but with the potential for market participants to find out where privacy improvements have the lowest impact on other business operations. This would give companies the flexibility to innovate while society at large would profit. Privacy – expressed as a target of privacy points that need to be achieved – becomes a constraint that needs to be met by markets, the same way as capping fuel consumption for car fleets increases the overall environmental quality without specifying details of how it is to be achieved.

3.3   Privacy Metrics

We do not invent new privacy metrics. We use existing privacy metrics and transform their scales to privacy points (cf. section 5). A collection of existing privacy metrics is given in section 2. Privacy points can be used in two ways: as an absolute measure of the level of privacy or to express privacy impact on a system after introduction of a privacy-impacting feature.

In the first (absolute) case, a system would have a number of privacy points. A system fulfilling today's legal privacy requirements would be valued with a certain arbitrary number, e.g., 42 privacy points; 0 privacy points would be an absolute minimum, i.e., no privacy at all.

We favour the second (relative) case, where we calculate the number of privacy points of a system before a change and after a change. The difference in privacy points is then the privacy impact of the new feature. A system with 100 users that had 42 privacy points per user before a change and that has 40 privacy points per user after a change, exhibits a net loss of 200 privacy points.

4   Regulation with Privacy Points

4.1   Compensatory Actions

A measure that decreases the level of privacy leads to a lower number of privacy points for the company. If the sum of privacy points drops below the regulatory goal, the company needs to establish compensatory actions so that it generates the requested number of privacy points. Alternatively, it could negotiate with another company to use their excess privacy points. Depending on the regulatory stance, compensation could be limited to compensation within the same user profile, the same user identity, the same user group, the same company, the same sector, the same country, the same type of feature, the same service. A regulator may require that only a certain amount of privacy points can be compensated for by any specific measure, i.e., it might be advisable to distinguish between volume (number of privacy points) and details/constraints (the categories of compensatory actions).

Companies can integrate privacy points in their existing schemes for key performance indicators (KPIs). That way, also managers with no understanding of privacy, will be able to manage the business and meet goals for the overall level of privacy.

4.2   Goal Setting

Lawmakers would not focus on the individual minimum requirements for privacy. Instead, they would specify a desired number of privacy points above minimum requirements that a sector as a whole needs to deliver. There could be higher goals for sectors like healthcare, and there could be lower goals for small companies or social networks with consenting adults.

The baseline of 0 privacy points would be the existing minimum requirements. Lowering minimum requirements would generate privacy points for all companies. Raising minimum requirements for everybody would reduce privacy points in the market and create a need for some market participants to improve to meet thenew (and higher) minimum requirements. It would be enticing for lawmakers to just raise the numeric goal of privacy points for a given year instead of embarking on lengthy debates on the economic and technical impact of legislation specifying new improvements in detail.

5   Implementation Aspects

5.1   Agreement on Numerical Values

Privacy metrics assign values to privacy impacts. These values need to be transformed into privacy points, usually using multiplication wih a scalar or by using a table. If impact is measured per user, the total number of privacy points is the sum of privacy points per user impact. We draw on experience with "eco-points" where the area under consideration is split into areas of same ecological value. The total number of eco-points is the sum of eco-points for the sub-areas. Eco-points for a sub-area are its size in square metres multiplied by the number of eco-points for a square metre area of the respective ecological value.

Agreement on numerical values assigned to privacy-impacting measures is not a hard science, but will involve a political standardisation process. Experience from biotope value procedures with eco-points shows that there is considerable disagreement on details, but that numerical value statements for complex habitats work acceptably well in practice. To our knowledge (at least in Germany), different systems are used by different municipalities, different states, and in different sectors (e.g. building construction, road works).

5.2 Privacy Impact Assessment and Audit

Privacy impact is determined by a privacy impact assessment [7] using privacy metrics. Measurement results are then converted to privacy points and reported by the company. Reporting can be done by any lightweight mechanism, e.g., p23r.de, allowing automatic checking against regulatory goals. Enforcement can be integrated into existing systems, e.g., as part of balance sheet audits. The challenges here are the same as with eco-point reporting in costruction projects or with emission trading, and can be solved in the same (existing) ways.

6 Consequences

6.1 Risk: Decreased Attention for Privacy

A phenomenon that has shown with "eco-points" in assessment of environmental impact is that compensation takes precedence over local minimsation of impact. The same could happen with privacy. If it is easy to compensate for privacy-impacting features, companies might create many of them. Compensation would happen on a purely quantitative basis. As an example, *Facebook* could compensate for a single debated feature with a number of several minor features or by paying *LinkedIn* for an improvement of privacy for their users.

6.2 Pricing of Privacy Measures

Privacy points would support a market for privacy if companies would be allowed to trade privacy points, similar to emission trading. In the context of environmental impact in building codes, such a (limited) market has grown in recent years. There exist exchanges (cf. http://www.ausgleichsagentur.de) to connect property developers and developers of compensatory areas.

An effect we also observe with respect to environmental impact is the use of large volume low quality compensatory actions. Destruction of a lake is compensated for by large areas of simple grassland. Privacy impact could also tend to be compensated for by paying for large volume low quality privacy features, e.g., by introducing large numbers of features that are rarely used. This will be a challenge for any points scheme. Limiting a market in size or collecting (and compensating) points in different categories might be alternative approaches.

7   Conclusions

We have presented an innovative regulatory framework to assess and to compensate for privacy-impacting measures. Similar to established procedures in building codes for environmental impact, privacy impact could be expressed as "privacy points" to quantify the amount of compensation needed to keep the overall level of privacy. In future work we envision to address concerns of individual privacy protection and to validate our approach in a case study.

Acknowledgment. Tobias Mahler and Sebastian Meyer gave helpful feedback.

References

1. Google's Schmidt warns regulators against killing innovation (2012),
   http://www.physorg.com/news/2012-02-google-schmidt.html
2. Bezzi, M.: Expressing privacy metrics as one-symbol information. In: Proceedings of the 2010 EDBT/ICDT Workshops, EDBT 2010, pp. 29:1–29:5 (2010)
3. Bruns, E.: The evaluation and accounting methods used in the mitigation and compensation regulation. In: An Analysis and Systematization of the Proceedings and Approaches Used at the Federal and State Levels. Dissertation, TU Berlin (2007)
4. Buchanan, T., Paine, C., Joinson, A.N., Reips, U.-D.: Development of measures of online privacy concern and protection for use on the internet. Journal of the American Society for Information Science and Technology 58(2), 157–165 (2007)
5. Dayarathna, R.: Taxonomy for information privacy metrics. Journal of International Commercial Law and Technology 6(4) (2011)
6. Diaz, C.: Anonymity metrics revisited. In: Dolev, S., Ostrovsky, R., Pfitzmann, A. (eds.) Anonymous Communication and its Applications, Dagstuhl, Germany. Dagstuhl Seminar Proceedings, vol. 05411 (2006)
7. Gellert, R., Kloza, D.: Can Privacy Impact Assessment Mitigate Civil Liability? A Precautionary Approach. In: IRIS 2012 Proceedings of the 15th International Legal Informatics Symposium, pp. 497–505 (2012)
8. Herrmann, D.S.: Complete Guide to Security and Privacy Metrics: Measuring Regulatory Compliance, Operational Resilience, and ROI (2007)
9. ICO. Privacy impact assessment (PIA) handbook, Version 2.0 (2009),
   http://www.tbs-sct.gc.ca/pol/doc-eng.aspx?id=12451
10. Landesamt für Natur, Umwelt und Verbraucherschutz Nordrhein-Westfalen. Numerische Bewertung von Biotoptypen für die Eingriffsregelung in NRW (2008)
11. Pfitzmann, A., Hansen, M.: A terminology for talking about privacy by data minimization: Anonymity, unlinkability, undetectability, unobservability, pseudonymity, and identity management, v0.34 (August 2010),
    http://dud.inf.tu-dresden.de/literatur/Anon_Terminology_v0.34.pdf
12. Reiter, M.K., Rubin, A.D.: Crowds: anonymity for web transactions. ACM Trans. Inf. Syst. Secur. 1(1), 66–92 (1998)
13. Shokri, R., Freudiger, J., Jadliwala, M., Hubaux, J.-P.: A distortion-based metric for location privacy, pp. 21–30 (2009)
14. Sweeney, L.: k-anonymity: a model for protecting privacy. Int. J. Uncertain. Fuzziness Knowl.-Based Syst. 10(5), 557–570 (2002)
15. Wright, D.: Should privacy impact assessments be mandatory? Commun. ACM 54(8), 121–131 (2011)

On the Security of the Non-Repudiation of Forwarding Service

Rainer Schick and Christoph Ruland

Chair for Data Communications Systems, University of Siegen,
Hoelderlinstr. 3, 57076 Siegen, Germany
{rainer.schick,christoph.ruland}@uni-siegen.de
http://www.uni-siegen.de/fb12/dcs/

Abstract. Nowadays, digital data can be protected by several security services. For example, confidentiality can be provided using encryption mechanisms and authentication can be realized by digital signatures. However, it is usually assumed that only unauthorized users want to manipulate data or attack the system. Often the attacks committed by allegedly trusted users are neglected.

A question following secured transmissions is addressed by the non-repudiation of forwarding service: How to find the responsible person if a data leak comes up? The service provides traceability of confidential data via multiple recipients. Unique tracking data are added to the message each time it is forwarded, and these data are used to generate evidence in case of a conflict. This paper deals with the security aspects of the non-repudiation of forwarding service and explains how the tracking data are protected against targeted manipulations.

Keywords: Security Service, Non-Repudiation, Data Tracking, Privacy, Digital Watermarking, Data Protection.

1 Introduction

Valuable data can be protected against unauthorized access or manipulations using different security services like *confidentiality, authentication, data integrity* and *access control*. However, often an important question is neglected: What happens, if allegedly trustworthy receivers misbehave? How to find out who is the data leak? The non-repudiation of forwarding service (NRFS) is an approach to solve this problem and has been introduced in [1, 2]. Previous work concerning the NRFS did not consider the security aspects of the tracking data in detail. The new service deals with the topics of *Endpoint Security* and *Data Leakage Protection* [3]. Currently, one of the largest security problems of companies is the unauthorized use of private devices at work. Large amount of data can be stored on insecure devices and the damage may be huge if such a device gets lost or forwarded to an unauthorized person. The NRFS collects so-called tracking data from multiple recipients and provides traceability of data protected by the service. These tracking data are used to prove the forwarding and updated each

S. Fischer-Hübner, S. Katsikas, G. Quirchmayr (Eds.): TrustBus 2012, LNCS 7449, pp. 167–178, 2012.

time the protected message is sent to the next authorized receiver. In case of a dispute, tracking data are used to generate evidence and the traitor cannot deny the forwarding. The conflict resolution after the evidence generation phase is out of scope of the NRFS.

This paper is organized as follows: This introduction is followed by an overview about related work in the next chapter. Chapter 3 provides a general overview about non-repudiation services and summarizes the basic idea of the NRFS. Additionally, the Data Tracking Protocol (DTP) is resumed, which is designed to realize the NRFS. The DTP must ensure that the tracking data are protected against various attacks, so that these protection mechanisms are explained in chapter 4. Finally, chapter 5 presents some conclusions and an outlook to future work is given.

2   Related Work

The ISO/IEC 13888 standards describe eight different non-repudiation services [4–6]. General information about non-repudiation services are provided in ISO 13888-1, symmetric and asymmetric examples are given in ISO 13888-2 and ISO 13888-3, respectively. Roughly spoken, non-repudiation services protect a party against another party falsely denying the involvement in a particular action or event [7]. For example, a sender of sensitive private data requests evidence of receipt by the designated recipient. The recipient in turn requests evidence of sending from the sender. The proof of a certain action is done by the generation of non-repudiation token (NRT). In contrast to other non-repudiation services, **one** NRT generated by the NRFS provides evidence of **multiple** (trans-)actions and proves the **forwarding** of protected information by allegedly trustworthy users.

Non-repudiation services and their underlying protocols usually should be **fair** [9]: No party should get an advantage over another party. The NRFS exchanges tracking data between communicating parties. These tracking data can be considered as token, which are updated and processed by a security module. The use of such a module implies that no party can trick another party, so that the aspect of fairness does not need to be considered in the NRFS. Instead, false positives must be prevented by the NRFS: Attackers shall not be able to tamper tracking data such that innocent users are falsely suspected. Evidence generated by the NRFS shall be unambiguous and unforgeable. Manipulations that prevent the expose of an attacker can be tolerated, but shall be prevented, if possible.

Another approach to provide traceability of data is digital watermarking [10]. Using watermarks, copyright holders want track data leaks if an unauthorized copy is found. In general, digital watermarks can be embedded visible or invisible (or better: imperceptible) and have to cope with different problems: The embedding capacity is limited in relation to the size of its carrier and the embedding algorithms strongly depend on the file format. However, as far as pirated material of multimedia data is concerned, the attackers do not care if the copied content is authentic or not. They manipulate the material, such that the watermark is destroyed or removed. This problem led to stricter solutions, the Digital Rights Management (DRM) technologies.

The idea behind DRM is to prevent unauthorized copies of protected data. This is usually achieved by the installation of proprietary software and online activation mechanisms. During the video playback, the software checks if the content is authentic and if the user has permission to watch it. DRM is considered controversially, and many experts claim that unauthorized copies cannot be prevented. The authors partially share this opinion - also the NRFS cannot prevent the unauthorized forwarding of plaintext information. However, depending on the non-repudiation policy, a data originator can determine certain authorized recipients, precluding everyone else. If still an unauthorized copy is found, it tries to find the data leak and prevent further damage.

3   Non-Repudiation of Forwarding

3.1   Notation

The following terms and notations apply for this paper:

- $X\|Y$: Result of the concatenation of data X and Y in that order.
- M: The confidential message to be protected by the NRFS.
- KH: Key Header containing the secret keys required to realize the NRFS.
- CD: Specific configuration data generated during the initialization phase.
- M': Concatenation of $KH\|M\|CD$.
- $\sigma_{SK}(X)$: Returns the signature over data X using private key SK.
- M^*: $M'\|\sigma_{SK}(M')$.
- $\varepsilon_{SK}(X)$: Returns encrypted data of input data X using secret key SK.
- $\mathcal{O}$: Initial sender (= originator) of data M.
- $A/B/N$: First/Second/n-th recipient of data M.
- PID_N: Personal identifier of user N.
- FID: Unique identifier of data M as specified by a TTP.
- TID_N: Unique transaction identifier of the transmission of data M between users N and $N+1$.
- TS_N: Timestamp of transaction TID_N.
- TDU_N: Tracking data unit as inserted by user N.
- TD_N: Total tracking data after insertion of TDU_N by sender N.
- TD_N^*: $TD_N^* = TD_N\|\sigma_{SK}(TD_N)$.

3.2   General Information about Non-Repudiation Services

Non-repudiation services can be divided into four main phases [8, 9]:

1. Evidence generation: The critical action occurs and evidence is generated.
2. This phase includes the transfer, storage and request of the evidence.
3. The evidence is verified by a trusted authority.
4. Dispute resolution: Evidence is retrieved from storage, presented and again verified to resolve the dispute.

If symmetric techniques are used, the token generated by such a service must necessarily be verified by a Trusted Third Party (TTP) in case of a dispute. Using asymmetric techniques, the TTP is not mandatory. Nevertheless, the authenticity of the applied public keys must be guaranteed. Moreover, non-repudiation policies may enforce that only TTPs are allowed to generate the token. A URL pointing to the applied policy is then part of the generated NRT. A non-repudiation service must permit a trusted authority to verify if a given signature was applied to given data. This authority checks if the private signature key corresponds to a given valid certificate.

Each sender and recipient adds certain information to the protected data [1, 2]. Spoken clearly, for each action unique tracking data are added to the confidential message. These tracking data are used to generate evidence if an allegedly trusted user repudiates the forwarding.

3.3   The Non-Repudiation of Forwarding Service

The main goals of the NRFS are as follows:

- The service *shall* provide traceability for confidential data over multiple recipients.
- The originator *shall* be able to prove to be the source of the information.
- All recipients *shall* be able to verify the source and the authenticity of the received data.
- The protected message *shall not* be accessible by the recipient unless his or her unique tracking data are indelible added.
- If the received information is not provable authentic, it *shall not* be output the the recipient.
- The plaintext data output to the recipient *shall* be accompanied by unique tracking data. These tracking data *shall not* be erasable. At least any manipulation of these data *shall* be recognized reliably.

A security module is needed to realize the NRFS. This module is mandatory for different reasons: It provides access control and ensures that the confidential message is output to the user only if the embedded tracking data are authentic. Most importantly, the required private and secret keys can be securely stored. The Data Tracking Protocol (DTP) is specified to realize the NRFS. Protocol Data Units (PDUs) are transmitted between the security modules of the users. Figure 1 shows, that the NRFS is accessed via Service Access Points (SAP) and the users do not need to have knowledge about the underlying protocol(s). Service primitives abstractly describe the functions provided by the service without considering implementation details.

The default application scenario for the NRFS implies a closed group of recipients (e.g. a company network). In this case, the TTP may be represented by the initial sender $\mathcal{O}$. The TTP should not be involved in each transaction, so that the role of the TTP is *off-line*. Digital signatures and trusted timestamps [11] are used to generate and provide the evidence. Thus, the NRFS is an asymmetric non-repudiation service.

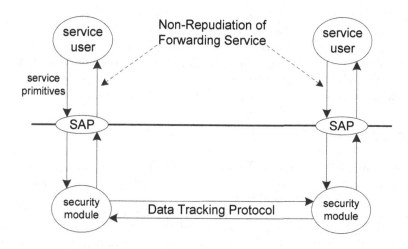

Fig. 1. Service primitives of the non-repudiation of forwarding service

3.4   Structure of the Non-Repudiation of Forwarding Token

Non-repudiation of forwarding token (NRFT) can be generated in two different ways, depending on the source of evidence.

Firstly, NRFT may be generated based on the tracking data of user N using the security module. These token are specified as follows:

$$NRFT = \left(FID, Z_{TD_{N-1}}, \sigma_{SK_N}\left(Z_{TD_{N-1}}\right)\right) \tag{1}$$

$$Z_{TD_{N-1}} = Pol\|f_{fwd}\|TD_{N-1}\|Imp(M) \tag{2}$$

with Pol as the non-repudiation policy applied for this token and f_{fwd} as the flag indicating the non-repudiation of forwarding service. $Imp(M)$ is the imprint of the message, e.g. a hashed value of M. Note that $N-1$ in TD_{N-1} is correct, because the tracking data have been inserted by the user $N-1$ at the time of forwarding to user N. Token as shown in equation 1 provide evidence about the forwarding by all users, whose tracking data are contained in TD_{N-1}. That is, the users with identifier $PID_{\mathcal{O}}\|PID_A\|\dots\|PID_{N-1}$ cannot repudiate the forwarding of M.

Secondly, tracking data are also inserted into the plaintext when output to the recipient. As already stated in section 2, watermarks cope with two main problems. For this reason, only the information about the last recipient N is embedded. In the current state, the DTP supports only JPEG (images) and PDF (documents) as file format (see chapter 4.7).

NRFT as generated based on digital watermarks are specified as follows:

$$NRFT = \left(FID, Z_{WM_N}, \sigma_{SK_N}\left(Z_{WM_N}\right)\right) \tag{3}$$

$$Z_{WM_N} = Pol\|f_{fwd}\|PID_N\|TS_{N-1}\|Imp(M) \tag{4}$$

with $WM_N = PID_N \| FID \| TID_{N-1} \| TS_{N-1}$. This time N is correct, because the tracking data are inserted by the security module of user N based on TDU_N when the data are output to the recipient. These data contain only information about the current user N. Thus, token as shown in equation 3 prove that N was the last authorized recipient of that copy of M. It is worth to mention that this NRFT does not prove that N has published the data unauthorized.

3.5   Data Tracking Protocol

Goals of the Data Tracking Protocol. The DTP is designed to fulfill the requirements specified in chapter 3.3 und thus to realize the non-repudiation of forwarding service as described in [1, 2].

A Public-Key Infrastructure (PKI) is a basic requirement of the DTP. The implementation and detailed processes of a PKI are out of scope of the protocol description. It is assumed, that digital certificates are verified, Certificate Revocation Lists (CRL) checked periodically and the *nonRepudiation* bit in the *keyUsage* extension of X.509v3 certificates is set [12].

The functions provided by the security module must ensure that the tracking data cannot be manipulated or removed targeted. In the following, the service primitives provided by the module are shortly described and the protection mechanisms are described in more detail.

Tracking Data. The tracking data are used to track the way of M if a dispute arises. Due to the fact that they service as evidence, the trackingdata have to be both unambiguous and provable authentic. Figure 2 shows the structure of the tracking data. Also, the difference between $TDU_{\mathcal{O}}$ and other tracking data units $TDU_A \dots TDU_N$ is figured out.

The tracking data must be protected from several attacks, because they are used to generate evidence. This includes protection from targeted manipulations, traffic flow analyses and privacy aspects (concerning the unique user identifer). The protection mechanisms are described in chapter 4.

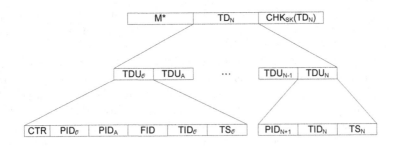

Fig. 2. Structure of the tracking data

4 Security of the Non-Repudiation of Forwarding Service

4.1 The Service Primitives

The tracking data are used to generate evidence, so that nobody shall be able to tampere or manipulate them. To achieve this, a security module is mandatory for different reasons: Firstly, the required private and secret keys must be generated and stored in a secure environment. The user must not be able to access these keys; otherwise he or she would be able to access data without permission. Secondly, the confidential message M must not be output to the receiver if any manipulation is detected. In case of an error, the security module must stop data processing and signalize an error message. Thirdly, the tracking data must be added to M **before** the receiver gets access to it. The authenticating signatures must be generated and verified by the security module. Hence, the module must provide the following service primitives:

1. **Initialize:** $\mathcal{O}$ configures the DTP and prepares the data for the forthcoming actions. The required keys are also generated by this function.
2. **Send:** Checks if the data are in good condition, adds the tracking data of the current user and outputs protected data. These data must be sent to the next receiver.
3. **Receive:** Processes the received protected data. If all verifications succeed, the watermarked message and encrypted storage data are output.
4. **Evidence-TD:** This service primitive generates the NRFT based on the tracking data accompanying the protected storage message. Additionally, the course of M can be shown to the recipient.
5. **Evidence-WM:** This function generates the NRFT based on the tracking data read out from the digital watermark.

The tracking data must be protected when during storage (**Initialize, Receive**) and transmission (**Send**). The following protection mechanisms are proposed for the DTP:

1. Anonymizing the user identifier PID.
2. Using group policies for data access.
3. Setting expiry dates.
4. Protection against traffic flow analyses.
5. Confusion of the tracking data.

4.2 Anonymization of User Identifier

This mechanism considers privacy aspects in the DTP and affects the $PIDs$ that are shown to the recipient. Whenever a user receives a confidential message, he or she may be interested in the history of that copy. The **Receive**-function provides the possibility to watch the history of the data. This history contains the $PIDs$ of involved parties and transaction timestamps. Obviously, not all users should be able to see the real PID.

For that reason, the DTP can be configured such that the $PIDs$ of the users are anonymized when they are output. During the initialization phase, $\mathcal{O}$ configures group policies. If a security module does not have appropriate rights to see the real identifier, the $PIDs$ are anonymized when they are shown to the user. Anonymization in this case means, that the $PIDs$ are replaced by a placeholder, i.e. the value '0'. The timestamps of corresponding transactions do not need to be anonymized. Therefore, the user knows that someone had access to the protected data and he or she knows the time of forwarding. Nevertheless, the recipient does not know **who** has been the user. Note that this mechanism only affects the $PIDs$ that are output to the users. For signature generation and for data processing the real $PIDs$ are used.

4.3   Using Group Policies for Data Access

During the initialization phase, $\mathcal{O}$ configures group policies to define access rights. These policies are part of CD and have to be analyzed by the security module. If the module does not have appropriate rights to output the message M, the data will not be output to the recipient in plaintext.

Nevertheless, the user may still be allowed to forward M, and therefore serve as a delivery authority. The tracking data are also updated by the information about that user, even if he or she does not have permission to watch the information. Recipients with appropriate rights then know that the delivery authorities received and forwarded the protected data. Therefore, the NRFS also supports to track authorized users that do not have sufficient rights to watch the data.

4.4   Setting Expiry Dates

Besides the configuration of group policies, $\mathcal{O}$ can set a certain timestamp until which the information is valid. This setting is part of the configuration data CD and always accompanies M. If this date has expired, this copy of M may neither be sent nor received anymore. The security module of the user checks if the date has expired. If so, it stops processing and outputs an error message. If no expiry date is set (i.e. the timestamp is set to '0' by default), no time limitation exists. This setting does not affect the watermarked data output by the *Receive*-function, because once it is output, the data can be watched unlimited.

4.5   Preventing Traffic Flow Analyses

When the DTP is initialized, $\mathcal{O}$ defines a maximum number of allowed forwardings. The tracking data are filled with dummy data $X^{\#}$ dependent on this setting. The setting is inserted as CTR into $TDU_{\mathcal{O}}$. The size of the tracking data units is known in advance, because the tags shown in figure 2 have a fixed length. Therefore, the size of the dummy data is known and can be inserted. An untrustworthy eavesdropper will not be able to find out how many $TDUs$ are already inserted.

Duting the **Send**-function, the security module decrements CTR. If that value becomes zero, the data may not be forwarded anymore and an appropriate error message is output. If the new TDU_N is inserted by user N (which means that the dummy data $TDU_N^\#$ of that position are replaced by real values), CTR in $TDU_\mathcal{O}$ is updated and the resulting tracking data TD_N are signed by the security module. Finally, TD_N must be protected and the resulting data M_N are sent to the next receiver $N+1$. Concerning the signature $\sigma_{SK}(TD_N)$ of the tracking data, only the real $TDUs$ are considered. The dummy data are not included in the signature calculation.

	M*					
Initialize:	M*	$TDU_\mathcal{O}^\#$	$TDU_A^\#$	$TDU_B^\#$	...	$TDU_N^\#$	$\sigma(TD^\#)$
Send ($\mathcal{O}$):	M*	$TDU_\mathcal{O}$	$TDU_A^\#$	$TDU_B^\#$	...	$TDU_N^\#$	$\sigma_{SK_\mathcal{O}}(TD_\mathcal{O})$
Send (A):	M*	$TDU_\mathcal{O}$	TDU_A	$TDU_B^\#$	...	$TDU_N^\#$	$\sigma_{SK_A}(TD_A)$
Send (B):	M*	$TDU_\mathcal{O}$	TDU_A	TDU_B	...	$TDU_N^\#$	$\sigma_{SK_B}(TD_B)$
Send (N):	M*	$TDU_\mathcal{O}$	TDU_A	TDU_B	...	TDU_N	$\sigma_{SK_N}(TD_N)$

Fig. 3. Prevention of traffic flow analyses by dummy data insertion

4.6   Data Confusion

The Data Confusion Mechanism (DCM) is applied, so that an eavesdropper will not be able to analyze encrypted data targeted [13]. In combination with the insertion of dummy data as shown in chapter 4.5, it also provides very good security against traffic flow analyses.

The DCM is applied prior to the encryption and confuses data without respect to block sizes. Symmetric block ciphers (normally) permute data well enough - but encrypted data remains in the same block as it has been before the encryption was applied.

A secret value is needed to initialize the confusion mechanism of the DTP. This value is used as a seed for the pseudo random number generator (PRNG) and specified by $\mathcal{O}$ during the initialization of the protocol. For each byte of the selected data, the PRNG selects a new byte position in the resulting confused data (with the same total size). When the mechanism has finished, the data are permuted (pseudo-)randomly. The security module of the receiver reads out the secret confusion value and reverses the changes - first the tracking data are decrypted and the inverse function of the DCM is applied. As far as the DTP is concerned, only TD_N^* is confused, so that the protection function is completely independent from the size of the protected data.

4.7   Protection of Digital Watermarks

The digital watermark $WM_N^* = WM_N \| \sigma_{SK}(WM_N)$ must be protected when it is inserted into the source data M. If the message $M_{WM_N^*}$ including the digital

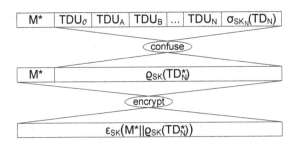

Fig. 4. Confusion of the tracking data prior to the encryption

watermark is found in an unexpected place, no unauthorized person should be able to extract the watermark targeted. Only users who know the secret embedding key must be able to extract the watermark and generate the NRFT. In the DTP, this key is generated by the security module of $\mathcal{O}$ during the initialization phase. While the readout of the watermark cannot be avoided in all cases, manipulations of that data must be detected at all costs. This is why a digital signature is generated by the security module. The signature authenticates the watermark WM_N and thus the contained tracking data of the last authorized recipient.

If the extraction (by an authorized user) succeeds and the signature σ_{SK} (WM_N) contained in WM_N^* can be validated, the NRFT as shown in formulae (3) and (4) can be generated. The NRFT must be sent to and verified by a TTP in order to approve the evidence.

The tool *OutGuess* is used by the DTP to embed the tracking data into M [14]. OutGuess is still the state-of-the-art steganographic tool and is (mostly) independent of the source data as long as there exists a data specific handler. By default, the tool supports JPEG images (and the rather rare format PNM) and can embed any kind of data into the data source. A seed (the secret embedding key) can be used to modify the embedding procedure.

4.8   Example

The following example explains how the protection mechanisms work and when they will be applied. In the example, the application of the previously mentioned protection mechanisms on the tracking data TD_N^* is represented by $\varrho_{SK}(TD_N^*)$. It does not include a detailed description of all data processing parts of the DTP.

After the initialization, the protected data must be stored by $\mathcal{O}$. These data contain the configured amount of $TDUs$, so that the dummy data $TD_N^\#$ are already inserted. Then the data are protected applying the DCM and finally $M^* \| \varrho_{SK}(TD_N^\#)$ is encrypted using a secret storage key known only to the security module of $\mathcal{O}$. At the time of forwarding, $\varepsilon_{SK}(M^* \| \varrho_{SK}(TD_N^\#))$ is decrypted with the same secret key and the DCM is reversed. In the next step, $TDU_\mathcal{O}^\#$ is replaced by $TDU_\mathcal{O}$ and the new tracking data are signed and the DCM is applied again in order to protect the tracking data. Finally, the resulting data $\varepsilon_{SK}(M_{\mathcal{O}})$ are sent to the first receiver A.

A decrypts the received data and reverses the protection functions. The signatures must then be verified by the security module. If no manipulation is detected, the user obtains two outputs: Firstly, the encrypted data for local storage $\varepsilon_{SK}(M^* \| \varrho_{SK}(TDU_{\mathcal{O}} \| TDU_A^{\#} \| \ldots \| TDU_N^{\#} \| \sigma_{SK}(TDU_{\mathcal{O}})))$ are output and encrypted with a secret storage key known only to the security module of A. Secondly, the watermarked plaintext $M_{WM_A^*}$ is output to the recipient. If the protected information should be sent to B, $\varepsilon_{SK}(M_{\mathcal{O}})$ is input into the security module and once again checked for manipulations. After that, TDU_A is inserted and the counter CTR in $TDU_{\mathcal{O}}$ is decremented. The resulting tracking data are signed and protected again. Finally, $\varepsilon_{SK}(M_A)$ is sent to B.

After some time, user N receives $\varepsilon_{SK}(M_{N-1})$. These data have to be decrypted and the DCM must be reversed, so that the security module can calculate the verification functions $VER(\sigma_{SK}(M^*), PK)$ and $VER(\sigma_{SK}(TD_{N-1}), PK)$. These functions return either positive or negative. If no manipulation is detected (both functions return postitive), N gets $\varepsilon_{SK}(M_{N-1})$ and $M_{WM_A^*}$ as output data. When N wants to forward the confidential message M, $\varepsilon_{SK}(M_{N-1})$ must be inserted into the security module. If all verifications succeed, TDU_N replaces $TDU_N^{\#}$ and CTR is decremented, so that its value becomes '0'.

In the end, user $N+1$ receives $\varepsilon_{SK}(M^* \| \varrho_{SK}(TD_N) \| \sigma_{SK}(TD_N))$ and is able to decrypt and watch the plaintext data $M_{WM_{N+1}^*}$. Since the maximum number of allowed forwardings has been reached, user $N+1$ is not allowed to forward M again. The security module stops data processing and signalizes that the limit has reached.

5   Conclusions

The non-repudiation of forwarding service can be used to track the way of data via multiple recipients. It provides evidence about all users that got access to confidential information. The service consists of two parts, where the first part uses a security module for data processing and the other part provides reasonable security to the plaintext output data using a digital watermark.

The tracking data used by the Data Tracking Protocol are used to generate the non-repudiation of forwarding token. Therefore, these data have to be protected from targeted manipulation and unauthorized access. In this paper, mechanisms that provide protection against traffic flow analyses and unauthorized eavesdropping are shown. Furthermore, privacy aspects are considered when the tracking data are shown to the recipient. Digital watermarks are applied to the output plaintext data, and these watermarks are also protected.

The DTP combines different protection functions with particular emphasis on the security of the tracking data. Although digital watermarking has to deal with some negative aspects, this technique provides reasonable security to protect confidential plaintext data.

As far as the support of different input file formats is concerned, the watermarking part should be improved in future work. This is planned by broadening the OutGuess tool, which can be extended by data specific handlers. Finally, at least the most common human-readable media files should be supported.

Acknowledgements. This work is funded by the German Research Foundation (DFG) as part of the research training group GRK 1564 - 'Imaging New Modalities'.

References

1. Schick, R., Ruland, C.: Document Tracking - On the Way to a New Security Service. In: Conference on Network and Information Systems Security. Conference Proceedings, pp. 89–93 (2011)
2. Schick, R., Ruland, C.: Data Leakage Tracking – Non-Repudiation of Forwarding. In: Abd Manaf, A., Zeki, A., Zamani, M., Chuprat, S., El-Qawasmeh, E. (eds.) ICIEIS 2011, Part I. CCIS, vol. 251, pp. 163–173. Springer, Heidelberg (2011)
3. InfoWatch, Global Data Leakage Report (2011),
   http://infowatch.com/sites/default/files/report/
   InfoWatch_global_data_leakage_report_2011.pdf
4. International Organization for Standardization, 13888-1: Information technology - Security techniques - Non-repudiation - Part 1: General (2009)
5. International Organization for Standardization, 13888-2: Information technology - Security techniques - Non-repudiation - Part 2: Mechanisms using symmetric techniques (2010)
6. International Organization for Standardization, 13888-3: Information technology - Security techniques - Non-repudiation - Part 3: Mechanisms using asymmetric techniques (2009)
7. Zhou, J., Gollmann, D.: Evidence and Non-Repudiation. Journal of Network and Computer Applications 20, 267–281 (1997)
8. International Organization for Standardization, 10181-4: Information technology - Open Systems Interconnection - Security frameworks for open systems: Non-repudiation framework (1997)
9. Zhou, J., Gollmann, D.: A Fair Non-Repudiation Protocol. In: IEEE Symposium on Security and Privacy, pp. 55–61. IEEE Press (1996)
10. Cox, I., Miller, M., Bloom, J., Fridrich, J., Kalker, T.: Digital Watermarking and Steganography, 2nd edn. Elsevier (2008)
11. Network Working Group, Internet X.509 Public Key Infrastructure - Time-Stamp Protocol, TSP (2001)
12. Network Working Group, Internet X.509 Public Key Infrastructure - Certificate and Certificate Revocation List (CRL) Profile (2008)
13. Schick, R., Ruland, C.: Introduction of a New Non-Repudiation Service to Protect Sensitive Private Data. In: Advances in Information and Communication Technologies, pp. 71–76. Conference Proceedings (2011)
14. Provos, N.: A universal steganographic tool (2001), http://www.outguess.org

Profitability and Cost Management of Trustworthy Composite Services

Hisain Elshaafi, Jimmy McGibney, and Dmitri Botvich

TSSG, Waterford Institute of Technology
Waterford, Ireland
{helshaafi,jmcgibney,dbotvich}@tssg.org

Abstract. Building business solutions may require combining multiple existing services. In SOA paradigm this can be achieved using composite services. Composite services may be in turn recursively composed with other services into higher level solutions. The number of component services that need to be aggregated may be large and dynamically changing. Additionally, the component services may vary in their trustworthiness and cost and in their importance to the value of the composite service. Therefore, determining and maintaining the optimal composition in terms of its short-term and long-term profitability and building and expanding consumer base for composite service providers are challenging goals especially in the competitive business service environments. This paper addresses how to create profitable, consumer-focused and trust worthy composite services through optimising pricing and managing the cost and the trustworthiness of those services. The techniques described support consumer differentiation, prioritisation of offered services and dynamic capacity-dependent component charging.

1 Introduction

Service Oriented Architecture (SOA) is increasingly popular, with increased attention from industry. A key concept is that services can be dynamically or statically composed to create new services. Services are described, published, discovered, and assembled, providing distributed business processes exposed externally as *composite services (CSs)*. A composite service may be used directly by a service consumer or recursively incorporated in further service compositions.

The composition techniques must be able to provide the most profitable, cost-efficient and trustworthy composite services for competitive services environments. Profitability over the short- and long-term is achieved through a number of measures including optimal pricing, cost efficiency and trustworthiness of the provided service. Consumers do not necessarily buy the service with the highest trustworthiness or lowest price. Therefore, attractiveness of a CS to the consumer should be based on consumer market segments by providing multiple levels of trustworthiness and price targeting each segment. Cost efficiency improves profitability directly by creating a more flexible margin for profit and indirectly by affording to offer the service at lower prices and hence more effectively compete as well as build the consumer base.

S. Fischer-Hübner, S. Katsikas, G. Quirchmayr (Eds.): TrustBus 2012, LNCS 7449, pp. 179–191, 2012.

Establishing and maintaining the trustworthiness supports consumer confidence and provides a safe environment for carrying out transactions. Security mechanisms such as encryption, authentication, and confidentiality are necessary steps to establish trust. For example, authentication assures the consumer that the service provider is who it claims it is. However, the service may not behave in the way it is required or expected in terms of reliability, availability, reputation, etc. We define *trust* as a relationship between a consumer (or its agent) and a service that indicates the contextual expectations from an entity towards another in relation to reliance in accomplishing a certain action at a certain quality. *Trustworthiness* of a service is the level of trust that a consumer or its agent has in that service. *Reputation* of a service is the perception of its users through usage ratings. These definitions are in line with existing approaches considering trust as a multidimensional concept as in [1–4].

Composite service providers (CSPs) aggregate component services and offer them to consumers as higher level business services. CSPs have access to pools of component services of which many may provide the same functionality but with different levels of trustworthiness and cost. The roles of the CS components can also vary in their importance to its reputation. Additionally, CSPs may select a component service for multiple offered composite services. Therefore, CSPs require the management and balancing of the component demand and admission taking into consideration market segments and priority of CSs in terms of their profitability. This paper addresses enhancing profitability of those CSPs through novel approaches to the interrelated issues of competitive CS pricing, cost efficiency and trustworthiness.

The paper is structured as follows: Related work is described in Section 2. Section 3 describes an illustrative service composition scenario. Optimisation of the pricing of composite services is described in Section 4. Section 5 introduces capacity dependent charging of component services and capacity determination based on factors that include those related to profitability such as consumer differentiation. Section 6 describes aggregation of trustworthiness properties of a CS to determine its trustworthiness. Section 7 discusses simulation and experiments. Conclusions and future work are discussed in section 8.

2   Related Work

Service composition is similar in some aspects to product bundling by companies serving their consumers with heterogeneous preferences. Bundling has been studied in terms of consumer behaviour, economics and marketing. The literature on bundling focuses mainly on reasons and contexts adequate for bundling. Bitran and Ferrer [5] address the problem of determining the components and price of a bundle to maximise the total expected profit in a competitive environment. A scalar is used for the price response function which is not realistic since demand may change differently at different price changes. Attractiveness is considered an attribute of a bundle in addition to price. Chung and Rao [6] developed a model to find market segments for bundles with heterogeneous products to estimate willingness to pay and to determine optimal prices for market segments.

B. Wu et al. [7] describe an approach to improve the Quality of Service (QoS) of a static CS workflow with a common resource pool. The work does not consider issues such as dynamic services, admission control, distributed resources or feedback to component providers. In [8] García et al. discuss requirements definition and analysis that the control mechanisms must fulfil in service exchange between enterprises including consumer differentiation and protection from overload.

In the past decade there has been much activity in the area of computational trust and reputation in a variety of applications [10–12]. The terms *trust* and *trust models* are also used in Web service standards – e.g. WS-Trust [13] – but they are limited to the context of being able to trust the identity of the service [2]. However, establishing a service identity is not sufficient to determine if the service is trustworthy. For instance, an authenticated service may be unreliable or unavailable. Takabi et al. [3] discuss the barriers and possible solutions to providing trustworthy services in cloud computing environments. They describe the need of multiple service providers to collaborate and compose value-added enterprise services. They propose that a trust framework should be developed to allow to efficiently capture parameters required for establishing trust and to manage evolving trust and sharing requirements.

In [14] Maximilien and Singh present an agent based trust model for Web service reputation that enables rating of individual services as well as providers. A probabilistic model for aggregation of reputation and QoS in service workflows was described by Hwang et al. [9]. In [1] Malik and Bouguettaya introduce a framework for establishing trust in service environments named RATEWeb. Reputation ratings from consumers are aggregated in a P2P fashion. However, it does not consider the computation of trustworthiness in a composite service. In dynamic service compositions the capability of a CSP to maintain trustworthiness of component services helps to stabilise the CS over time. We discussed trustworthiness in service compositions in our previous work [15]. We introduced a trustworthiness monitoring and prediction software module that receives data on trustworthiness properties including QoS metrics, user ratings and security events. The data which indicates violations or adherence to service contracts is used to predict services' trustworthiness.

3   Multi-composite Service Provider Scenario

Composition of business services is one of the main features of SOA, where existing services can be used to build higher level enterprise solutions. In many business cases, services are only competitive as part of an overall portfolio. In other cases, integrating new services increases profitability. Additionally, business innovations are frequently based on service integrations. Service composition has other advantages as well [16], including simplification of usage, enhancing reusability and improving partitioning and change management.

Figure 1 shows an illustrative example of a set of composite services in an e-commerce product purchasing scenario. The composite services are offered by a single CSP but similar composite services are also offered by competing

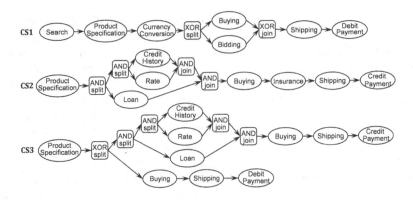

Fig. 1. Example e-Commerce Composite Services

providers. These CSs are different in their structure, business models, product categories and target consumers. They contain twelve abstract component services providing for the various tasks of the workflow with most of the components shared between two or three CSs. The service labels are generally self-explanatory. For example, *Product Specification* is a service provided by one component vendor for multiple categories of products. CS1 supports bidding on prices and debit payment while CS2 supports product insurance and only credit payments are possible. CS3 consumer can choose to buy by credit payment service. Credit payment requires applying for a loan and checking for consumer credit history and loan rate. Alternatively, the consumer can purchase the product through a debit payment. The CSs interact with the consumers in a black-box fashion and the component services providers are invisible to the consumers.

The component services are invoked in a business process with multiple constructs as indicated in the figure including sequence, parallel (AND split/AND join) and exclusive choice (XOR Split/XOR join). The aggregation of the execution time, trustworthiness level, and cost of composite services depends on the structure of its workflow. The construct types and their language and product support are investigated in other works such as Workflow Patterns Initiative [17].

The CSP can select the component services from a pool of services some of which offer the same functionality but with varying costs and trustworthiness. The aim of the CSP is to optimise its profitability from the composite services through optimal management of pricing, costs and trustworthiness. The CSP can adapt the composite services if an unfavourable change to a component service occur by replacing it with another. However, it provides measures to maintain the trustworthiness of the component services through determining the required component capacities and the management of request admissions.

4   Optimisation of Prices of Composite Services

Let us assume that n competing composite services are offered by competitors including one from our CSP. Each composite service k $(k = 1, .., n)$ has a trustworthiness T and a price P. Consumers can choose between available compositions and make an overall evaluation of each CS based on a set of attributes by using *utility maximisation*. Attributes may differ in types and expected values between consumers depending on factors such as personal preferences. Bitran and Ferrer [5] classify utility into deterministic utility and stochastic utility; where deterministic utility is based on measurable choice such as in our case trustworthiness and price. Stochastic utility refers to independent factors such as incomplete information or errors in consumer perception. The deterministic utility is given by function $U_k(P, T, \alpha)$ where P is the price of the composite service k, T is its trustworthiness ($0 \leq T \leq 1$), α is the *price response function* [18]. The price response function determines how demand changes as a function of price and it indicates price sensitivity. α is unique for each service composition and market segment.

Price response function is based on assumptions about consumer behaviour. One of the models for consumer demand is called *willingness to pay*, which indicates the maximum price a consumer is willing to pay for a service at a particular trustworthiness. A consumer who decides not to pay for a CS will choose one from a competitor or may not purchase any. Commonly a negative value (e.g. $\alpha=-0.07$) is used to represent a price response function as in [5]; however, the function is typically not linear and tends to take the shape of a downward sloping curve. The slope of the curve at a given point may be affected by other factors in addition to the price change such as the distribution of the consumers' willingness to pay, the trustworthiness of the CS, and the availability of alternative CSs from competitors. The two most common measures of price sensitivity [18] are:

- *Slope* of the price response function measures how demand changes due to a price change. It is equal to the change in demand divided by the change in price. The quality of this measurement reduces with larger changes in price as it assumes linearity of the price response function.
- *Elasticity* of the price response function is the ratio of percentage change in demand to the percentage change in price. Elasticity changes at different prices and tends to be highest around the market price.

The deterministic utility U_k for a composition k is calculated from its utility variables:

$$U_k = T + \alpha \cdot P \tag{1}$$

Multinomial Logit (MNL) is commonly used in economics as a consumer choice model. Using MNL in our case, the probability ρ of choosing the CSP's service instead of that of its competitors is as follows:

$$\rho = e^{U_1} \bigg/ \sum_{k=1}^{n} e^{U_k} \tag{2}$$

where U_1 is the deterministic utility of the composite service from our CSP. Although ideally equation (2) would include all competing providers, in practice it may be satisfactory to only consider a limited number of major competitors.

Finding the optimal price is an optimisation problem as follows:

$$\max\left((P-C)\rho\right) \tag{3}$$

where C is the cost of the composite service including the aggregated cost of its component services.

To create a new CS, the CSP may first select its market segments which determine the prices and the required trustworthiness. Affordable trustworthiness and cost balance varies for each market segment. In that case, the CS can be offered at multiple price/trustworthiness levels and the probability of purchase ρ_j for market segment j can be computed as follows:

$$\rho_j = e^{U_{j1}} \Big/ \sum_{k=1}^{n} e^{U_{jk}} \tag{4}$$

where $\sum_{k=1}^{n} e^{U_{jk}}$ is the sum of utilities for the CS and competing compositions for j.

5   Profitability and Cost in CS Provision

5.1   Capacity-Dependent Cost

We propose a dynamic component capacity management and capacity dependent component charging approach where:

- the component provider may adjust its component capacity according to dynamic capacity update requests from the CSP.
- the CSP pays for each component according to the capacity made available by the component provider (dynamic cost) in addition to its usage (fixed cost).

This approach can offer advantages compared to only per use based approach including: First, the ability of the CSP to manage request admissions based on service availability, CS prioritisation and consumer differentiation. Consequently, it makes it easier to control pricing and profitability of composite services. Second, it can be more cost efficient to the CSP if discounting on capacity sizes is supported and more cost efficient to the component providers since they can provide capacity adequate to the workload. Finally, it helps maintain the trustworthiness of the CS since the capacity required and offered is known to the CS and component providers respectively.

We calculate the cost c_s of a component service s as the sum of its fixed cost and dynamic cost; the fixed cost is based on usage u_s and the dynamic cost is based the provided capacity $\hat{y}_s$, as follows:

$$c_s = u_s \cdot c_u + \hat{y}_s \cdot c_y \tag{5}$$

where c_u is the fixed cost per usage and c_y is the cost of the capacity at $\hat{y}_s$.

5.2 Priority-Based Capacity Determination and Admission

The CSP in the scenario described in Section 3 may take several factors into consideration during the determination of capacity and admission of consumer requests. These factors include:

- The currently *ongoing and waiting executions* u_s and q_s of each component service s respectively according to the admitted requests.
- The existing *total capacity* $\hat{y}_s$ of each component service in terms of the number of possible concurrent executions as a component of one or more composite services. The capacity of component services in a composite service $\hat{y}_s$ are divided to two allocations; a shared capacity y_{sh} , and exclusive capacities assigned for each composite service y_{sk}. The goal of the allocations is to allow sharing of available resources while permitting priorities among CSs in admission when resources become scarce.
- The *maximum allowed execution time* $\hat{t}$ of the CS according to, for instance, a service level agreement, and the *execution time* t_s of each component in order to predict the time of execution of all subsequent components in the CS workflow.
- The *constructs* in the CS workflow e.g. sequence, parallel, exclusive choice. A construct may contain two or more components running simultaneously. For example, in a parallel construct the minimum capacity of its components is taken as the capacity of the construct.
- The *choice of execution* of each component in the CS workflow. This may depend on the characteristics, interdependence or limited supply of some component services. For example, in an emergency composite service a fire service, an ambulance service or both may be required in certain executions. An example of limited capacity is where a highly trustworthy car rental service has limited supply. In that case more demand requires additional supply from other car rental service providers.
- The *priority of the requested CS* among offered composite services based for example on profitability. A prioritised composite service k is exclusively allocated a proportion y_{sk} of the capacity of each component.
- *Consumer differentiation* through ranking that can be based on market segments, loyalty, or other criteria. A minimum allocation of a component service capacity can be assigned to a consumer rank. In this paper we consider 3 ranks *Gold (G)*, *Silver (V)* and *Bronze (B)*. y_{Gmin} and y_{Vmin} are fractions of CS exclusive capacities y_{sk} to maintain minimum capacities available exclusively to ranks G and V respectively. Note that $y_{sk} \geq (y_{Gmin} + y_{Vmin})$.
- *Component weighting*. Component services may vary in their importance to the CS as a whole. For example, in a travel service a user may not appreciate all components to the same extent such as car rental, health insurance, and flight booking. Therefore, component services differ in their contribution to the reputation of the CS. Each component s has a weight ω_s based on its importance. The weighting is useful when a component capacity is in full usage or close to becoming so. In that case a non-critical component can be excluded from the CS execution. This is particularly useful if the request

Table 1. Conditions for Request Admission

Rank	Admission	Conditions
Gold (G)	Immediate	$\forall s \in S_k : \{u_s < y_{sh} \text{ OR } u_{sk} < y_{sk}\}$
	Queue	$\forall s \in S_k : \{u_s \geq y_{sh} \text{ AND } u_{sk} \geq y_{sk} \text{ AND } q_s < Q_k\}$
Silver (V)	Immediate	$\forall s \in S_k : \{u_s < y_{sh} \text{ OR } u_{sk} < (y_{sk} - y_{Gmin})\}$
	Queue	$\forall s \in S_k : \{u_s \geq y_{sh} \text{ AND } u_{sk} \geq y_{sk} \text{ AND } q_s < (Q_k - q_{Gmin})\}$
Bronze (B)	Immediate	$\forall s \in S_k : \{u_s < y_{sh} \text{ OR } u_{sk} < (y_{sk} - y_{Gmin} - y_{Vmin})\}$
	Queue	$\forall s \in S_k : \{u_s \geq y_{sh} \text{ AND } u_{sk} \geq y_{sk} \text{ AND } q_s < (Q_k - q_{Gmin} - q_{Vmin})\}$

would otherwise be rejected or when low remaining capacity can be saved for higher ranks. A threshold Ω_k is specified for the minimum weight of a component to be considered in the request admission decision. S_k is the set of components in the composite service k where $\omega_{sk} \geq \Omega_k$.

A request is either admitted immediately to execution, added to the execution queue, or possibly rejected depending on the above factors. Table 1 describes conditions for admission of a request immediately or to the queue.

As indicated in Table 1, G rank request for composite service k is admitted if one of the following conditions are met for every component in k:

- current overall usage of a component service u_s is less than the overall shared capacity i.e. $u_s < y_{sh}$, or
- availability in the capacity currently assigned exclusively to k i.e. $u_{sk} < y_{sk}$.

For ranks V and B, in addition to previous conditions for G, y_{sk} is reduced to allow minimum available capacity for higher ranks e.g. y_{Gmin}.

A request may be admitted to the queue if access was not given for immediate execution. In order to admit a request of rank G to the queue, the shared and the exclusive allocations of component services at the time of their execution (taking durations of executions of preceding components) must be in full use. Additionally, the queue for the component q_s should be less than the queue threshold for the composite service Q_k. The queue threshold depends on the maximum allowed time for the CS execution $\hat{t}$, its actual execution duration t_k, and the capacities of each construct in the composite service as follows:

$$Q_k = y_k \cdot (\hat{t} - t_k)/\hat{t} \tag{6}$$

where y_k is the average capacity of sequential constructs in the composite service. A construct may contain two or more components running simultaneously e.g. parallel executions, as described in Section 3. The minimum capacity of components running in parallel is taken as the capacity of the construct. Subsequently, the resulting sequential construct capacities are averaged. For ranks V and B the queue threshold is reduced by a proportion allocated to higher ranks e.g. q_{Gmin} and q_{Vmin} for rank B.

6   Trustworthiness of a Service Composition

We classify data used to evaluate trustworthiness of CSs into properties. Properties defining trustworthiness in a particular service might not have the same significance depending on the type of service and the environment e.g. healthcare vs. financial services. For example, security properties in a financial service may have more priority than performance properties where a service having high security and medium performance is preferable to one with medium security and high performance which may be different in health services. A similar analogy applies to the variations of services environments e.g. high degree of maliciousness requires more security. Therefore, different properties can be given different weights depending on those circumstances.

In this paper we consider reputation, reliability, and security properties as the trustworthiness properties. Reputation is the information available about a service from user ratings. Reliability refers to the percentage of successful executions of a service within a time limit. Security properties include a number of properties such as confidentiality, authentication, and encryption. In the paper we focus on how the trustworthiness level is aggregated from that of its components. A security property d for a service is a boolean $d \in \{0, 1\}$ with 1 representing the fulfilment of the property and 0 for its non-fulfilment. For other trustworthiness properties the value may be scalar as in the case of reputation r and reliability l where $0 \leq r, l \leq 1$.

In a CS with z security properties $\sigma_j \in \{\sigma_1, \sigma_2, ..., \sigma_z\}$, the score of σ_j follows the weakest link approach. Therefore, we calculate σ_j for a composite service k with m components as follows:

$$\sigma_j = \min_{i=1}^{m} \sigma_{ji} \tag{7}$$

The level of security d_k of a CS based on z security properties where each property σ_j has a weight γ_j ($\gamma_j \geq 0$) is calculated as follows:

$$d_k = 1 - e^{-\sum_{j=1}^{z} (\gamma_j \cdot \sigma_j)} \tag{8}$$

This means the bigger γ_j value for the property the more the property's change affects the security level and consequently the trustworthiness. The sum of γ_j for the security properties should be set to a value where for compositions satisfying all those properties $d_k \approx 1$. A threshold for the minimum allowed security level e.g. $d_k \geq 0.95$ must also be set.

The reputation and reliability are calculated as a product of that of interdependent components e.g. sequence, parallel, with the component weight ω considered in the case of reputation as in equation (9). Component weighting is discussed in Section 5.

$$r_k = \prod_{i=1}^{m} r_i^{\omega_i} \tag{9}$$

We calculate the trustworthiness level T_k of a composite service k from its trustworthiness properties - which in our case are security, reliability and reputation - as a product of the aggregated values of the properties as in equation (10).

$$T_k = d_k \cdot r_k \cdot l_k \tag{10}$$

The optimal selection of component services for a service composition is a maximisation problem given by:

$$\max \left(\tau \cdot T_k + \frac{\varsigma}{C_k} \right) \tag{11}$$

where C_k is the cost of the CS; and τ and ς are constants used to normalise the values and customise priority of trustworthiness and cost respectively.

7   Simulation and Experiments

We simulated three composite services with outsourced component services based on those illustrated in Figure 1. The existence of components in multiple composite services results in the need to coordinate the usage of the shared resources taking into consideration various factors described in Section 5. The overall pattern of requests for each CS is based on datasets on the request for popular web pages [19]. Each pattern is applied to requests in a specific consumer rank for one CS. The rate of requests usually fluctuates between 10 to 50 requests per sec but the patterns particularly for the rank B include peaks at certain time durations reaching up to 150-250 requests per sec. Poisson distribution is used to simulate the request arrivals. The execution duration for a CS depends on that of its components and on how they are constructed. The execution time for each component is set at 100 msec on average. The $\hat{t}$ for each CS is set at 25% more than average execution time t_k. $\hat{t}$ is important in controlling the dynamic queue threshold as described in Subsection 5.2 and consequently affects the usage/capacity relationship.

Figures 2 and 3 show the results of the operation for a component service that exists in the three CSs. The capacity required is sent to the component provider which dynamically adjusts the capacity. In Figure 2 the resources of the component provider are flexible and the capacity can be adjusted for up to the maximum required. In case of Figure 3 the capacity is limited to a maximum of 300 concurrent executions. This results in the adjustment of the capacity of the CSs to that of its weakest link and consequently the rejection of excess requests of B and to a lesser extent of V rank. y_{Gmin} and y_{Vmin} are set at 30 and 15% of y_{sk}, and y_{sh} at 50% of $\hat{y}_s$.

Figure 4 depicts denied requests for each of the CSs with exclusive capacities at 70, 20 and 10% of total nonshared component capacities for CS1, CS2, and CS3 respectively. Despite high exclusive capacity of CS1 there is still denied requests since a trade off is to be made between maximising usage of existing capacity v.s. denying some requests of higher priority CSs. Another option is the

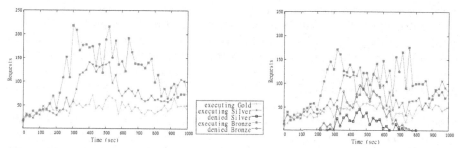

Fig. 2. Usage in Flexible Capacity   **Fig. 3.** Usage in Limited Capacity

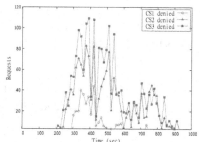   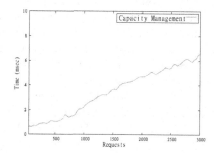

Fig. 4. Denied Requests Per CS in   **Fig. 5.** Performance of Capacity Man-
Limited Capacity   agement Operations

preemption or abandoning of ongoing low priority executions to admit higher
priority requests in order to avoid denying prioritised requests.

Figure 5 shows the performance of the coordinated capacity determination
and related resource management operations in msec taken for the processing of
requests. As in the figure there is a mild increase in the processing times as the
rate of requests increases. However, the times do not seem to increase to a level
that can cause a problem to the accuracy of the operations within moderate to
high rate of requests.

8   Conclusion and Future Work

We presented novel approaches to managing short- and long-term profitability of
composite services (CSs) and maintaining as well as expanding consumer base
in a competitive service environment where consumers purchase a composite
service that maximises their utility. The management of cost and trustworthiness
and the optimal pricing of the CS are made in view of compositions it will be
competing with in the market.

The paper described a technique for component service charging that is dependent on the capacity available to the composite service provider. The technique

allows better management of costs and trustworthiness by the composite service provider (CSP) and consequently a better control of its profitability. The admission of requests can be prioritised based on the capacity available for the rank of request and the priority of the requested CS. The aim is to help enhance profitability of the CSP especially in cases of limited availability due to high request rates or low capacities.

Establishing and maintaining service trustworthiness supports consumer confidence and provides a safe environment for businesses to dynamically interact and carry out transactions. We discussed techniques to determine the trustworthiness of component services. Additionally, the communication of the capacity requirements to component service providers helps maintain the most trustworthy and cost efficient composite service.

In the future we will extend this work to allow the integration of the described cost efficiency and trustworthiness techniques in composite services with security access control policies and mechanisms. The aim is to extend the trustworthiness maintenance to include other security aspects in composite services.

Acknowledgement. The research leading to these results has received funding from the European Union Seventh Framework Programme (FP7/2007-2013) under grant n° 257930 (Aniketos) [20].

References

1. Malik, Z., Bouguettaya, A.: Trust Management for Service Oriented Environments. Springer (2009)
2. Singhal, A., Wingrad, T., Scarfone, K.: NIST Guide to Secure Web Services. Nat. Inst. of Standards and Technology (August 2007)
3. Takabi, H., Joshi, J., Ahn, G.: Security and Privacy Challenges in Cloud Computing Environments. IEEE Security & Privacy 8(6), 24 (2010)
4. Chang, E., Hussain, F., Dillon, T.: Trust and Reputation for Service-Oriented Environments: Technologies For Building Business Intelligence And Consumer Confidence. John Wiley & Sons (2005)
5. Bitran, G., Ferrer, J.-C.: On Pricing and Composition of Bundles. Production and Operations Management 16(1), 93 (2007)
6. Chung, J., Rao, V.: A Generic Choice Model for Bundles with Multiple Category Products: Application to Market Segmentation and Optimal Pricing for Bundles. J. of Marketing Research 40(2), 115 (2003)
7. Wu, B., Chi, C., Chen, Z., Gu, M., Sun, J.: Workflow-based resource allocation to optimize overall performance of composite services. Future Generation Computer Systems J. 25(3), 199 (2009)
8. García, D., García, J., Entrialgo, J., García, M., Valledor, P., García, R., Campos, A.: A QoS Control Mechanism to Provide Service Differentiation and Overload Protection to Internet Scalable Servers. IEEE Trans. on Services Computing 2(1), 3 (2009)
9. Hwang, S., Wang, H., Tang, J., Srivastava, J.: A probabilistic approach to modeling and estimating the QoS of web-services-based workflows. Information Science J. 177(23), 5484 (2007)

10. Xiong, L., Liu, L.: PeerTrust: Supporting Reputation-Based Trust for Peer-to-Peer Electronic Communities. IEEE Trans. on Knowledge and Data Engineering 16(7), 843 (2004)
11. Huynh, T., Jennings, N., Shadbolt, N.: An integrated trust and reputation model for open multi-agent systems. J. of Autonomous Agents and Multi-Agent Systems 13(2), 119 (2006)
12. McGibney, J., Botvich, D.: A Trust Overlay Architecture and Protocol for Enhanced Protection against Spam. In: Proc. 2nd Int. Conf. on Availability, Reliability, and Security (2007)
13. WS-Trust specification document (February 2009), http://docs.oasis-open.org/ws-sx/ws-trust/v1.4/ws-trust.html
14. Maximilien, E., Singh, M.: Agent-based trust model involving multiple qualities. In: Proc. 4th Int. Conf. on Autonomous Agents and Multi-Agent Systems (2005)
15. Elshaafi, H., Mcgibney, J., Botvich, D.: Trustworthiness Monitoring and Prediction of Composite Services. In: Proc. 17th IEEE Symposium on Computers and Communications (2012)
16. Arsanjani, A.: Toward a pattern language for Service-Oriented Architecture and Integration. IBM DeveloperWorks (2005)
17. Workflow Patterns Initiative, http://www.workflowpatterns.com
18. Philips, R.: Pricing and revenue optimization. Stanford Business Books (2005)
19. Trending Topics, http://www.trendingtopics.org/
20. Aniketos (Secure and Trustworthy Composite Services), http://www.aniketos.eu

Query Auditing for Protecting Max/Min Values of Sensitive Attributes in Statistical Databases

Ta Vinh Thong and Levente Buttyán

Laboratory of Cryptography and System Security (CrySyS)
Budapest University of Technology and Economics, Hungary
{thong,buttyan}@crysys.hu
http://www.crysys.hu

Abstract. In this paper, we define a novel setting for query auditing, where instead of detecting or preventing the disclosure of individual sensitive values, we want to detect or prevent the disclosure of aggregate values in the database. More specifically, we study the problem of detecting or preventing the disclosure of the maximum (minimum) value in the database, when the querier is allowed to issue average queries to the database. We propose efficient off-line and on-line query auditors for this problem in the full disclosure model, and an efficient simulatable on-line query auditor in the partial disclosure model.

Keywords: Privacy, query auditing, online auditor, offline auditor, simulatable auditor, probabilistic auditor, statistical database.

1 Introduction

Query Auditing is a problem that has been studied intensively in the context of disclosure control in statistical databases [1]. The goal of a query auditing algorithm is to detect (off-line query auditing) or to prevent (on-line query auditing) the disclosure of sensitive private information from a database that accepts and responds to aggregate queries (e.g., average value of an attribute over a subset of records defined by the query). To the best of our knowledge, in all existing works on query auditing, the private information whose disclosure we want to detect or prevent consists of the sensitive fields of individual records in the database (e.g., the salery of a given employee). The reason may be that statistical databases are mainly used for computing statistics over certain attributes of human users (e.g., the average salary of women employees), and in such applications, each database record corresponds to an individual person. In this paper, we define a novel setting for query auditing, where we want to detect or prevent the disclosure of *aggregate* values in the database (e.g., the maximum salary that occurs in the database).

The motivation behind our work comes from a project[1], called CHIRON, where we use body mounted wireless sensor networks to collect medical data

---

[1] www.chiron-project.eu

S. Fischer-Hübner, S. Katsikas, G. Quirchmayr (Eds.): TrustBus 2012, LNCS 7449, pp. 192–206, 2012.
© Springer-Verlag Berlin Heidelberg 2012

(e.g., ECG signals, blood pressure measurements, temperature samples, etc.) from a patient, and we use a personal device (e.g., a smart phone) to collect those data and provide controlled access to them for external parties (e.g., hospital personnel, personal coach services, and health insurance companies). In this context, the records stored in the database on the personal device all belong to the same patient, and individual values (i.e., sensor readings) may not be sensitive, whereas aggregates computed over those values (e.g., the maximum of the blood pressure in a given time interval) should be protected from unintended disclosure. The reason is that some of those aggregates (extreme values) can be used to infer the health status of the patient, and some of the accessing parties (e.g., health insurance companies) should be prevented to learn that information.

More specifically, in this paper, we study the problem of detecting or preventing the disclosure of the maximum value in the database, when the querier is allowed to issue average queries to the database. We propose efficient off-line and on-line query auditors for this problem in the full disclosure model, and an efficient simulatable on-line query auditor in the partial disclosure model. As for the organization of the paper, we start with an overview of the query auditing problem domain, introduce some terminology, review the state-of-the-art, and then present our model and algorithms together with their detailed analysis. Finally, we note that due to space limitations, we only sketch the proofs, and we focus on the main results of our work. More illustrating examples, explanations and more detailed proofs can be found in our technical report [13].

2   Query Auditing Problems

Query auditing problems can be classified according to the characteristics of the auditor and the attacker model that they resist [1]. In case of offline auditing, the auditor is given a set of t queries $q_1, \ldots, q_t$ and the corresponding answers $a_1, \ldots, a_t$, and its task is to determine offline if a breach of privacy has occurred. In contrast, an online auditor prevents a privacy breach by denying to respond to a new query if doing so would lead to the disclosure of private information. More specifically, given a sequence of $t-1$ queries $q_1, \ldots, q_{t-1}$ that have already been posed and their corresponding answers $a_1, \ldots, a_{t-1}$, when a new query q_t is received, the online auditor denies the answer if it detects that private information would be disclosed by $q_1, q_2, \ldots, q_t$, and $a_1, a_2, \ldots, a_t$, otherwise it gives the true answer a_t.

Let n denote the total number of records in the database. $X = \{x_1, x_2, \ldots, x_n\}$ is the set of the private attribute values in the records. $q = (Q, f)$ is an aggregate query, where Q specifies a subset of records, called the *query set* of q. f is an aggregation function such as MAX, MIN, SUM, AVG, MEDIAN. Finally, let $a = f(Q)$ be the result of applying f to Q, called the answer. In the following, we give an overview of the disclosure models, as well as the notion and concept of simulatable auditor.

In the full disclosure model, the privacy of some data x breaches when x has been uniquely determined.

Definition 1. *Given a set of private values* $X = \{x_1, x_2, \ldots, x_n\}$, *a set of queries* $\mathcal{Q} = \{q_1, q_2, \ldots, q_t\}$, *and corresponding answers* $\mathcal{A} = \{a_1, a_2, \ldots, a_t\}$, *an element* x_i *is fully disclosed by* $(\mathcal{Q}, \mathcal{A})$ *if it can be uniquely determined, that is,* x_i *is the same in all possible data sets* X *consistent with the answers* A *to the queries* $\mathcal{Q}$.

One may think that the full disclosure model defines a weak notion of privacy since a private value can be deduced to lie in a tiny interval or even a large interval where the distribution is heavily skewed towards a particular value, yet it is not considered a privacy breach. To deal with this problem, a definition of privacy has been proposed that gives bounds on the ratio of the posteriori probability that an individual value x_i lies in an interval I given the queries and answers to the apriori probability that $x_i \in I$. This is also known as probabilistic (partial) disclosure model [10], which we will introduce next.

Consider an arbitrary data set $X = \{x_1, \ldots, x_n\}$, in which each x_i is chosen independently according to the same distribution $\mathcal{H}$ on $(-\infty, \infty)$. Let $\mathcal{D} = \mathcal{H}^n$ denote the joint distribution. Next we introduce the notion of λ-safe and AllSafe. We say that a sequence of queries and answers is λ-safe for an entry x_i and an interval I if the attacker's confidence that $x_i \in I$ does not change significantly upon seeing the queries and answers.

Definition 2. *The sequence of queries and answers,* $q_1, \ldots, q_t$, $a_1, \ldots, a_t$ *(denoted by* $\wedge_1^t(q_j, a_j)$*) is said to be λ-safe with respect to an x_i and an interval* $I \subseteq (-\infty, \infty)$ *if the next Boolean predicate evaluates to 1:*

$$Safe_{\lambda, i, I}(\wedge_1^t(q_j, a_j)) = \begin{cases} 1 \text{ if } 1/(1+\lambda) \leq \frac{Pr_{\mathcal{D}}(x_i \in I | \wedge_{j=1}^t (f_j(Q_j) = a_j))}{Pr_{\mathcal{D}}(x_i \in I)} \leq (1+\lambda) \\ 0 \text{ otherwise} \end{cases}$$

Definition 3. *Predicate AllSafe evaluates to 1 if and only if* $q_1, \ldots, q_t$, $a_1, \ldots, a_t$ *is λ-safe for all x_i's and all ω-significant intervals.*

$$AllSafe_{\lambda, \omega}(\wedge_1^t(q_j, a_j)) = \begin{cases} 1 \text{ if } Safe_{\lambda, i, J}(\wedge_1^t(q_j, a_j)) = 1, \forall J, \forall i \in [n] \\ 0 \text{ otherwise} \end{cases}$$

We say that an interval J is ω-significant if for every $i \in [n]$, $Pr_{\mathcal{D}}(x_i \in J)$ is at least $1/\omega$, and we will only consider the change of probabilities with respect to these intervals. The definition of a randomized auditor for the case of partial disclosure model is as follows.

Definition 4. *A randomized auditor is a randomized function of queries* $q_1, \ldots, q_t$, *the data set X, and the probability distribution $\mathcal{D}$ that either gives an exact answer to the query q_t or denies the answer.*

Below we introduce the notion of the (λ, ω, T)-privacy game and the $(\lambda, \delta, \omega, T)$-private auditor. The (λ, ω, T)-privacy game is a game between an attacker and an auditor, where each round t (for up to T rounds) is defined as follows:

1. In each round t $(t \leq T)$, the attacker poses a query $q_t = (Q_t, f_t)$.
2. The auditor decides whether to respond to q_t or not. The auditor replies with $a_t = f_t(Q_t)$ if q_t is allowed, and denies the response otherwise.
3. The attacker wins if $AllSafe_{\lambda,\omega}(\wedge_1^t(q_j, a_j)) = 0$.

Definition 5. *An auditor is $(\lambda, \delta, \omega, T)$-private if for any attacker A,*

$$Pr\{A \text{ wins the } (\lambda, \omega, T)\text{-privacy game}\} \leq \delta.$$

The probability is taken over the randomness in the distribution $\mathcal{D}$ and the coin tosses of the auditor and the attacker.

Unfortunately, in general an offline auditor cannot directly solve the online auditing problem because even denials can leak information if in choosing to deny, the auditor uses information that is unavailable to the attacker (i.e., the answer to the current query). We refer the reader to the extended report of this paper [13] for an illustrating example. In order to overcome this problem, the concept of *simulatable auditor* has been proposed. Taking into account the crucial observation above, the main idea of simulatable auditing is that the attacker is able to simulate or mimic the auditor's decisions to answer or deny a query. As the attacker can equivalently determine for himself when his queries will be denied, she obtains no additional information from denials. For these reasons denials *provably* leak no information. The definition of simulatable auditor in the full disclosure model is given in Definition 6.

Definition 6. *An online auditor B is simulatable, if there exists another auditor B' that is a function of only $\mathcal{Q} \cup \{q_t\} = \{q_1, q_2, \ldots, q_t\}$ and $\mathcal{A} = \{a_1, a_2, \ldots, a_{t-1}\}$, and whose answer to q_t is always equal to that of B.*

When constructing a simulatable auditor for the probabilistic disclosure model, the auditor should ignore the real answer a_t and instead make guesses about the value of a_t, say a_t', computed on randomly sampled data sets according to the distribution $\mathcal{D}$ conditioned on the first $t-1$ queries and answers. The definition of simulatable auditor in the probabilistic case is given in Definition 7.

Definition 7. *Let $\mathcal{Q}_t = \{q_1, \ldots, q_t\}$, $\mathcal{A}_{t-1} = \{a_1, \ldots, a_{t-1}\}$. A randomized auditor B is simulatable if there exists another auditor B' that is a probabilistic function of $\langle \mathcal{Q}_t, \mathcal{A}_{t-1}, \mathcal{D} \rangle$, and the outcome of B on $\langle \mathcal{Q}_t, \mathcal{A}_{t-1} \cup \{a_t\}, \mathcal{D} \rangle$ and X is computationally indistinguishable from that of B' on $\langle \mathcal{Q}_t, \mathcal{A}_{t-1}, \mathcal{D} \rangle$.*

A general approach for constructing simulatable auditors works as follows: The input of the auditor is the past $t-1$ queries along with their corresponding answers, and the current query q_t. As mentioned before, the auditor should not consider the true answer a_t when making a decision. Instead, to make it simulatable for the attacker, the auditor repeatedly selects a data set X' consistent with the past $t-1$ queries and answers, and computes the answer a_t' based on q_t and X'. Then, the auditor checks if answering with a_t' leads to a privacy breach. If a privacy breach occurs for any consistent data set (full disclosure model) or for a large fraction of consistent data sets (partial disclosure model), the response to q_t is denied. Otherwise, it is allowed and the true answer a_t is returned.

While ensuring no information leakage, a simulatable auditor has the main drawback that it can be too strict, and deny too many queries resulting in bad utility.

3   Related Works

We note that *the related works discussed below are concerned with protecting the privacy of individual values, and not aggregated values* that we are addressing in this paper. In case of the full disclosure model, efficient simulatable online auditors have been proposed for SUM [3], MAX, MIN and the combination of MAX and MIN queries [6], [10]. In all these cases the values of private attributes are assumed to be unbounded real numbers. For effectiveness, the MAX and MIN auditors assume that there is no duplication among $x_1, \ldots, x_n$ values.

In the full disclosure model, effective offline auditors have been proposed for SUM, MAX, MIN, and the combination of MAX and MIN queries over unbounded real values and under the same conditions as in the online case above [3], [4]. Additionally, SUM auditors have also been proposed for boolean values [7], but the authors proved that the online sum auditing problem over boolean values is coNP-hard. It has been shown that the problem of offline auditing the combination of MAX and SUM (MIN and SUM, MIN and MAX and SUM) queries in the full disclosure model is NP-hard [3].

In [14] an offline SUM auditor has been proposed in which sensitive information about individuals is said to be compromised if an accurate enough interval is obtained into which the value of the sensitive information must fall. In [2] the authors consider the problem of auditing queries where the result is a distance metric between the query input and some secret data.

Similarly, simulatable SUM, MAX, MIN and the combination of MAX and MIN auditors have been proposed for the probabilistic disclosure model [3], [4]. In all cases the private attributes are assumed to take their values randomly accorinding to uniform and log-concave distributions, from an unbounded domain. In [8] the notion of simulatable binding has been proposed that provides better utility than simulatable auditor, but requires more computations.

Targeting the problem of mutable databases, which allow for deleting, modifying, and inserting records, auditors have been proposed in the full disclosure model for MIN, MAX, MIN and MAX, and SUM queries [11].

Next we review a bit more in details the offline SUM auditor proposed in [3] because it is referred to during discussing our method. The main concept of the method is that each query is expressed as a row in a matrix with a 1 wherever there is an index in the query and a 0 otherwise. If the matrix can be reduced to a form where there is a row with one 1 and the rest 0s then some value has been compromised. To make it simulatable, the transformations of the original matrix are performed via elementary row and column operations by ignoring the answers to the queries.

4   Our Contributions

We address a new auditing problem by considering an *aggregation* value of a data set to be sensitive and concentrating on protecting the privacy of aggregation values. In contrast to the previous works, we assume that the domain of sensitive values is bounded, which leads to some new problems. We note that in each case below, without loss of generality and for simplicity, we transform each equation $\frac{\sum_1^k x_i}{k} = a$ induced by each AVG query and its answer to the form $\sum_1^k x_i = ak$.

In the rest of the paper, we denote the auditor that receives average queries and protects the privacy of the max (min) value as $\text{Auditor}_{avg}^{max}$ ($\text{Auditor}_{avg}^{min}$), and we denote $\max\{x_1, \ldots, x_n\}$ by MAX. We note that in the paper we mainly focus on the privacy of the maximum values, however, auditors can be constructed for minimum values in an equivalent way.

4.1   Offline and Online $\text{Auditor}_{avg}^{max}$ in the Full Disclosure Model

I. The Proposed Offline Auditor: Let us consider t queries $q_1, \ldots, q_t$ over the stored data set $X = \{x_1, \ldots, x_n\}$ and their corresponding answers $a_1, \ldots, a_t$. Each query q_i is of form (Q_i, AVG), where $i \subseteq [n]$, and the value of each x_i is assumed to be a real number that lies in a finite interval $[\alpha, \beta]$, where $\beta > \alpha$. The task of the offline auditor is to detect if the value of MAX is fully disclosed.

Let us refer to the algorithm proposed in [3] as $\mathcal{A}_{sum}$. Using $\mathcal{A}_{sum}$ is not sufficient in our case because it does not consider the bounds of each x_i, as well as the values of the answers. For the purpose of illustration, let us take the following example: let $X = \{x_1, x_2, x_3\}$ and $\forall x_i \in [20, 90]$, let $q_1 = (\{x_1, x_2\}, \text{AVG})$, $q_2 = (\{x_1, x_2, x_3\}, \text{AVG})$ and the corresponding answers $a_1 = 45$, $a_2 = 60$. Finally, let the stored values be $x_1 = 40$, $x_2 = 50$, $x_3 = 90$. According to $\mathcal{A}_{sum}$ the value of MAX is not fully disclosed, because the answers and the bounds of x_i's are not considered. We only know that x_3 can be uniquely determined, but nothing about its value. However, in fact MAX is fully disclosed because by involving the answers we additionally know that the value of x_3 is 90, which at the same time is the value of MAX since 90 is the upperbound of any x_i.

Hence, we have to consider a method that also takes into account the bounds of x_i's and the answers. For this purpose, we propose the application of the well-known linear optimization problem as follows: The t queries are represented by a matrix $\bar{A}$ of t rows and n columns. Each row $r_i = (a_{i,1}, \ldots, a_{i,n})$ of $\bar{A}$ represents the query set Q_i of the query q_i. The value of $a_{i,j}$, $1 \leq i, j \leq n$, is 1 wherever x_j is in the query set Q_i, and is a 0 otherwise. The correponding answers are represented as a column vector $\bar{b} = (b_1, \ldots, b_t)^T$ in which b_i is the answer for q_i.

Since each attribute x_i takes a real value from a bounded interval $[\alpha, \beta]$ we obtain the following special linear equation system, also known as *feasible set*, which includes equations and inequalities:

$$\mathcal{L} = \begin{cases} \bar{A}\bar{x} = \bar{b}, \text{where } \bar{x} \text{ is the vector } (x_1, \ldots, x_n)^T. \\ \alpha \leq x_i \leq \beta, \forall x_i : x_i \in \{x_1, \ldots, x_n\} \end{cases}$$

Then, by appending each objective function $maximize(x_i)$ to $\mathcal{L}$, we get n linear programming problems P_i, for $i \in \{1, \ldots, n\}$. Let $x_i^{max} = maximize(x_i)$, then the maximum value of $x_1, \ldots, x_n$ is the maximum of the n maximized values, $x^{opt} = max\{x_1^{max}, \ldots, x_n^{max}\}$. Let us denote the whole linear programming problem above for determining the maximum value x^{opt} as $\mathcal{P}$. Note that x^{opt} returned by $\mathcal{P}$ is the exact maximum value if (i) $\mathcal{L}$ has a unique solution or (ii) $\mathcal{L}$ does not have a unique solution but there exist some x_i that can be derived to be equal to x^{opt}. To see the meaning of point (ii), let us consider the specific case of $\mathcal{L}$ in which $n = 4$, $\alpha = 0$, $\beta = 5$, and $\bar{A} = \begin{pmatrix} 1 & 1 & 0 & 0 \\ 0 & 0 & 1 & 1 \end{pmatrix}$, $\bar{b} = \begin{pmatrix} 6 \\ 10 \end{pmatrix}$. In this example, $\mathcal{L}$ does not have a unique solution but the exact maximum still can be derived such that $x_3 = x_4 = 5$.

Otherwise, x^{opt} is the best estimation of the exact maximum. We note that in our case $\mathcal{L}$ always has a solution, because one possible solution is actually the values stored in the database.

Based on this linear programming problem, our offline auditor will follow the next steps. Given t queries $q_1, \ldots, q_t$ over $X = \{x_1, \ldots, x_n\}$ and their corresponding answers $a_1, \ldots, a_t$, the value of MAX is fully disclosed in any of the following two cases:

- (F1) In case $\mathcal{L}$ has a unique solution, the value of MAX is equal to x^{opt}.
- (F2) In case $\mathcal{L}$ does not have a unique solution: If by following the solving procedure of $\mathcal{L}$ (e.g., basic row and column operations), there exist some x_i that can be uniquely determined such that $x_i = x^{opt}$, then the value of MAX is x_i. This is because x^{opt} is always at least as large as the value of MAX.

Otherwise, the attacker cannot uniquely deduce the value of MAX. The complexity of the auditor is based on the complexity of $\mathcal{P}$. It is well-known that there are polynomial time methods to solve $\mathcal{P}$, for instance, the path-following algorithm [12], which is one of the most effective method with complexity $O(n^3 L)$. Here n is the number of variables while L is the size of the input in bits, and the number of rows is assumed to be $O(n)$. Therefore, our offline auditing method has a polynomial time complexity in the worst case.

II. The Proposed Online Auditor: Let us consider the first $t - 1$ queries and answers over the data set similarly defined as in the offline case above. When a new q_t is posed, the task of the online auditor is to make a decision in *real-time* whether to answer or deny the query. More specifically, our goal is to propose an auditor that detects if answering with true a_t causes full disclosure of MAX.

First of all, we discuss the construction of a simulatable auditor for this problem, and we will show the limitation of simulatable auditors in this case. Thereafter, we introduce another method that gets around this limitation. Based on the concept shown in Section 2 and the linear programming problem, the simulatable auditor for this problem is shown in Algorithm 1.

Algorithm 1. Simulatable online auditor Auditor$_{avg}^{max}$

Inputs: $q_1, \ldots, q_t, a_1, \ldots, a_{t-1}, \alpha, \beta$;

for each consistent data set X' **do** compute the AVG a'_t based on Q_t and X';

    Let $\mathcal{L}_t$ be the feasible set formed by the t queries/answers;

    if $\mathcal{L}_t$ yields an exact maximum **then** output DENY; **endif**

endfor

output a_t;

Algorithm 2. Online auditor Auditor$_{avg}^{max}$

Inputs: $q_1, \ldots, q_t, a_1, \ldots, a_t, d_{tr}, \alpha, \beta$;

Let $\mathcal{L}_t^*$ be the feasible set formed by the t queries/answers

Let x_t^{opt} be the returned maximum by solving $\mathcal{P}$ with $\mathcal{L}_t^*$

if $|x_t^{opt} - MAX| > d_{tr}$ AND $(MAX - max_t) > d_{tr}$ **then** output a_t; **endif**

else if $|x_t^{opt} - MAX| \leq d_{tr}$ OR $(MAX - max_t) \leq d_{tr}$ **then** output DENY; **endif**

Note that in Algorithm 1, based on the concept of simulatable auditor in Section 2, by ignoring the true answer a_t we examine every data set X', consistent with the past queries and answers, and check if it causes the full disclosure of MAX. This means that the answer a'_t computed based on X' and Q_t, is included in the analysis. The auditor is simulatable because it never looks at the true answer when making a decision. The main drawback, however, of using simulatable auditor in our problem is the bad utility. In order to see this, consider any AVG query q that specifies a subset $\{x_{i1}, x_{i2}, \ldots, x_{ik}\}$ of X as the query set. There always exist a data set X' for which this query is not safe to respond, namely, the data set where $x_{i1} = x_{i2} = \ldots = x_{ik} = \beta$, as in this case, the true response would be β, and the querier can figure out that all values in the query set must be equal to β. This essentially means that all queries should be denied by a simulatable auditor.

To achieve better utility, hence, we propose a method (Algorithm 2) that is not simulatable but we show that it still ensures, in the full disclosure model, the privacy of the maximum value. Let us denote $|x^{opt} - MAX|$ as the absolute distance between x^{opt} and MAX. Let max_t be the maximum of the first t answers. Let $\mathcal{L}^*$ be the feasible set that is similar to $\mathcal{L}$ but the constraint $\alpha \leq x_i \leq \beta$ is involved only for such x_i's that occurs in the first t queries, and not for all the n variables. Namely, in $\mathcal{L}^*$ the second line of $\mathcal{L}$ is changed to $\alpha \leq x_i \leq \beta$, for all i such that x_i occurs in in the first t queries. Note that we use $\mathcal{L}^*$ instead of $\mathcal{L}$ in our online auditor because by doing this the auditor leaks less information to the attacker either when answering or denying.

The online auditor works as follows: Recall that $\mathcal{L}^*$ is defined over t queries and answers. Whenever a new query q_t is posed, the auditor computes the true answer a_t, and then it solves the problem $\mathcal{P}$ with $\mathcal{L}^*$, obtaining x^{opt}. If for a given treshold value d_{tr}, $|x^{opt} - MAX| > d_{tr}$ and $(MAX - max_t) > d_{tr}$ then the true answer a_t is provided. Otherwise, if $|x^{opt} - MAX| \leq d_{tr}$ or $(MAX - max_t) \leq d_{tr}$ the auditor denies.

Lemma 1. *The online auditor implemented by the Algorithm 2 provides the privacy of MAX in the full disclosure model.*

Proof. (Sketch) Let $f_{att}(d_{tr}, q_1, \ldots, q_t, a_1, \ldots, a_{t-1}, \alpha, \beta)$ represent the attacker's based on the input parameters, and returning as output a deny or an answer. We prove that our online auditor does not leak information about MAX, in the full disclosure model by showing that the number of the data sets and the parameter sets for which f_{att} returns deny or answer is always larger than 1. In other words, in every possible scenario, for the attacker the number of possible maximum values will always be greater than 1, hence, the value of MAX cannot be uniquely determined. We apply mathematical induction in each case.   □

The utility of the auditor can be measured based on the number of denies. This is controlled by the treshold value d_{tr}. Broadly speaking, if d_{tr} is large then the expected number of denies is greater, while when d_{tr} is small the degree of privacy provided decreases, because the estimated maximum can be very close to the real maximum (MAX). The more specific choice of d_{tr} to achieve a good trade-off between utility and privacy level for the specific application scenarios is an interesting question, for which we will find the answer in our future work.

The worst-case complexity of the online auditor depends on the worst-case complexity of $\mathcal{P}$ and the number of posed queries. We can assume that the number of queries is $O(n)$, where n is the size of the data set. In this case, by applying one of the polynomial time linear program solver methods, the whole complexity remains polynomial.

4.2   Simulatable Auditor$_{avg}^{max}$ in the Partial Disclosure Model

We propose a simulatable auditor that prevents the probabilistic disclosure of MAX. By transforming the AVG queries to SUM queries we can adapt one part of the auditor given in [6],[5], but our problem is different from those in [6],[5], because we consider bounded intervals and MAX. Hence, the methods proposed for SUM auditors cannot be used entirely in our case, and although using similar terminology, the proofs are not the same (see [13]).

We assume that each element x_i is independently drawn according to a distribution $\mathcal{G}$ that belongs to the familiy of log-concave distributions over the set $\mathbb{R}$ of real numbers between $[\alpha, \beta]$. Note that we consider the class of log-concave distribution because it covers many important distributions including the guassian distribution. In addition, our online simulatable auditor is based on random sampling, and we want to apply directly the method of Lovasz [9] on effective sampling from log-concave distributions. The main advantage of the sampling method in [9] is that it is polynomial-time and produces only small error.

A distribution over a domain D is said to be log-concave if it has a density function f such that the logarithm of f is concave. Due to the lack of space we only sketch the proofs in this section, but the full proofs can be found in [13].

Lemma 2. *Next we give some relevant points that will make the method in [9] applicable in the construction of our auditor.*

1. *The truncated version of log-concave distribution is also log-concave.*
2. *If $\mathcal{G}$ is a log-concave distribution then the joint distribution $\mathcal{G}^n$ is also log-concave.*
3. *Let the joint distribution $\mathcal{G}^n$ conditioned on $\wedge_{j=1}^t (avg(Q_j) = a_j)$, be $\mathcal{G}_t^n$. If $\mathcal{G}$ is a log-concave distribution then $\mathcal{G}_t^n$ is also log-concave.*

Proof. (Sketch)

1. Let the density and the cumulative distribution function of a variable Y be $f(y)$ and $F(y)$, respectively. The truncated version of $f(y)$, $f(y|Y \in I)$, is equal to $\frac{f(y)}{\int_I f(y)dy}$. By assumption, $f(y)$ is log-concave and the denominator is a constant, it follows that $f(y|Y \in I)$ is log-concave. Hence, returning to our problem, each x_i is taken according to a truncated log-concave distribution, which is log-concave.

2. Because the logarithm of the product of log-concave functions is a concave function we get that the product of log-concave distributions is also log-concave. From this the second point of the Lemma follows.

3. Similar to the truncated distribution density function, the density of $\mathcal{G}_t^n$ is as follows: $f_{\mathcal{G}_t^n}(*) = \frac{f_{\mathcal{G}^n}(*) I_{\mathcal{P}}(*)}{Pr(x \in \mathcal{P})}$, where $f_{\mathcal{G}^n}(*)$ is the density of the joint distribution, $I_{\mathcal{P}}(*)$ is an indicator function that returns 1 if x are in the convex constraint $\mathcal{P}$ induced by the t queries and answers, and 0 otherwise. The denominator contains the probability that x being within $\mathcal{P}$, which is a constant value for a given $\mathcal{P}$. According to second point and based on the similar argument as the case in the first point, it follows that $f_{\mathcal{G}_t^n}(*)$ is log-concave.   □

In our case, the predicate λ-Safe and AllSafe is a bit different from the traditional definitions discussed in Section 2, because we are considering the maximum of n values instead of single values. Specifically, in $Safe_{\lambda,I}(\wedge_1^t(q_j, a_j))$ we require $\frac{P_{\mathcal{G}_{post}^t}(MAX \in I|\wedge_{j=1}^t(avg(Q_j)=a_j))}{Pr_{\mathcal{G}_{max}}(MAX \in I)}$ to be within the bound $\left[\frac{1}{1+\lambda}, 1+\lambda\right]$, where $\mathcal{G}_{post}^t$ is the distribution of the posteriori probability, and $\mathcal{G}_{max}$ is the distribution of MAX. The definition of AllSafe, $AllSafe_{\lambda,\omega}(\wedge_1^t(q_j, a_j))$ is then given over all ω-significant intervals J of $[\alpha, \beta]$. Here the notion of ω-significant interval is defined over the maximum value instead of individual values: An interval J is ω-significant if $P_{\mathcal{G}_{max}}(MAX \in J) \geq \frac{1}{\omega}$. The definitions of (λ, ω, T)-privacy game and $(\lambda, \delta, \omega, T)$-privacy auditor remains unchanged.

In [9] the authors proposed the algorithm $Sample(D, \epsilon)$ for sampling from an arbitrary log-concave distribution D (defined in $\mathbb{R}^n$) with the best running time of $O^*(n^5)$, such that the sampled output follows a distribution D' where the total variation distance between D and D' is at most ϵ. The notation $O^*()$ is taken from [9], and indicates that the polynomial dependence on $\log n$, and the error parameter ϵ are not shown. We make use of this algorithm for constructing our auditor.

The next question is that what kind of, and how many intervals I we need to consider when examining the AllSafe predicate. Of course, in practise, we cannot examine infinitely many sub-intervals in $[\alpha, \beta]$. Following the approach in [6], we show that it is enough to check only finite number of intervals.

Let us consider the quantiles or quantile function in statistics. Informally, a p-quantile has the value x if the fraction of data smaller than x is p. A quantile function is the inverse of a distribution function. We use the methods for finding quantiles in case of $\mathcal{G}_{max}$ and divide the domain into γ sub-intervals, $I_1, \ldots, I_\gamma$ such that $P_{\mathcal{G}_{max}}(MAX \in I_i) = \frac{1}{\gamma}$, for $1 \leq i \leq \gamma$ (this is related to the inverse distribution function in order statistics). In Lemma 3 we show that if AllSafe evaluates to 1 in case of the γ intervals for a smaller privacy parameter $\widetilde{\lambda}$ (i.e., stricter privacy) then it evaluates to 1 in case of ω-significant intervals as well.

Lemma 3. *Suppose $Safe_{\widetilde{\lambda}, I} = 1$ for each interval I of the γ intervals, and $\widetilde{\lambda} = \frac{\lambda(c-1)-2}{c+1}$, where c is any integer greater than $1 + 2/\lambda$. Then, $Safe_{\lambda, J} = 1$ for every ω-significant interval J.*

Proof. (Sketch)
Based on the intuition we use during our proof (see the three cases discussed below) and to achieve that $\widetilde{\lambda}$ is smaller than λ, we set $\widetilde{\lambda}$ such that $\frac{c+1}{c-1}(1 + \widetilde{\lambda})$ $= (1 + \lambda)$. Further, to make $\widetilde{\lambda}$ be positive, based on the setting of $\widetilde{\lambda}$ above we choose the parameter c to be larger than $1 + 2/\lambda$. In addition, γ is set to be larger than ω, namely, to $\lceil c\omega \rceil$, where the brackets represent ceiling. Finally, let J be a ω-significant interval and denote $P(MAX \in J)$ as P_J^{max}, and let $d = \lceil \gamma P_J^{max} \rceil$. Note that with these settings of γ and d we have $d \geq c$ and $\frac{d+1}{d-1} \leq \frac{c+1}{c-1}$.

Our goal is to prove that the sequence $\wedge_1^t(q_i, a_i)$ is λ-Safe for each ω-significant interval, and to do this, we prove a stronger privacy notion. Specifically, we show that if the sequence $\wedge_1^t(q_i, a_i)$ is $Safe_{\widetilde{\lambda}, I} = 1$ for each interval I, then it is $(\frac{d+1}{d-1}(1 + \widetilde{\lambda}) - 1)$-Safe for every interval J. This is a stronger privacy requirement because $\frac{d+1}{d-1}(1 + \widetilde{\lambda}) - 1 \leq \frac{c+1}{c-1}(1 + \widetilde{\lambda}) - 1 = \lambda$. To prove this we examine three possible cases, and we show that this holds in all these cases: (Case 1) J is contained in the union of $d + 1$ consecutive intervals, say $I_1, I_2, \ldots, I_{d+1}$, of which J contains the intervals $I_2, I_3, \ldots, I_d$; (Case 2) J is contained in the union of $d + 2$ consecutive intervals, say $I_1, I_2, \ldots, I_{d+2}$, of which J contains the intervals $I_2, I_3, \ldots, I_{d+1}$; (Case 3) J is contained in the union of $d + 1$ consecutive intervals, say $I_1, I_2, \ldots, I_{d+1}$, of which J contains the d intervals $I_1, I_1, \ldots, I_d$. □

Now we turn to the construction of the simulatable auditor. According to Definitions 2 and 3, first, we provide the method (Algorithm 3) for checking if the predicate AllSafe is 1 or 0, and then we construct the simulatable auditor (Algorithm 4) based on the concept shown in Section 2 and the definition of (λ, δ, ω, T)-privacy game.

We give the algorithm $\overline{\text{AllSafe}}$, which is an *estimation* of the predicate AllSafe$_{\lambda, \omega}$. This is because the algorithm makes use of the sampling algorithm $Sample(\mathcal{G}_t^n, \epsilon)$ for estimating the posteriori probability, and instead of examining all the ω-significant intervals, we make an estimation by only taking into account γ intervals: $\overline{\text{AllSafe}}$ takes as inputs (1) the sequence of queries and answers $q_1, \ldots,$ $q_t, a_1, \ldots, a_t$; (2) the distribution $\mathcal{G}$; (3) a probability η of error for computing

ϵ; (4) the trade-off parameter c such that $\gamma = \lceil c\omega \rceil$, and $\tilde{\lambda} = \frac{\lambda(c-1)-2}{c+1}$, where $\lceil\ \rceil$ represents ceiling; (5) the parameter ω; and (6) the size n of the data set.

The parameter choice is made such that the Lemma 4 holds. In other words, if we modify the privacy parameters in Lemma 4 we have to modify the parameters above as well. Moreover, the intuition behind the parameter choice resides in the proof technique. In our proofs we apply the well-known definitions and theorems related to the Chernoff-bound, Union bound, and some basic statements in statistics and probability theory. Roughly speaking, these parameters have been chosen such that the Chernoff-bound and Union-bound can be applicable. We emphasize that the choice of these specific parameters is only for better illustrating purposes. These specific values of the parameters are one possible choice but not the only one. The general form of parameters is provided in [13].

One drawback of Lemma 3 is that the reverse direction is not necessarily true. Thus, to make claims on the AllSafe = 0 case, we cannot use directly the privacy parameter $\tilde{\lambda}$. Instead, in the algorithm $\overline{\text{AllSafe}}$ we consider an even more stronger privacy notion with a smaller parameter $\lambda' = \tilde{\lambda}/3$. We note that λ' can be any value that is smaller than $\tilde{\lambda}$ (see the proof in [13]), but then we have to modify the privacy parameters in Lemma 4 accordingly. In our case, however, we choose it to be $\tilde{\lambda}/3$ for easier discussion and illustrating purposes. The error ϵ of the algorithm $Sample(\mathcal{G}_t^n, \epsilon)$ is set to be $\frac{\eta}{2N}$. (see [13] for details)

Algorithm 3. AllSafe $(q_1, \ldots, q_t, a_1, \ldots, a_t, \mathcal{G}, \eta, \omega, \lambda, n, c)$

Let AllSafe = TRUE;
for each of the γ intervals I in $[\alpha, \beta]$ **do**
    Sample N data sets according to $\mathcal{G}_t^n$, using $Sample(\mathcal{G}_t^n, \epsilon)$;
    Let N_{max}, $N_{max} \subseteq N$, be the number of data sets for which MAX $\in I$;
    if $\left(\frac{\gamma N_{max}}{N} \notin \left[\frac{1}{1+\lambda'}, 1+\lambda' \right] \right)$ **then** Let AllSafe = FALSE; **endif**
endfor
return AllSafe;

Algorithm 4. Simulatable probabilistic auditor

Inputs: $q_1, \ldots, q_{t-1}, a_1, \ldots, a_{t-1}$, a new query q_t, $\mathcal{G}, \delta, \eta, \lambda, \gamma, n, T, c$;
Let $\epsilon = \delta/10T$;
for $\frac{80T}{9\delta} \ln \frac{T}{\delta}$ times **do**
    Sample a consistent data set X' according to $\mathcal{G}_{t-1}^n$ using $Sample(\mathcal{G}_{t-1}^n, \epsilon)$;
    Let $a'_t = avg_{X'}(Q_t)$; **call** $\overline{\text{AllSafe}}(q_1, \ldots, q_t, a_1, \ldots, a'_t, \mathcal{G}, \eta, \omega, \lambda, n, c)$;
endfor
if the fraction of data sets X' for which $\overline{\text{AllSafe}}$=FALSE is greater than $\frac{9\delta}{20T}$ **then**
    return DENY; **else return** a_t;
endif;

In Algorithm 3, N denotes the total number of data sets $(x_1, \ldots, x_n)$ sampled according to $Sample(\mathcal{G}_t^n, \epsilon)$, and N_{max}, $N_{max} \subseteq N$, denotes the number of the data sets satisfying $MAX \in I$. Hence, the posteriori probability is estimated by the ratio $\frac{N_{max}}{N}$. In addition, the apriori probability is $\frac{1}{\gamma}$, and according to Definition 2 the probability ratio $\frac{\gamma N_{max}}{N}$ is required to be close to 1.

.

Intuitively, the steps in Algorithm 3 are as follows: By Lemma 3 instead of checking infinite ω-significant intervals with the privacy parameter λ we check the Safe predicate for each of the γ intervals and the smaller privacy parameter λ'. To estimate the posteriori probability that $MAX \in I$, we sample sufficient number (N) of data sets according to the distribution $\mathcal{G}_t^n$, and compute the fraction (N_{max}) of the data sets for which the maximum value falls in the interval I. Intuitively, by sampling according to $\mathcal{G}_t^n$ we get the data sets that satisfy the condition $\wedge_{j=1}^t(avg(Q_j) = a_j)$. If the ratio of the posteriori and apriori probabilities is outside the required bounds then the algorithm returns FALSE, otherwise TRUE is output.

Next we discuss how good estimation Algorithm 3 provides. In the ideal case, we would like that if the predicate AllSafe$_{\lambda,\omega}$ returns 0 (1) then the algorithm $\overline{\text{AllSafe}}$ returns FALSE (TRUE). However, we cannot make these claims for the next reasons: (i) we do not check all (infinitely many) ω-significant intervals for privacy and instead check only γ intervals; (ii) we estimate the posteriori probability using sampling, which has some error. Hence, instead of achieving the ideal case we provide the following claims:

Lemma 4. *1. If AllSafe$_{\lambda,\omega}(q_1, \ldots, q_t, a_1, \ldots, a_t) = 0$ then Algorithm $\overline{\text{AllSafe}}$ returns FALSE with probability at least $1 - \eta$.*

2. If AllSafe$_{\tilde{\lambda}/9,\gamma}(q_1, \ldots, q_t, a_1, \ldots, a_t) = 1$ then Algorithm $\overline{\text{AllSafe}}$ returns TRUE with probability at least $1 - 2\gamma\eta$.

Proof. (Sketch) The proof and the parameter setting for this Lemma is based on the application of the well-known Chernoff-bound and Union-bound. Let $X_1, \ldots, X_n$ be independent Bernoulli trials (or Poisson trials), with $P(X_i = 1) = p$ (or $P(X_i = 1) = p_i$ in case of Poisson trials). Let X be $\sum_1^n X_i$ with μ be $E[X]$, and $\theta \in (0, 1]$. The Chernoff-bound says: $P(X \leq \mu(1 - \theta)) \leq e^{-\mu\theta^2/2} \leq e^{-\mu\theta^2/4}$, and $P(X \geq \mu(1 + \theta)) \leq e^{-\mu\theta^2/4}$. The Union-bound says that if we have the events $e_1, \ldots, e_n$ then by applying the Chernoff-bound we can give a bound for the union of these events, that is, $P[e_1 \cup \cdots \cup e_n] \leq \sum_1^n P[e_i] \leq \sum_1^n bound_i$. $\square$

Intuitively, with probability close to 1, whenever AllSafe$_{\lambda,\omega} = 0$ the algorithm $\overline{\text{AllSafe}}$ also returns FALSE, and for a smaller privacy parameter $\tilde{\lambda}/9$ whenever AllSafe$_{\tilde{\lambda}/9,\gamma} = 1$ then $\overline{\text{AllSafe}}$ returns TRUE. For the region in between, no guarantees can be made. We note that in the general case, by choosing properly the input parameters, in the second point of the Lemma, we can choose any privacy parameter smaller than $\tilde{\lambda}$. The question is that, with these chosen parameters, how large should N be? We show that, based on the Chernoff-bound (see [13]), setting $N = \frac{9\gamma^2 ln(2/\eta)}{\tilde{\lambda}^2} * (1 + \lambda')^2 * max((1 + \tilde{\lambda})^2, (3 + \lambda')^2)$ is suitable for fullfiling the claims in the Lemma.

Now that we have an algorithm that evaluates the predicate AllSafe$_{\lambda,\omega}$, we turn to discuss the construction of the simulatable auditor itself. During the auditor construction, besides making use of the algorithm $\overline{\text{AllSafe}}$ we also take into account the notion of the T-round privacy game discussed in Section 2.

In Algorithm 4, beyond the parameters used in $\overline{\text{AllSafe}}$, additional parameters δ and T are concerning the (λ, ω, T)-privacy game and the $(\lambda, \delta, \omega, T)$-privacy auditor, and ϵ is the sampling error. Intuitively, the auditor repeatedly samples, according to the distribution $\mathcal{G}_{t-1}^n$, a data set X' that is consistent with the previous $t-1$ queries and answers. Then the corresponding answer a_t' is computed based on X' and the query set Q_t of the query q_t. Thereafter, we call the algorithm $\overline{\text{AllSafe}}$ with the previous queries and answers, along with q_t and a_t'. If the *fraction* of data sets for which $\overline{\text{AllSafe}}$ returns FALSE is larger than $9\delta/20T$ then the auditor denies, otherwise it returns the true answer a_t. The reason of choosing $9\delta/20T$ is that we want to fullfil the definition of $(\lambda, \delta, \omega, T)$-privacy auditor. The proof that Algorithm 4 implements a $(\lambda, \delta, \omega, T)$-privacy auditor is based on the well-known theorems of the Chernoff bound and Union bound over T rounds of the privacy game.

Theorem 1. *Algorithm 4 implements a $(\lambda, \delta, \omega, T)$-private simulatable auditor, and its running time is $N\gamma\frac{80T}{9\delta}\ln\frac{T}{\delta}T_{samp}(\mathcal{D}_c, \epsilon)$, where $T_{samp}(\mathcal{D}_c, \epsilon)$ is the running time of the algorithm $Sample(\mathcal{D}_c, \epsilon)$, and $\mathcal{D}_c$ represents either $\mathcal{G}_{t-1}^n$ or $\mathcal{G}_t^n$. Finally, the running time of the simulatable auditor after t queries is $t\gamma N\frac{80T}{9\delta} log\frac{T}{\delta}T_{samp}(\mathcal{D}_{cond}, \epsilon)$.*

Proof. (Sketch) Again, the proof of the first point is based on the Chernoff-bound and Union-bound. The running time results from the fact that we check γ intervals and sample N data sets in each of the $\frac{80T}{9\delta}\ln\frac{T}{\delta}$ round, using the algorithm Sample. Finally, this process is executed totally t times after t queries. □

Since the running time of the algorithm Sample is polynomial [9], the running time of the Algorithm 4 is polynomial. We assume that our simulatable auditor does not include the quantile computation procedure, however, note that there is a large class of $\mathcal{G}$ for which the quantile computation is polynomial-time.

5   Conclusion

We defined a novel setting for query auditing, where instead of detecting or preventing the disclosure of individual sensitive values, we want to detect or prevent the disclosure of aggregate values in the database. As a specific instance of this setting, in this paper, we studied the problem of detecting or preventing the disclosure of the maximum value in the database, when the querier is allowed to issue average queries to the database. We proposed efficient off-line and on-line query auditors for this problem in the full disclosure model, and an efficient simulatable on-line query auditor in the partial disclosure model. Our future work is concerned with looking at other instances (e.g., other types of aggregates in the queires) and prototypical implementation of our algorithms for experimentation in the context of the CHIRON project.

Acknowledgments. The work presented in this paper has been carried out in the context of the CHIRON Project (www.chiron-project.eu), which receives funding from the European Community in the context of the ARTEMIS Programme (grant agreement no. 225186). The authors are also partially supported by the grant TAMOP - 4.2.2.B-10/12010-0009 at the Budapest University of Technology and Economics.

References

1. Aggarwal, C.C., Yu, P.S. (eds.): Privacy-Preserving Data Mining - Models and Algorithms. Advances in Database Systems, vol. 34. Springer (2008)
2. Chen, Y., Evans, D.: Auditing information leakage for distance metrics. In: 3rd IEEE International Conference on Privacy, Security, Risk and Trust, pp. 1131–1140. IEEE (2011)
3. Chin, F.: Security problems on inference control for sum, max, and min queries. J. ACM 33, 451–464 (1986)
4. Chin, F., Ozsoyoglu, G.: Auditing for secure statistical databases. In: Proceedings of the ACM 1981 Conference, New York, USA, pp. 53–59 (1981)
5. Kenthapadi, K.: Models and algorithms for data privacy. Ph.D. Thesis, Computer Science Department, Stanford University (2006)
6. Kenthapadi, K., Mishra, N., Nissim, K.: Simulatable auditing. In: 25th Symposium on Principles of Database Systems (PODS), pp. 118–127 (2005)
7. Kleinberg, J., Papadimitriou, C., Raghavan, P.: Auditing boolean attributes. Journal of Computer and System Sciences, 86–91 (2000)
8. Zhang, L., Jajodia, S., Brodsky, A.: Simulatable Binding: Beyond Simulatable Auditing. In: Jonker, W., Petković, M. (eds.) SDM 2008. LNCS, vol. 5159, pp. 16–31. Springer, Heidelberg (2008)
9. Lovász, L., Vempala, S.: The geometry of logconcave functions and sampling algorithms. Journal Random Struct. Algorithms 30, 307–358 (2007)
10. Nabar, S.U., Marthi, B., Kenthapadi, K., Mishra, N., Motwani, R.: Towards robustness in query auditing. In: Proceedings of the 5th VLDB Workshop on Secure Data Management, pp. 151–162 (2006)
11. Nabar, S.U., Marthi, B., Kenthapadi, K., Mishra, N., Motwani, R.: Towards robustness in query auditing. Technical Report, Stanford University (2006)
12. Renegar, J.: A polynomial-time algorithm, based on Newton's method, for linear programming, 1st edn. Mathematical Sciences Research Institute, Berkeley (1986)
13. Thong, T.V., Buttyán, L.: Query auditing for protecting max/min values of sensitive attributes in statistical databases (2012),
    http://www.crysys.hu/members/tvthong/QA/ThB12QATech.pdf
14. Li, Y., Wang, L., Sean Wang, X., Jajodia, S.: Auditing Interval-Based Inference. In: Pidduck, A.B., Mylopoulos, J., Woo, C.C., Ozsu, M.T. (eds.) CAiSE 2002. LNCS, vol. 2348, pp. 553–567. Springer, Heidelberg (2002)

Verification of Security Coherence
in Data Warehouse Designs

Ali Salem[1], Salah Triki[1,2], Hanêne Ben-Abdallah[1],
Nouria Harbi[2], and Omar Boussaid[2]

[1] Laboratory Mir@cl
University of Sfax
Route de l'Aéroport Km 4 – 3018 Sfax, BP. 1088
{Salah.Triki,Hanene.BenAbdallah}@Fsegs.rnu.tn,
Salem.Aly@gmail.com
[2] Laboratory ERIC
University of Lyon 2,
5 avenue P. Mendès France 69676 Bron, Cedex, France
{Nouria.Harbi,Omar.Boussaid}@univ-lyon2.fr

Abstract. This paper relies on a UML profile with a graphical concrete syntax
for the design of secure data warehouses. The UML extensions define security
concepts to adopt the RBAC and MAC standards, to define conflicts of interests, and to model multidimensional schemas. In addition, this profile has formal semantics defined in Prolog that provides for the verification of both the
design well-formedness and the coherence of security policies of data warehouse designs.

Keywords: Data warehouse, Security, Coherence, RBAC, MAC.

1 Introduction

A data warehouse (DW) contains large volumes of data that trace the enterprise's
daily activities, *e.g.,* financial information, medical records, customer information,
etc. In other words, a DW includes customer personal and enterprise proprietary
information whose disclosure may jeopardize the enterprise existence. In fact, several governments passed laws for the protection of the citizens' private lives; *cf.,* the
Health Insurance Portability and Accountability Act (HIPAA[1]), the Gramm-Leach-
Bliley Act[2], etc. Consequently, enterprises are forced to put in place strict security
means to comply with these laws.

Indeed, the need for securing a DW was felt long ago, *cf.* [2, 3]. Similar to information system security, several proposed approaches tackled the DW security problem at the requirement (*cf.* [7]), design (*cf.* [4, 5, 9]) or physical (*cf.* [8]) levels. To
provide for access control, several notations ([1, 5, 7]) were proposed to model access

---

[1] http://www.hhs.gov/ocr/privacy/index.html
[2] http://www.gpo.gov/fdsys/pkg/PLAW-106publ102/content-detail.html

S. Fischer-Hübner, S. Katsikas, G. Quirchmayr (Eds.): TrustBus 2012, LNCS 7449, pp. 207–213, 2012.
© Springer-Verlag Berlin Heidelberg 2012

rights according to the MAC ("Mandatory Access Control") and RBAC ("Role Based Access Control") standards. However, these notations are ambiguous since they are textual and graphical notations. One objective of this paper is to propose a formal framework for the specification and automatic verification of a secure DW design.

This work is a continuation of that presented in [10]. Here, we tackle two types of security problems in a DW: data access control and data inference. More specifically, our proposition consists of a UML profile that extends UML with multidimensional and security concepts. In addition, we propose a graphical, concrete syntax for our UML profile that facilitates the specification of DW security constraints. Moreover, we propose a formal semantics in PROLOG. This semantics provides for a rigorous analysis of DW designs to ensure both its well-formedness (as a multidimensional model) and its coherence in terms of security constraints.

2   SECDW-UML: A UML Profile for the Design of Secure DW

We propose SecDW-UML, an UML profile to design secured data warehouses. We use two UML extension mechanisms to customize the generic UML concepts. First, we use the stereotypes to define the roles of RBAC and the levels of MAC and conflicts of interest. Secondly, we use tagged values to add security information to stereotypes. Fig.1 shows these extensions whose description is given in Table 1.

Table 1. Descriptions of the security stereotypes

Name	Description
COI	Association that represents conflict of interest between two elements.
MM	Binary association that represents conflict of interest between two measures.
DD	Binary association between two dimensions indicates that are in conflict.
PP	Binary association between two parameters indicates are in conflict.
DDM	Indicates two dimensions are in conflict for a given measure.
PPM	Indicates that two parameters are in conflict for a given measure.
EXCEPT	Ternary association between two elements and one role. Indicates that the given role is allowed to combine these two elements in conflict.
H-RBAC	Binary oriented association between two RBAC roles to define a hierarchy.
SSD	Indicates static separation of duties constraint between two RBAC roles [10].
MAC-Link	Binary association between two MAC level.
RBAC	Role in RBAC model.
MAC	Level in MAC model.

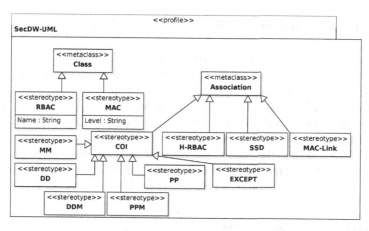

Fig. 1. SecDW-UML profile

We define a graphical, concrete syntax for the SecDW-UML profile. This syntax has two advantages: it facilitates the definition of security information, and it does not complicate the multidimensional model. The elements of the graphical syntax are detailed in Table 2.

In addition to modelling RBAC and MAC concepts, SecDW-UML can be used to model conflicts of interest. These arise when the decision makers could infer data that make their decisions partial and biased.

Table 2. Elements of the graphical, concrete syntax of SecDW-UML

Graphics	Stereotypes
◀┄(COI)┄▶	MM, DD, PP
◀┄(COI)┄▶ (with solid line below)	DDM and PPM. The two arrows point two the dimensions or two the parameters whereas the solid line is attached a measure
◀┄(EXCEPT)┄▶ (with solid line below)	EXCEPT. The two arrows directed to the multidimensional elements whereas the solid line is attached to a role.
↑	H-RBAC. The arrow is directed to the parent role.
(ROLE)	RBAC
◀┄(SSD)┄▶	SSD
↓	MAC-Link. The arrow is directed to the lower security level
Level	A MAC level is represented by a colored rectangle

3   Formal Verification of a SecDW-UML Design

The formal verification of a SecDW-UML model ensures the satisfaction of the well-formedness rules. Our formal verification framework is defined in Prolog as follows.

The fact is formalized as a predicate composed its name, set of measures and set of dimensions: *fact/3*. The dimension is formalized as a predicate characterized by the pair name and set of hierarchies: *dimension/2*. A hierarchy concept is formalized as a predicate characterized by the triplet name, set of parameters and the set of attributes: *hierarchy/3*. We define the *weakAtt/2* relationship that assigns the descriptive attributes to their parameters. Finally, we define the *weight/2* relationship which associates the weight *identifier*, *parameter*, *all* or *weak* to any attribute.

3.1   Security Constraint Propagation

SecDWUML includes three categories of constraints COI, RBAC and MAC. The objective of the coherence verification is to ensure that the propagation does not introduce any conflict.

COI Constraints. To formalize the COI binary relations of Table 1, we define the following dynamic predicates to enrich the knowledge base of Prolog by propagation.

-   *conflictM/2* denotes that the two measures *M1* and *M2* are in conflict.
-   *conflitP/2* expresses that the two parameters *P1* and *P2* are in conflict.
-   *conflitPM/3* denotes that the two parameters *P1* and *P2* are in conflict for the given measure *M*.
-   *conflictD/2* expresses that two dimensions *D1* and *D2* are in conflict.
-   *conflictDM/3* denotes that the two dimensions *D1* and *D2* are in conflict for a given measure *M*.

Given the above dynamic predicates, the rules for the propagation of COI are:

-   If two parameters are in conflict, then this conflict is propagated to the finest parameters.
    conflictPp(P1,P2):-hierarchy(H1,Param1,Att1),member(P1,Param1),
          hierarchy(H2,Param2,Att2),member(P2,Param2),H1\=H2,
          member(P3,Param2), conflictP(P1,P3),
          nth0(IndP2,Param2,P2), nth0(IndP3,Param2,P3),
          IndP2<IndP3, \+ member(P2,Param1).
-   If two dimensions d1 and d2 are in conflict then all d1 parameters are in conflict with the d2 parameters.
    conflitPp2(P1,P2):-dimension(Dim1,Hier1),dimension(Dim2,Hier2),
          conflictD(Dim1,Dim2),
          hierarchy(H1,Param1,Att1),hierarchy(H2,Param2,Att2),
          member(H1,Hier1),member(H2,Hier2),
          member(P1,Param1),member(P2,Param2).
-   Symmetry constraint indicates that all conflicts predicates are symmetric.
    constConfMs(M2,M1):-conflictM(M1,M2), \+ conflictM(M2,M1),

assert (conflictM(M2, M1)).
constConfDMs(D2,D1,M):-conflictD(D1,D2,M),\+ conflictD(D2,D1,M),
assert(conflictD(D2,D1,M)).
constConfDs(D2,D1):-conflictD(D1,D2),\+ conflictD(D2,D1),
assert(conflictD(D2,D1)).
constConfPMs(P2,P1,M):-conflictP(P1,P2,M),\+ conflictP(P2,P1,M),
assert(conflictP(P2,P1,M)).
constConfPs(P2,P1):-conflictP(P1,P2),\+ conflictP(P2,P1),
assert(conflictP(P2,P1)).

Now, we define the propagation predicates:

ConstConfPp1(P1,P2):- conflictPp1(P1,P2),\+ conflictP(P1,P2),
assert(conflictP(P1,P2)).
ConstConfPp2(P1,P2):- conflictPp2(P1,P2),\+ conflictP(P1,P2),
assert(conflictP(P1,P2)).

RBAC Constraints. They highlight the relationship between the roles of different users. They are based on an inheritance constraint and a mutual exclusion (ssd) constraint:

herit(Role1,Role2).   *ssd(Role1,Role2).*

-   If a role $R1$ inherits from role $R2$ then all inheriting roles $R3$ from $R1$ inherits from $R2$:
    heriteP(R1,R3):-herite(R1,R2),herite(R2,R3).
-   Mutual exclusion is propagated by the inheritance relationship:
    excluionMuP(R1,R2):-ssd(R3,R4),herite(R3,R1),herite(R4,R2).
-   Mutual exclusion is symmetric. This constraint is defined as above. We need to enrich the Prolog knowledge base by excluding required axioms:
    constExcRs(R2,R1):-ssd(R1,R2),\+ ssd(R2,R1),assert(ssd(R2,R1)).

MAC constraints. They describe the levels of security. We distinguish four levels of security: top secret, secret, confidential, unclassified. We define the list *secLev* combining these security levels in decreasing order: *secLev ([ts, se, conf, uncl]).*

Moreover, we define the predicate *AttributSecur* which expresses the security level of a parameter: *AttributSecur(Param, secLevElem).*

3.2   Coherency Constraints

In Prolog, when a predicate is not satisfied, the verifier produces either "*No*" if no element satisfies the predicate, or the *subset* of elements for which the predicate holds. This information lacks a specific explanation that assists the designer in correcting their model. For this reason, we opted to formalize the incoherence of each consistency constraints as a predicate.

COI Constraints
  COIRule 1: No COI between two parameters in the same hierarchy.
  incoherConflit(P1,P2):-hierarchy(H, Param, Att),
          member(P1,Param),member(P2,Param), conflictP(P1,P2).

We define the predicate *assignRoleElem* which assigns a role to an element MD.
assignRoleElem(Role, elem).

COIRule 2: If there is a COI between two multidimensional elements, then these elements must be assigned to roles in mutual exclusion.

The *COIRule2* rule is divided into two predicates. The first concerns parameters and the second concerns the dimensions. Moreover, we must define the predicates except for exception handling between roles and two elements. *"except/3."*

(COIRule2): *incoherParamRole(P1, Role1, P2, Role2):-conflictP(P1,P2),*
    assignRoleElem(Role1, P1), assignRoleElem(Role2, P2),
    \+ exclusionMu(Role1,Role2),\+ (except(Role1,P1,P2);except(Role2,P1,P2)).

(COIRule2'): *incoherDimRole(D1, Role1, D2, Role2):-conflictD(D1,D2),*
    assignRoleElem(Role1, D1), assignRoleElem(Role2, D2),
    \+ exclusionMu(Role1,Role2),\+ (except(Role1,D1,D2);except(Role2,D1,D2)).

RBAC Constraints [6] :

RBACRule 1 : Two roles in mutual exclusion cannot inherit one from the other.
    incoherExHer(R1,R2):- ssd(R1,R2), herite(R1,R2).

RBACRule 2: No role can inherit from two roles in mutual exclusion.
    incoherHerEx(R):-herite(R1,R), herite(R2,R), ssd(R1,R2).

RBACRule 3: No inheritance cycle among roles.
    incoherHerite(R1,R2):- herite(R1,R2), herite(R2,R1).

RBACRule 4: A role cannot be in mutual exclusion with itself (Irreflexivity) .
    incoherIrref(R1,R2):-herite(R1,R2), R1==R2.

MAC Constraints :

MACRule 1: The security level of a parameter (or a descriptive attribute) must be greater than or equal to the security level of the parameter that precedes it in the hierarchy

incoherSecur(P1, Sec1, P2, Sec2):-hierarchie(H,Param,Att),
    member(P1,Param), securParam(P1,Sec1), nth0(IndP1,Param,P1),
    member(P2,Param),securParam(P2,Sec2), nth0(IndP2,Param,P2),
    nth0(IndSec1, secLev,Sec1),nth0(IndSsec2, secLev,Sec2),
    IndP1<IndP2, IndSec1>IndSec2.

MACRule 2: The default security level is the lowest level. It is automatically checked during verification of the previous constraint.

4   Conclusion

A DW securing process should begin early in the data warehouse lifecycle, produce clear model, and verify formally the model. In this paper, we have proposed for the DW design an UML profile with a graphical concrete syntax. The profile offers, in addition to the multidimensional concepts, security concepts pertinent to RBAC and MAC. Its graphical syntax proposes clear and intuitive notations for these concepts.

We have also proposed for the coherence verification of the DW model a formal framework using Prolog.

References

1. Kirkgöze, R., Katic, N., Stolba, M., Tjoa, A.M.: A Security Concept for OLAP. In: DEXA 1997. IEEE Computer Society, Washington, DC (1997)
2. Bhargava, B.K.: Security in Data Warehousing (Invited Talk). In: Kambayashi, Y., Mohania, M., Tjoa, A.M. (eds.) DaWaK 2000. LNCS, vol. 1874, pp. 287–288. Springer, Heidelberg (2000)
3. Pernul, G., Priebe, T.: Towards OLAP security design - survey and research issues. In: Proc. of DOLAP 2000, Washington, DC, pp. 114–121 (2000)
4. Steger, J., Günzel, H.: Identifying Security Holes in OLAP Applications. In: Proc. DBSec 2000, August 21-23 (2000)
5. Villarroel, R., Fernández-Medina, E., Piattini, M., Trujillo, J.: A UML 2.0/OCL extension for designing secure data warehouses. Journal of Research and Practice in Information Technology 38(1), 31–43 (2006)
6. Ferraiolo, D.F.D., Kuhn, D.R., Chandramouli, R.: Role-Based Access Control, 2nd edn. Artech Print on Demand (2007)
7. Soler, E., Stefanov, V., Mazón, J.-N., Trujillo, J., Fernández-Medina, E., Piattini, M.: Towards comprehensive requirement analysis for data warehouses: Considering security requirements. In: Proc. of ARES 2008, Barcelone, Espagne, pp. 104–111. IEEE Computer Society (2008)
8. Cuzzocrea, A.: Privacy Preserving OLAP and OLAP Security. Encyclopedia of Data Warehousing and Mining, 1575–1581 (2009)
9. Blanco, C., Fernández-Medina, E., Trujillo, J., Jurjens, J.: Towards the Secure Modelling of OLAP Users' Behaviour. In: Jonker, W., Petković, M. (eds.) SDM 2010. LNCS, vol. 6358, pp. 101–112. Springer, Heidelberg (2010)
10. Triki, S., Ben-Abdallah, H., Feki, J., Harbi, N.: Modeling Conflict of Interest in the design of secure data warehouses. In: Proc. of KEOD 2010, Valencia, Espagne, pp. 445–448 (2010)

Towards the Secure Provision
and Consumption in the Internet of Services*

Luca Viganò

Dipartimento di Informatica, Università di Verona, Italy

Abstract. In this short paper, we describe the SPaCIoS ("Secure Provision and Consumption in the Internet of Services") project, illustrating its main objectives, the results obtained so far and those that we expect to achieve, in particular the development of the SPaCIoS Tool, an integrated platform that takes as input a formal description of the system under validation, the expected security goals, and a description of the capabilities of the attacker, and automatically generates and executes a sequence of test cases on the system through a number of proxies.

The vision of the Internet of Services (IoS) entails a major paradigm shift in the way ICT systems and applications are designed, implemented, deployed and consumed: they are no longer the result of programming components in the traditional meaning but are built by composing services that are distributed over the network and aggregated and consumed at run-time in a demand-driven, flexible way. In the IoS, services are business functionalities that are designed and implemented by producers, deployed by providers, aggregated by intermediaries and used by consumers. However, the new opportunities opened by the IoS will only materialize if concepts, techniques and tools are provided to ensure security.

State-of-the-art security validation technologies, when used in isolation, do not provide automated support to the discovery of important vulnerabilities and associated exploits that are already plaguing complex web-based security-sensitive applications, and thus severely affect the development of the IoS. Moreover, security validation should be applied not only at production time but also when services are deployed and consumed.

Tackling these challenges is the main objective of the SPaCIoS project, which has been laying the technological foundations for a new generation of analyzers for automated security validation at service provision and consumption time, thereby significantly improving the security of the IoS. This is being achieved by developing and combining state-of-the-art technologies for penetration testing, security testing, automatic learning, model checking and related automated reasoning techniques.

---

* The work presented in this paper was supported by the FP7-ICT-2009-5 Project no. 257876, "SPaCIoS: Secure Provision and Consumption in the Internet of Services" (http://www.spacios.eu/). SPaCIoS is a 3-year STREP project that started on October 1, 2010. I thank all the members of the SPaCIoS Consortium, which comprises: the Universities of Verona and Genova (IT); ETH Zurich (CH); Grenoble INP (FR), KIT, TUM, SAP and Siemens (DE), and IeAT (RO).

S. Fischer-Hübner, S. Katsikas, G. Quirchmayr (Eds.): TrustBus 2012, LNCS 7449, pp. 214–215, 2012.

More specifically, in SPaCIoS we have been developing both techniques for *property-driven security testing*, a variant of testing that applies techniques that make security properties (e.g., confidentiality and authentication) testable, and techniques for *vulnerability-driven testing*, where tests or test strategies are derived from vulnerabilities (e.g., XSS) that are likely to invalidate the security goals. Automated support to these testing activities is being achieved by generating test cases with *model checking* and related automated reasoning techniques, applied to a (possibly inferred) model of the *system under validation (SUV)*, the security goals, and a model of the attacker.

These techniques are all being implemented and integrated into the SPaCIoS Tool, whose architecture is depicted in Fig. 1. The tool takes as input a formal description of the SUV, the expected security goals, and a description of the capabilities of the attacker, and automatically generates and executes a sequence of test cases on the SUV through a number of proxies (e.g., http-proxies).

We have been applying the tool as a proof of concept on a set of security testing problem cases drawn from industrial and open-source IoS application scenarios, thereby paving the way to transferring project results successfully to industrial practice (e.g., to SAP's and Siemens' business units) and to standardization bodies and open-source communities.

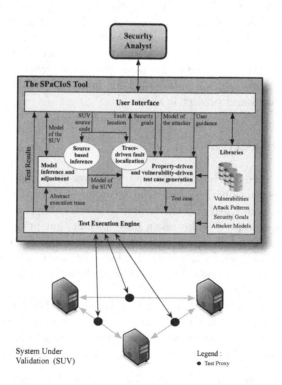

Fig. 1. The SPaCIoS Tool and its interplay with the Security Analyst and the SUV

WebSand: Server-Driven Outbound Web-Application Sandboxing*

Martin Johns[1] and Joachim Posegga[2]

[1] SAP Research, Germany
martin.johns@sap.com
[2] ISL, University of Passau, Germany
jp@sec.uni-passau.de

1 Motivation

The Web started in 1990 as a simple, stateless delivery mechanism for static hypertext documents; it evolved over time into a fully-fledged run-time environment for distributed, multi-party applications. Even today, new features and capabilities are added continuously, which drives the Web's chaotic evolution.

Security became increasingly important, in particular with the commercialization of the Web around 2000; but even today security is typically only an afterthought in the Web's evolutionary process. Today's primarily server-centric solutions provide a rich and stateful client-centric paradigm, but barely any manageable security: Data and services from multiple heterogeneous domains, aggregated both on the server-side and on an end-user's clients, demand a novel, comprehensive security solution, addressing fundamental security requirements. This is what the Websand project is about.

2 Project Objective

WebSand tackles security beyond dealing with low-level vulnerabilities at a higher level of abstraction: The technical strategy is to deal with security in a server-driven fashion. Clearly, security preferences and requirements from end-users at the client-side need to be taken into account, but primarily service developers at the server-side have the required expertise and context information to define adequate policies to be enforced. Moreover, server-driven security can be deployed relatively easily, since the need for updating the client-side platform is minimized.

Since WebSand strands for "Server-driven Outbound *Web*-application *Sand*-boxing", the project's overall goal is –along with this strategy– to empower web application developers, service providers, and users in designing, implementing, and running secure applications: Developers and service providers can develop

* WebSand is funded by the EU under FP7-256964. The WebSand consortium consists of SAP AG, Katholieke Universiteit Leuven, Chalmers Tekniska Hoegskola AB, University of Passau, Siemens AG. http://websand.eu

S. Fischer-Hübner, S. Katsikas, G. Quirchmayr (Eds.): TrustBus 2012, LNCS 7449, pp. 216–217, 2012.

and deploy secure web applications on their application servers; users will benefit from the project's results by transparently receiving a suitable security platform for their applications. WebSand aims to deliver this non-disruptively, i.e. by building upon existing web application technologies wherever possible to allow a seamless, immediate adoption of results in existing and future web applications.

3   Approach, Organisation, and Challenges

Websand identified three main focal areas for it's technical objectives:

Secure Web Interaction: The public interface of a Web application consists of the set of incoming HTTP request that it handles. Consequently, security properties, such as authentication and authorization, are directly linked to properties of incoming HTTP traffic. However, the original one-to-one browser/server relationship of early Web applications has been replaced recently with application scenarios spanning multiple clients and severs, interacting within one application context. The established concepts for authentication, cross-domain interaction, and control-flow integrity must hence be revisited and adapted to meet the security challenges of the evolving Web application interaction.

Secure Composition: Web 2.0 applications –unlike any other application model– frequently mix data and executable code from different service providers. Web browsers were initially not designed to cater for such scenarios, and application developers frequently encounter situations whore the currcnt trust mudel of the Web browser's same-origin Policy is insufficient: it only allows either full or no trust at all between components. WebSand's secure composition policies are much more expressive, allowing to specify privileges of each component, including behavioral capabilities and interaction constraints. This enables least-privilege composition and the enforcement of secure multi-origin policies.

Secure Information Flow Control: If application components from different sources are executed in a shared context, as in multi-party, mash-up driven Web applications, unintended and potentially insecure flow of sensitive information can occur. Information flow control governs sensitive and public data, possibly originating from multiple content providers in multiple trust domains; such data can be used in data aggregations or client-side and server-side processing as typically seen in mashups. Particular challenges for this task arise from Web browser's flexible nature and JavaScript's dynamic characteristics.

4   Summary

WebSand aims at developing a foundation for developers to build multi-party Web applications with robust security guarantees in non-trivial settings. The project defines fine-grained security policies and applies novel sandboxing techniques to the application, to enable a client-side enforcement of the given security policies. Whenever applicable, WebSand will build upon emerging Web standards; for its novel contributions, WebSand targets compatibility to such standards. This should enable the use of WebSand techniques together with these standards and support future inclusion of WebSand's contributions.

Attribute-Based Credentials for Trust (ABC4Trust)

Ahmad Sabouri, Ioannis Krontiris, and Kai Rannenberg

Goethe University Frankfurt,
Deutsche Telekom Chair of Mobile Business & Multilateral Security,
Grueneburgplatz 1, 60323 Frankfurt, Germany
{Ahmad.Sabouri,Ioannis.Krontiris,Kai.Rannenberg}@m-chair.net
https://www.abc4trust.eu

The rapid growth of communication infrastructures and enterprise software solutions has caused electronic services to penetrate into our everyday life. So it is not far from reality that many personal and trust-sensitive transactions happen online. In this regard, one of the biggest challenges to deal with will be proper user authentication and access control, as strong authentication and authorization techniques used nowadays are double-edged swords: while they can protect service providers by offering a satisfactory level of resilience against unauthorized accesses, most of these technologies have the drawback of threatening the clients' privacy.

As an example, X.509 certificates, which are one of the most common strong authentication mechanisms, contain a list of attributes of users attested and digitally signed by a trusted issuer in the domain. The static representation of these certificates makes it possible to trace users' online activities and link their various transactions . Furthermore, due to the nature of these certificates, the signature cannot be verified if a single modification occurs in the issued certificates. As a result, there is no choice for the users other than revealing all the attested attributes in their transactions even though some of them are not needed. Online techniques like SAML, OpenID, or WS-Federation can overcome this problem and offer selective disclosure of attributes, but they still suffer from other privacy breaches such as enabling the respective identity service provider to track the user's online transactions.

Privacy Preserving Attribute-Based Credentials (Privacy-ABCs) are elegant techniques to cope with these problems. They can offer strong authentication and a high level of security to the service providers, while users' privacy is preserved. Users can obtain certified attributes in the form of Privacy-ABCs, and later derive unlinkable tokens that only reveal the necessary subset of information needed by the service providers. However, inspite of the powerful features Privacy-ABCs provide, the diversity of the cryptographic schemes used in different existing implementations has so far hindered a satisfactory level of adoption.

The EC funded project Attribute-based Credentials for Trust (ABC4Trust) aims to bring all the common features of the existing Privacy-ABC technologies together under the same hood and provide a framework abstracted from the concrete cryptographic realization of the modules underneath. This gives software developers the flexibility to build Privacy-ABC enabled systems without

S. Fischer-Hübner, S. Katsikas, G. Quirchmayr (Eds.): TrustBus 2012, LNCS 7449, pp. 218–219, 2012.
© Springer-Verlag Berlin Heidelberg 2012

any concern about what cryptographic schemes will be employed at the bottom layer. As a direct result, the service providers are free to choose from those concrete cryptographic libraries that implement the ABC4Trust required interfaces, and plug them into their software solutions. This helps to avoid a lock-in with a specific technology, as the threat of a lock-in reduces the trust into an infrastructure.

The interchangeability of Privacy-ABC techniques in ABC4Trust framework is the outcome of its layered architecture design. Figure 1 depicts a cropped view of the high level ABC4Trust architecture where two of the main actors, namely User and Verifier, interact in a typical service request scenario. The core of the architecture is called ABCE (ABC Engine) layer; it provides the necessary APIs to the application layer residing on the top and utilizes the interfaces offered by the bottom layer called CE (Crypto Engine). To complete the picture an XML-based language framework has been designed so that ABCE peers from different entities of the system, e.g. the User and the Verifier, can communicate in a technology-agnostic manner. Putting all the pieces together, the application layer follows the corresponding steps defined in the protocol specification [1], calls the appropriate ABCE APIs, and exchanges the given messages with the other parties. Further down in the layers, upon receiving an API call, the ABCE performs technology-agnostic operations, such as matching the given access policy with the user's credentials, interacting with the user in case it is needed, and invoking crypto APIs from the CE in order to accomplish cryptographic operations. Finally the bottom layer CE is where the different realizations of Privacy-ABC technologies appear and provide their implementations for the required features.

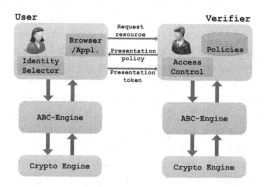

Fig. 1. ABC4Trust layerd architecture, User-Verifier interaction

Reference

1. Krontiris, I. (ed.): D2.1 Architecture for Attribute-based Credential Technologies Version 1, available at ABC4Trust project website

uTRUSTit – Usable Trust in the Internet of Things

Christina Hochleitner[1], Cornelia Graf[1],
Peter Wolkerstorfer[1], and Manfred Tscheligi[1,2]

[1] CURE – Center for Usability Research and Engineering, Vienna, Austria
{Hochleitner,Graf,Wolkerstorfer,Tscheligi}@cure.at
[2] ICT&S Center, University of Salzburg, Salzburg, Austria
Manfred.Tscheligi@sbg.ac.at

Abstract. In this paper we present uTRUSTit, a project with the goal to increase the users' understanding of trust in Internet of Things. The Internet of Things consists of complex technology that is often hard to understand for users. Most security properties are hidden in small devices and are not visible for users. Thus, uTRUSTit will display the underlying security implications to the users in order to create a justified level of trust in the Internet of Things.

Keywords: HCI, Privacy, Trust, IoT.

1 Overview

The Internet of Things (IoT) will connect a large number of communication and information systems. These systems will be part of everyday life in the same way mobile phones have become part of our lives. As systems become more ubiquitous and pervasive, the user loses track of which applications or "'things"' are connected to the Internet, how they are connected, what information is transmitted and who is receiving the information that is sent. uTRUSTit aims to provide users with tools that present this information and allow them to make informed trust-decisions. uTRUSTit is an international collaboration between six organizations from six different countries aiming at directly integrating the user in the trust chain, guaranteeing transparency in the underlying security and reliability properties of the IoT. The uTRUSTit consortium is composed of experienced security researchers, legal experts, practitioners, and simulation and usability laboratories from different parts of Europe.

The assessment of security functions and privacy implications is accomplished by developing a cognitive model of trust perception and an end-user evaluation with simulated and real systems. Based on this research, design guidelines help the industry to implement the Trust Feedback Toolkit (TFT) developed by uTRUSTit. Therefore, the general goals of uTRUSTit lie in the exploration, mapping, modeling and verification of user perception of trust and trustworthiness of IoT applications, as well as in the implementation of technological tools

S. Fischer-Hübner, S. Katsikas, G. Quirchmayr (Eds.): TrustBus 2012, LNCS 7449, pp. 220–221, 2012.

for building and testing trust visualizations in simulated and real IoT systems with end-user groups (including disabled users).

To achieve its goal, uTRUSTit is currently developing a trustworthy, legally compliant and accessible toolkit to close the loop of trust between the technological and psychological layers of the IoT. The TFT includes feedback mechanisms informing the user about the security and trustworthiness of applications and devices in the IoT and their connectivity to networks, the data to be transmitted, the security of the transmission and the trustworthiness of the recipient.

Furthermore uTRUSTit enables the user to get an overview of the "'things"' that are located in his/her environment and enable the user to locate them and to get information about the data these things are sending out to other devices. Assuming that in the future an increasing number of personal things will be capable of providing sensitive information to other networks, this function is a prerequisite for the development of an IoT that people can trust and believe in.

The prototypes that demonstrate the application of the TFT to an IoT environment are being iteratively developed, considering the needs and requirements of the targeted end-users. End-user inclusion is assured throughout the project by making use of the personas method, as well as continuous user-related activities, such as focus groups, online surveys or ad hoc interviews. As part of these activities, the consortium has developed a multi-faceted approach to measure traits and states of trust, e.g. through physiological measurements. At the same time, interaction workflows and interfaces depicting IoT application scenarios and providing trust feedback are developed.

As the IoT is a very complex environment that cannot be easily prototyped, the first iteration of IoT mock-ups was realized within a virtual environment. As part of this environment, two of the three key scenarios of uTRUSTit, smart home and smart office were realized as immersive virtual worlds the user could interact with and navigate within. Using these environments, 32 users experienced the scenarios and interaction workflows between the devices and the simulated IoT environment. The results of this first large-scale evaluation indicate that users perceived the environment as realistic and appreciated the provided feedback. Nevertheless, the combination of this new research field with the complex concept of trust has also raised several issues, such as the appropriate provision of feedback, that have to be considered within the next iteration of interfaces.

Within the upcoming development steps, the results from the first evaluation phase are integrated in order to provide more intuitive and efficient feedback on the system's trustworthiness. The resulting prototypes will again be iteratively evaluated with end-users and further refined in order to provide efficient trustworthiness feedback within the IoT.

Acknowledgments. This work was funded by the European Union Seventh Framework Programme (FP7/2007-2013) under grant 258360 (uTRUSTit; see http://www.utrustit.eu/).

Challenges for Advanced Security Monitoring – The MASSIF Project

Roland Rieke[1], Elsa Prieto[2], Rodrigo Diaz[2],
Hervé Debar[3], and Andrew Hutchison[4]

[1] Fraunhofer Institute SIT, Darmstadt, Germany
[2] Atos Research & Innovation, Spain
[3] Institut Télécom, France
[4] T-Systems, South Africa

Abstract. The vision of creating a next-generation Security Information and Event Management environment drives the development of an architecture which provides for *trustworthy and resilient collection of security events* from source systems, processes and applications.

A number of novel inspection and analysis techniques are applied to the events collected to provide *high-level situational security awareness*, not only on the network level but also at the service level where high-level threats such as money laundering appear. An *anticipatory impact analysis* will predict the outcome of threats and mitigation strategies and thus *enable proactive and dynamic response*.

Research Challenges and Emerging Trends. The vision of the Future Internet already created a paradigm which promises to largely enrich our ability to create new applications and businesses within this new environment. However, this enables new threats and scales up the risks of financial and also physical impact. In many cases, the information itself will be the essential product which deserves to be protected. In the Internet of Things however, real and virtual Cyber-physical resources deserve our attention. *Security Information and Event Management (SIEM)* is a key concept to identify security threats and mitigate their malicious impact. A SIEM system collects and examines security related events and provides a unifying view of the monitored systems' security status. There are a number of highly regarded SIEM solutions available commercially, and most SIEM solutions have the ability to identify, collect and correlate security events from a heterogenous ICT environment including end-user devices, servers, network elements and various security appliances such as firewalls. The main constraint of current systems is the restriction of SIEM to infrastructure, and the inability to interpret events and incidents from other layers such as the service view, or the business impact view, or from a viewpoint of the service itself. Furthermore, there are a number of other constraints such as the inability of systems to consider events from multiple organisations (thus identifying security threats that are emerging from one entity but yet to affect other entities), or the ability to provide high degrees of trustworthiness or resilience in the event collection environment (thus ensuring the non-repudiation of the event source). A further issue is the scalability of current solutions, to provide

S. Fischer-Hübner, S. Katsikas, G. Quirchmayr (Eds.): TrustBus 2012, LNCS 7449, pp. 222–223, 2012.

comprehensive posture of the environments under consideration when considering global deployment of ICT infrastructure. Current solutions depend largely on centralised rule processing with the constraint that single nodes process the full event traffic, bounding the capacity of the system to the capacity of a single node. Here, we consider challenges for advanced SIEM systems, which are derived from the analysis of four industrial domains: (i) the management of the Olympic Games information technology infrastructure; (ii) a mobile phone based money transfer service, facing high-level threats such as money laundering; (iii) managed IT outsource services for large distributed enterprises; and (iv) an IT system supporting a critical infrastructure (dam). The project MASSIF (http://www.massif-project.eu/), a large-scale integrating project co-funded by the European Commission, addresses these challenges. The vision of creating a next-generation SIEM environment drives the development of an architecture which provides for trustworthy and resilient collection of security events from source systems, processes and applications.

Approach and Key Results. MASSIF combines a wide set of innovations in different areas to progress beyond the state of the art in SIEM technology. *Cross-layer correlation* of security events from network and security devices and service infrastructure, and multi-level security event modelling will provide a holistic solution to protect the service infrastructures of the Future Internet. *Predictive security monitoring* will enable to fight attacks proactively by predicting their future actions. The SIEM infrastructure will be protected against accidental (e.g. node crashes) and malicious failures (e.g. intrusions) with leading edge innovations in high availability and Byzantine fault tolerance. The former will enable to provide continuous availability of the SIEM in the face of accidental failures, by tolerating them and reintegrating failed components in an online non-disruptive manner. The latter will protect against intrusions and specific attacks to the SIEM infrastructure. The SIEM infrastructure will be holistically protected with unforgeability that will guarantee the authenticity of generated, processed and stored events, which will enable use of stored events as evidence for criminal/civil prosecution of attackers. Finally, the balance between the amount of processing, normalization, aggregation and analysis at *edge collectors* of an SIEM system, and the work done at the central *nerve centre* are also topics which have to be re-considered in the context of an Internet type deployment of an SIEM system. A scalable distribution of acquisition and parallel processing, and seamless function-splitting between core engines and edge collectors, such as the MASSIF architecture develops is an important first step in this direction.

In essence though, the evolving Internet provides many new questions for SIEM deployment, and from a SIEM perspective reinforces the importance of having an Internet with security and possibly differentiated service for *high priority* and *trustworthy* control traffic such as the events from an SIEM. The *commercial models also change* since a service fee needs to evolve to scale up/scale down and pay-per-use models. The MASSIF project is already addressing many issues which we have identified as necessary in the Future Internet vision which we have presented here.

Decentralized, Cooperative, Secure and Privacy – Aware Monitoring for Trustworthiness

DEMONS Project Consortium

www.fp7-demons.eu

1 Introduction

Trustworthiness, in terms of resilience to failures and malicious activities, is a key issue in today's data networks; its provision is very challenging due to the large geographical scale of network accidents (e.g., routing accidents and software faults), as well as from the presence of distributed and coordinated inter–domain infrastructures specifically set up for malicious activities (e.g., botnets). This scenario is even worsened by the extremely high volume of traffic flowing across the Internet which makes traditional intra–domain monitoring systems based on centralized storage and post–processing analysis inadequate. In addition, any approach designed to overcome such limitations will ultimately have to handle massive amounts of data about users; this creates serious privacy concerns, also surrounded by legal implications [6]. On the other hand, cooperative cross–domain monitoring mechanisms that involve data exchange among the collaborating partners, create the danger of disclosing business-critical information.

2 The DEMONS Approach

The starting point of DEMONS is represented by the recognition that large, globally distributed threats call for a distributed, highly efficient and cooperative inter–domain detection and mitigation infrastructure. From a top–down perspective, the DEMONS monitoring infrastructure allows rapid development and deployment of measurement and mitigation **applications** and incident response workflows by leveraging on the layered architecture depicted in Fig. 1. The **measurement layer** is in charge of measurement and analysis primitives and the means to compose them. The core of the measurement layer is represented by nodes running Blockmon [4], a novel and composable high performance measurement system that provides a set of units called *blocks*, each of them in charge of specific discrete processing actions. Blockmon blocks communicate with each other by passing *messages* via *gates*. Monitoring applications are therefore easily implemented by a *composition* of a set of inter–connected blocks.

The **coordination layer** combines such Blockmon nodes into a distributed data processing system that ultimately provides summarized results (exported through IPFIX protocol), possibly exchanged across domains by means of dedicated Interdomain eXchange Points (IXPs), as shown in Fig. 2. At a higher level,

S. Fischer-Hübner, S. Katsikas, G. Quirchmayr (Eds.): TrustBus 2012, LNCS 7449, pp. 224–226, 2012.

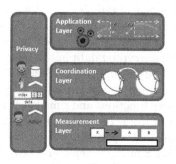

Fig. 1. The DEMONS architecture

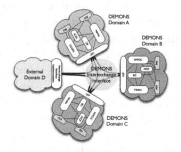

Fig. 2. High level view of DEMONS

Blockmon compositions are combined with other operations, such as mitigation ones, and form operational *workflows*; the latter constitute series of *tasks* with well-defined interaction patterns (both data– and control–flow) that are mapped to a service–oriented abstraction of the underlying architecture, thus enabling high–level management and control, as well as the coordination of privacy mechanisms enforcement. In fact, the coordination layer performs all actions subject to the constraints imposed by available capabilities, access rights and authorization permissions, data protection requirements, and any other application-specific workflow needs.

3   Privacy Preserving Techniques

In line with the *Privacy by Design* principle, DEMONS fosters network monitoring that is inherently privacy–aware, in the sense that data protection is built *into* the systems and operations. In that respect, privacy preservation is realized by a set of complementary mechanisms that combine a variety of features.

Intuitively, a privacy violation implies illicit access to data; in this context, DEMONS proposes an innovative privacy-aware access and usage control approach, in charge of regulating how data are accessed and used [7]. The approach has been conceived on the basis of network monitoring needs and the data protection legislation; it relies on a semantically rich *information model* that captures the associated concepts and enables the definition of contextual authorization policies at different abstraction levels. Moreover, it provides the means for the specification of privacy–aware workflows, by driving the automatic verification of workflows' compliance with the privacy principles and their enhancement with privacy features already at design–time [5].

For the protection of the data shared across different domains, DEMONS proposes a novel technique that permits the sharing of data if and only if other collaborative partners have observed the same or similar monitoring events [2]. For this purpose, the proposed approach leverages cryptographic primitives, particularly distributed threshold cryptosystems and Identity-Based Encryption techniques, to permit selective per-feed key escrow. This way, it ensures that each participant in the collaboration reveals fine-grained organized data only if a threshold number of other participants are ready to reveal similar data. Albeit collaborative, the proposed mechanism allows autonomous operation and requires no signalling; each participant releases the encrypted data independently.

Privacy–preserving cross-domain cooperation is also supported by Secure Multiparty Computation (SMC) techniques, where privacy is accomplished by permitting different administrative entities to compute functions and run algorithms over monitoring data without disclosing the input data, but only the results of such computation. DEMONS proposes two different approaches. The first is SEPIA [3], which is based on the Shamir's Secret Sharing scheme and provides a variety of basic as well as complex and composite operations for cooperative computation. The second is COMINDIS–private [1], enabling privacy–enhancing information exchange by means of conditional disclosure, and to conceal the identity of information publisher, thus protecting not only sensitive business information, but also the identities of the cooperative parties.

Acknowledgements. This work was partially supported by DEMONS, a research project supported by the European Commission under FP7 (contract no. 257315).

References

1. Berger, A., Cesareo, J., D'Alconzo, A.: Collaborative network defense with minimum disclosure. In: 2011 IEEE Global Telecommunications Conference, GLOBECOM 2011 (2011)
2. Bianchi, G., Rajabi, H., Sgorlon, M.: Enabling conditional cross-domain data sharing via a cryptographic approach. In: 2011 IEEE 5th International Conference on Internet Multimedia Systems Architecture and Application, IMSAA (2011)
3. Burkhart, M., Strasser, M., Many, D., Dimitropoulos, X.: SEPIA: Privacy-Preserving Aggregation of Multi-Domain Network Events and Statistics. In: 19th USENIX Security Symposium (2010)
4. Huici, F., Pietro, A.D., Trammell, B., Hidalgo, J.M.G., Ruiz, D.M., d'Heureuse, N.: Blockmon: A high-performance composable network traffic measurement system. In: Posters and Demos Session at ACM SIGCOMM 2012. ACM (to appear, 2012)
5. Koukovini, M.N., Papagiannakopoulou, E.I., Lioudakis, G.V., Kaklamani, D.I., Venieris, I.S.: A Workflow Checking Approach for Inherent Privacy Awareness in Network Monitoring. In: Garcia-Alfaro, J., Navarro-Arribas, G., Cuppens-Boulahia, N., de Capitani di Vimercati, S. (eds.) DPM 2011 and SETOP 2011. LNCS, vol. 7122, pp. 295–302. Springer, Heidelberg (2012)
6. Lioudakis, G.V., Gaudino, F., Boschi, E., Bianchi, G., Kaklamani, D.I., Venieris, I.S.: Legislation-aware privacy protection in passive network monitoring. In: Portela, I.M., Cruz-Cunha, M.M. (eds.) Information Communication Technology Law, Protection and Access Rights: Global Approaches and Issues. IGI Global (2010)
7. Papagiannakopoulou, E.I., Koukovini, M.N., Lioudakis, G.V., Garcia-Alfaro, J., Kaklamani, D.I., Venieris, I.S.: A Contextual Privacy-Aware Access Control Model for Network Monitoring Workflows: Work in Progress. In: Garcia-Alfaro, J., Lafourcade, P. (eds.) FPS 2011. LNCS, vol. 6888, pp. 208–217. Springer, Heidelberg (2012)

PASSIVE: Policy-Assessed System-Level Security of Sensitive Information Processing in Virtualised Environments

Panagiotis Rizomiliotis and Charalambos Skianis

Dep. of Inf. and Comm. Syst. Eng., University of the Aegean
Karlovassi GR-83200, Samos, Greece
{prizomil,cskianis}@aegean.gr

Abstract. PASSIVE is an EU funded ICT STREP project that aims to develop a framework for the secure deployment of virtualisation technology in e-Government scenarios.

Server Virtualisation technology promises to be a key enabler for the roll-out of privacy-sensitive applications in finance and e-Government, and in promoting green computing initiatives for governmental and large private-sector organisations. However, given the volume and sensitivity of information maintained by such organisations, existing virtualisation security technologies offer insufficient reassurance to permit full consolidation of computing facilities across, for example, entire governmental agencies and departments. In this context, PASSIVE, an EU funded ICT project, develops a technological framework and software implementation toward adequately resolving these security issues. PASSIVE's consortium consists of seven partners, three academic, one institute, two industrial and one SME. PASSIVE has four main scientific objectives. Namely,

1. the investigation of the unique virtualisation requirements for e-Government applications.
2. the identification of e-Government security requirements and propose solutions to security/privacy challenges that are hindering the adoption of virtualisation technologies by European governments and associated agencies.
3. the development of a framework for the secure deployment of virtualisation technology in e-Government scenarios, in consultation with the advisory board.
4. the enhancement of the state-of-the-art in virtualisation security by designing and creating a prototype implementation of a policy-based hypervisor security management tool.

To achieve these aims, the PASSIVE proposes and implements:

1. A policy-based Security architecture, to allow security provisions to be easily specified, and efficiently addressed.
2. Fully virtualised resource access, with fine-grained control over device access, running on an ultra-lightweight Virtual Machine Manager.

S. Fischer-Hübner, S. Katsikas, G. Quirchmayr (Eds.): TrustBus 2012, LNCS 7449, pp. 227–228, 2012.

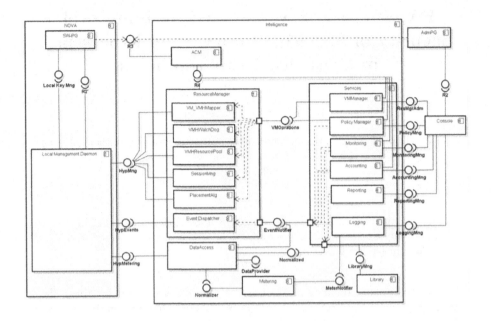

Fig. 1. PASSIVE architecture

3. A lightweight, dynamic system for authentication of hosts and applications in a virtualised environment.

The PASSIVE intelligence consists of the following modules: the policy manager, the resource manager, the Monitoring, accounting, reporting and logging components. The users are authenticated using credentials that are provided by a secure hardware and all the internal requests are approved by an access control module. In Fig. 1, the architecture of PASSIVE is shown. For the proof-of-concept, the PASSIVE intelligence has been implemented using Eclipse and NOVA as the hypervisor. Logging and accounting are resuing XDAS implementations on AOP framework, and more precisely Spring. For the interface between the hypervisor and the PASSIVE intelligence a adequately adapted version of the libvirt library is used.

For more details on the PASSIVE project please refer to the project's official webpage ([1]) and do not hesitate to contact any of the partners.

Acknowledgements. The work in this paper was sponsored by the EC Framework Programme as part of the ICT PASSIVE project.

Reference

1. PASSIVE project, `ict-passive.eu/`

Policy and Security Configuration Management[*]

Henrik Plate

SAP Research Sophia-Antipolis, 805 Avenue Dr. M. Donat, 06250 Mougins, France
henrik.plate@sap.com

Abstract. The PoSecCo project establishes a consistent, sustainable and traceable link between high-level security requirements and low-level security configurations, herewith aiming to support IT service providers in the effective and cost-efficient management and enforcement of security requirements.

Keywords: Security Management, Security Policy, Policy Refinement, Policy-Driven System Management.

1 Motivation

The PoSecCo project takes the perspective of providers of IT services realized by a composition of in-house and outsourced subservices working on different layers, from low-level infrastructure services such as for storage or bandwidth, up to high-level services for specific business functionality. The technical composition of such services, typically by means of Web technologies, is accompanied by a multitude of contractual, binding agreements on security and compliance aspects.

The success of such service providers depends on the pursuit and alignment of two interdependent goals: The profitable management and operation of its services, and, at the same time, the diligent implementation of each stakeholder's security requirements and compliance with regulatory requirements. However, achieving and maintaining the required security level and providing the necessary evidence in a cost-efficient manner is hindered by various issues: The multitude of security stakeholders that, on the one hand, express security requirements, and, on the other hand, contribute to their fulfillment at a security concept's design and runtime. The potential overlap and conflict at various levels, e.g., among security requirements or security mechanisms operating at various architecture layers. Last, the steady evolution and change of regulatory requirements, business relationships and IT systems.

Even today, where most organizations still operate bigger shares of their IT systems themselves, above issues lead to cost-intensive and error-prone security processes in which high-level requirements are formulated and maintained in prose and manually translated into lower-level, service-specific configuration settings [1, 2, 3]. These processes have a well-known impact on the trustworthiness of IT infrastructures, many times confirmed by studies such as [4], which found that "misconfiguration was the

---

[*] This work is partially supported by the FP7-ICT-2009.1.4 Project PoSecCo (no. 257129, http://www.posecco.eu).

S. Fischer-Hübner, S. Katsikas, G. Quirchmayr (Eds.): TrustBus 2012, LNCS 7449, pp. 229–231, 2012.

leading category of error contributing to data compromise". At the same time, organizations "cannot prove enforcement [of policies] or it is prohibitively expensive to do so" [5]. Besides creating exploitable security vulnerabilities, incorrect security configuration may have a significant impact on service availability, possibly violating corresponding service level agreements.

2   Project Objectives and Approach

The overall project goal is to increase and prove system compliance and security at reduced costs. Tools developed in the scope of the project support service providers in the design and enforcement of security policies, hereby addressing a variety of provider internal and external stakeholders, e.g., security managers, auditors, or administrators. To ensure the applicability of project results in real-life environments, policy enforcement will not require the installation of a dedicated software infrastructure, but solely rely on standard security mechanisms present in a given landscape. The interface towards the system landscape is mainly represented by common IT service management solutions that comprise system details and offer support for configuration provisioning, i.e., Configuration Management Systems (CMS) and Databases (CMDB) as defined in the IT Infrastructure Library (ITIL).

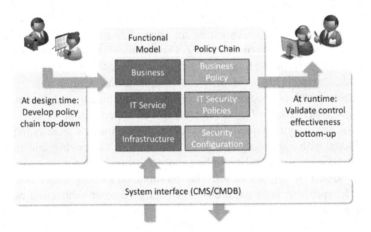

Fig. 1. The PoSecCo Policy Chain

Central to approaching above challenges is the so-called policy chain, a consistent, sustainable and traceable link between security artifacts of three abstraction levels (see Fig. 1). Business policies represent high-level security requirements imposed on service providers. Expressed in natural language, they address the service provider's business domain, e.g., the requirement to "ensure the confidentiality of invoice data". IT security policies describe how to meet the requirements considering the choreography of IT components, but do not yet prescribe a given enforcement mechanism (they specify, e.g., "the encryption of invoice data sent over a given channel". Modeled formally, they allow reasoning about dependencies and conflicts. A conflict-free set of such policies then triggers a policy refinement process that selects the most efficient enforcement mechanisms existing in the given IT system, based on security, cost and performance metrics associated to the system's security capabilities. Alternatives to enforce channel protection are, e.g., WS-Security or SSL/TSL. Security configurations implement IT security policies for a previously selected mechanism. They are specific to a class of enforcement mechanisms, e.g., firewalls, but abstract from vendor specific formats. The translation of such an abstract configuration to a concrete, deployable configuration required by a given product is left to the CMS.

The policy chain is built top-down during a security concept's design phase, by automated means where possible and offering decision support where human intervention is inevitable. Its construction depends on a complete functional model of a service provider's business and system. This model is similarly structured as the policy chain: The business model supports the elicitation of business policies with a description of, e.g., the service offering and the relevant stakeholders. The IT service model describes the choreography of software components designed to implement a given business service, hereby outlining their interfaces and the exchange and processing of data. The infrastructure model describes the system, e.g., its network topology or installed software components, as well as security capabilities that will be discovered, selected and configured during the policy refinement process.

Once built, the policy chain will be used at operations time to deal with continuous change on the level of requirements or system components, e.g., for the consideration of new requirements, change impact analysis, the comprehensive and automated validation of security configuration settings, or the scoping and execution of IT audits.

References

1. Chen, H., Al-Nashif, Y.B., Qu, G., Hariri, S.: Self-Configuration of Network Security. In: 11th IEEE International Enterprise Distributed Object Computing Conference (EDOC 2007), p. 97 (2007)
2. Oppenheimer, D.: The importance of understanding distributed system configuration. In: Proceedings of the 2003 Conference on Human Factors in Computer Systems Workshop (April 2003)
3. Patterson, D.A.: A simple way to estimate the cost of downtime. In: Proceedings of LISA: Sixteenth Systems Administration Conference, pp. 185–188. Usenix (2002)
4. Forrester Research, How To Manage Your Information Security Policy Framework (January 2006)
5. Verizon Business, Data Breach Investigations Report (2009)

Challenges and Current Results
of the TWISNet FP7 Project
(Extended Abstract)

Markus Wehner[1], Sven Zeisberg[1], Nouha Oualha[2], Alexis Olivereau[2], Mike Ludwig[3], Dan Tudose[4], Laura Gheorghe[4], Emil Slusanschi[4], Basil Hess[5], Felix von Reischach[5], and David Bateman[6]

[1] University of Applied Sciences Dresden, Dresden, Germany
{wehner,zeisberg}@htw-dresden.de
[2] CEA-LIST, Paris, France
{alexis.olivereau,nouha.oualha}@cea.fr
[3] Dresden Elektronik Ingenieurtechnik GmbH, Dresden, Germany
mike.ludwig@dresden-elektronik.de
[4] University Politehnica of Bucharest, Bucharest, Romania
{dan.tudose,laura.gheorghe,emil.slusanschi}@cs.pub.ro
[5] SAP Research CEC, Zurich, Switzerland
{basil.hess,felix.von.reischach}@sap.com
[6] Electricité de France, Paris, France
david.bateman@edf.fr

Abstract. Over the past years, the deployment of sensor networks in industrial environments has attracted much attention in several business domains. An increasing number of applications have been developed, ranging from defense, public security, energy management, traffic control to health care. Sensor networks are particularly interesting due to their ability to control and monitor physical environments. Nevertheless, several technical (e.g. remote management, deployment) and security (e.g. user's privacy, data confidentiality and reliability) challenges deter their integration in industrial processes. This extended abstract presents an overview of the current research results on an architecture aiming at supporting and securing the integration of sensor networks into large scale industrial environments. This work is carried out in the "TWISNet: Trustworthy Wireless Industrial Sensor Networks" project financially supported by the EC under grant agreement FP7-ICT-258280.

Keywords: wireless sensor networks, threat analysis, cybersecurity, authentication.

1 Challenges and Current Results – Extended Abstract

Many security concerns of wireless sensor networks raised by business applications have not been properly and efficiently addressed, particularly as far as industrial

S. Fischer-Hübner, S. Katsikas, G. Quirchmayr (Eds.): TrustBus 2012, LNCS 7449, pp. 232–233, 2012.

settings and multi-owner or mobile networks are concerned. The objective of TWIS-Net is to develop a platform supporting the integration of sensor networks in an efficient, secure and reliable way, considering the strong technical constraints of sensor networks. Project work started with the identification of four use cases in the area of nuclear plant facility management, supply and demand energy management, industrial process monitoring and control, and multi-owner environmental monitoring. For each of them, concerns of user's privacy, node authentication in multi-PAN environments and data confidentiality or reliability are addressed. All those security requirements must be fulfilled considering resource constraints on the nodes by means of security and trust mechanisms efficiency (e.g. battery, CPU, memory).

The architecture that masters the mentioned key challenges is categorized into the following six subjects. (i) Automatic configuration and reconfiguration is mandatory to ease sensor deployment in large industrial settings. This part includes mechanisms for secure bootstrapping as well as remote update of firmware resp. security credentials over the air. (ii) Identity management, authentication and access control is concerned with ensuring that no malicious node can masquerade as an honest node. The resource-constrained nature of sensor nodes and their mobility emphasize the need for fast re-authentication as the sensors have to periodically attach to a new PAN, and will be unable to transmit any contextual data. Pseudonymity is employed as the proposed authentication mechanism in TWISNet should not reveal the real identities of sensor nodes to an eavesdropper. (iii) Shared information and resources dealing with user's privacy is a major requirement for user acceptance of new solutions, so pseudonymity is also important in this context. Further, using communication and computation resources, for example by routing packets, may lead to obvious security threats which are focused here. (iv) Availability for communications, information and services are designed to guarantee certain levels of service quality in the presence of hardware and software failures. When network components are accidentally or maliciously damaged, the system pinpoints insecure nodes to ensure network availability. Based on the monitoring process, a secure and trusted system ensuring failure anticipation, prevention and detection is to be designed covering techniques for predicting and detecting failures as well as taking appropriate preventive steps. The service availability issue is also important for the scenario where the service information flows across heterogeneous administrative domains or from a private to a public domain, and vice versa. The goal behind this is to ensure that a satisfactory trust level can be established among network components from different administrative domains to ensure an inter-domain end-to-end service availability. Techniques for setting up backup options are considered when service continuity cannot be ensured because of access limitations to some network infrastructures. (v) Adaptive security is very important in the framework of sensor networking, where scarce resources and quickly changing environments make adaptive mechanisms attractive. TWISNet enhances its architecture by providing support for dynamicity and context dependency in the security services. (vi) Secure and trusted mediation layer ensures trustworthiness assessment of processed sensor data rather than ensuring that the sensor data is implicitly trustworthy. This includes algorithms for the detection of misbehaving nodes or malicious data from sensor nodes, trust and reputation systems and the application of a trust model that ranges from sensing the data on the sensor, through routing until final delivery to a business application component.

Aniketos: Challenges and Results

Miguel Ponce de Leon[1], Richard Sanders[2], Per Håkon Meland[2],
Marina Egea[3], and Zeta Dooly[1]

[1] TSSG, Waterford Institute of Technology, Cork Road, Waterford, Ireland
[2] SINTEF, Strindveien 4, 7465, Trondheim, Norway
[3] Atos, Calle Albarracin 25, 28037, Madrid, Spain

Abstract. This article gives a brief overview of Aniketos, a large EU-funded Integrated project [1], funded under the 7th Framework programme, that aims to establish and maintain trustworthiness and secure behaviour in todays constantly changing service environment. It is looking at ways to assess what level of trust should exist between entities. This offers users a fast and accurate way to decide if they can depend on an on-line service or data source. This automatic assessment will also provide ways to analyse and share information on preventing new threats and vulnerabilities.

Keywords: secure, trustworthy, service composition.

1 Aniketos Challenges and Results

Moving from todays static services, we will see service consumers that transparently mix and match service components depending on service availability, quality, price and security attributes. Contracts are cornerstones of service compositions, but current solutions focus mostly on availability and secure message exchange.

The Aniketos project is developing security service level contracts which makes it possible to express a wider range of security and trustworthiness requirements. Services will be able to expose their offered security contracts and can be composed by using them. There is also a need for mechanisms to ensure that contracts are fulfilled at both design-time and run-time, as we expect that there will be changes to both individual services and compositions from time to time.

1.1 Requirements and Architectural Approach

The requirements and architectural approach [2] provides the context of the Aniketos platform. The report presents the current state of the project requirements and is followed by the descriptions of the information, subsystems and interfaces within the Aniketos platform itself. Of particular interest is the set of practical use case scenarios for the Aniketos project which have been developed to define how Aniketos is envisioned to improve secure service composition.

There is also the Aniketos socio-technical security modelling language (STS-ml), and its support tool (STS tool) [3]. STS-ml captures security requirements at the organisational (business) level.

S. Fischer-Hübner, S. Katsikas, G. Quirchmayr (Eds.): TrustBus 2012, LNCS 7449, pp. 234–235, 2012.

1.2   Define, Establish and Maintain Trust

One of the main goals of Aniketos is to establish and maintain trust. The project has concentrated on three technologies in this space, Trustworthiness; Security-by-Contract; and Verification modules. The report D2.1 [4] describes models and methodologies for establishing and maintaining trust for services. A special focus of this research is on the compositional aspects of services as well as in their dynamic nature.

1.3   Secure Composition of Dynamic Services

The research behind the secure composition of dynamic services is producing software and algorithms that support design time and run-time secure service composition [5] . The project has looked at candidate techniques that are suitable to support the Aniketos requirements, such as formal analysis and verification, composable security policies of service security agreement and secure composition patterns.

1.4   Response to Changes and Threats

In this area Aniketos is dealing with the run-time reactions of the platform. Since the service composition environment targeted by Aniketos is in essence always changing, then the Aniketos platform must provide mechanisms to respond to changes and threats at run-time. The report D4.1 [6] describes tools that affect the satisfaction of the security and trustworthiness requirements, detect and observe changes or threats at run-time and notifies corresponding components when there is a change of the threat level. Finally there is a Threat Repository which is part of the community support module. It contains a repository of threats, dynamically updated, with information about the threat type and recommended response.

References

1. Aniketos Website, http://www.aniketos.eu
2. Meland, P.H.: Aniketos D1.2 First Aniketos architecture and requirements specification (2011)
3. Dalpiaz, F.: Aniketos D1.3 Initial version of the socio-technical security modelling language and tool (2011)
4. Elshaafi, H.: Aniketos D2.1 Models and Methodologies for Embedding and Monitoring Trust in Services (2011)
5. Brucker, A.: Aniketos D3.1 Design-Time Support Techniques for Secure Composition and Adaptation (2011)
6. Ayed, D.: Aniketos D4.1 Methods and design for the response to changes and threats (2011)

Ubiquitous Participation Platform for POLicy Making (UbiPOL): Security and Identity Management Considerations

Aggeliki Tsohou[1], Habin Lee[1], Yacine Rebahi[2], Mateusz Khalil[2], and Simon Hohberg[2]

[1] Brunel University, Business School, Uxbridge, UK
{Aggeliki.tsohou,Habin.Lee}@brunel.ac.uk
[2] Fraunhofer Fokus, Berlin, Germany
{Yacine.rebahi,Mateusz.khalil,Simon.hohberg}@fokus.fraunhofer.de

Facilitating citizen participation in policy making processes is vitally important for a sustainable policy implementation in the public sector. Governments have often expressed concern in the lack of engagement of citizens in the development of public policies. Motivating citizens to participate and engage in the policy making processes has been a challenging task and public authorities are yet to find satisfactory solutions [1]. Researchers have also highlighted the need for new governance models which will enable the wider and the deeper participation of citizens in policy making processes [2]. UbiPOL (Ubiquitous Participation Platform for Policy Making) is research project funded under the EU FP7 Programme that targets to address these issues. UbiPOL is an e-government platform that employs a new governance model in which citizens can participate in policy making processes in the middle of their everyday life overcoming spatial and time barriers. The core of the governance model is a ubiquitous participation platform that motivates its users to be involved in policy making processes. The system will utilise location-based notification services with the aim to alert citizens for consultation requirements about policies that are relevant to them when they are moving around physical places in their everyday life. Although location-based services have been used to influence citizen/consumer behaviors in many fields, such as tourism, marketing or education, they have not been used to engage citizens in the policy making processes. Moreover, UbiPOL retrieval services are designed to provide citizens only with the policies that are relevant to their personal preferences and necessities. Additionally, UbiPOL policy sharing services enable citizens to view other citizens' opinion on a specific policy issue without revealing their identity. Finally, the platform will provide policy tracking functionality via a workflow engine and opinion tag concept to improve the transparency of the policy making processes.

For the realisation of UbiPOL opinion tags represent a fundamental concept in attracting citizens in policy making processes. UbiPOL uses a policy making workflow (PMWf) model for representing policy making processes. Tasks in the PMWf model are classified into two categories: admin and opinion task. Admin tasks are executed by policy makers and usually are related with reviewing existing

S. Fischer-Hübner, S. Katsikas, G. Quirchmayr (Eds.): TrustBus 2012, LNCS 7449, pp. 236–237, 2012.

policies, contacting expert groups for identification of alternative policies, preparing public consultation, and responding to citizen opinions on policy issues and so on. Admin tasks are usually allocated to administration roles like 'town planning officer' and the role resolution is performed via linear mappings. On the other hand, opinion tasks are executed by mobile citizens. An opinion task has one or more opinion-tags that encapsulate policy issues, point-of-interests (POIs) to which the tags are attached, and role resolution rules that define who are qualified to participate to the policy issues. An opinion-tag is created by a policy maker and attached to one or more POIs on geographical maps. Any citizens who are located near the POIs can identify the opinion-tag and participate to the PMWf by adding their opinion on the tag which is shared with other citizens.

UbiPOL provides a security and identity management facility to ensure only authorised citizens can have access to relevant policies based on their roles in policy making processes. Among the objectives of UbiPOL the developed platform should:

–Ensure citizens privacy in filtering citizen opinions
–Secure the communication between the mobile device and the Ubipol platform
–Ensure the anonymity of the user in case of opinion casting. This means the association between the opinions records and the user identity must remain unknown
–Prevent multiple opinions casting
–Manage the Ubipol platform users identities and regulates the access to it according to the user role

The security and identity management framework consists of a certification authority, an authentication function, and an opinion casting function. User authentication in UbiPOL is realised using single sign on based on WS technologies (WS-Security, WS-Trust, WS-SecureConversation and WS-SecurityPolicy) [3]. Currently, user authentication can be realised with simple credentials (user name, password) but it is also possible with the new German eID cards.

References

1. Laurian, L.: Public participation in environmental decision making: Findings from communities facing toxic waste clean-up. Journal of the American Planning Association 70(1), 53–65 (2004)
2. Kanstrup, A.M., Rose, J., Torpe, L.: A Multi-Perspective Approach to eParticipation. In: Demo-Net – The Participation Network: European Research Workshop: in conjunction with the 7th Mediterranean Conference on Information Systems, Venice, Italy, pp. 3–6 (2006)
3. OASIS: Advancing open standards for the information society, http://www.oasis-open.org/ (access March 2012)

Secure Embedded Platform with Advanced Process Isolation and Anonymity Capabilities*

Marc-Michael Bergfeld[3], Holger Bock[5], Roderick Bloem[4], Jan Blonk[2],
Gregory Conti[1], Kurt Dietrich[4], Matthias Junk[5], Florian Schreiner[5],
Stephan Spitz[3], and Johannes Winter[4]

[1] ARM
[2] Brightsight
[3] Giesecke & Devrient
[4] Graz University of Technology
[5] Infineon

Mobile and embedded devices are increasingly popular: well over a million smartphones were sold *each day* in 2011. These devices have changed from simple single-purpose tools, to powerful multifunctional personal computers, providing the owner with functionality previously only available on much more powerful desktop computers.

This versatility allows devices to run convenient but security-critical applications including electronic banking, stock trading, and direct connections into corporate VPNs. In particular, recent payment applications make phones a very interesting target to attack.

Thus, while worms, viruses, and phishing attacks are no longer limited to "classical" personal computers, security critical applications increase the importance of strong protection. Users *and* service providers need to trust them: A platform should operate "securely, reliably and resilient to attacks and operational failures, while guaranteeing quality of service, protecting user data and ensuring privacy". Current mobile and embedded platforms, however, implement these characteristics imperfectly and are often susceptible to threats that prevent them from being used in applications with increased security demands.

Furthermore, the user has to have assurance that his assets and sensitive information stored on the mobile device are well protected. Providing this assurance of trustworthiness to the user requires establishment of trust in the protection mechanisms that are active when data is processed on the platform. Technical aspects of this goal can be addressed by providing secure, reliable and resilient support against attacks, using secure elements, processor and SoC extensions for process isolation, and process virtualisation on the platform. These, along with certification, are the goals of the SEPIA project.

Modern smartphones are essentially multi-tenant platforms on which untrustworthy downloaded apps co-exist with security critical applications such as mobile payment. In order to isolate the security critical parts from untrustworthy applications, SEPIA employs hardware virtualization and isolation techniques. These extensions provide strong separation between a *secure* and a *normal* world,

---

* This work was supported by the EU under grant 257433 (SEPIA).

S. Fischer-Hübner, S. Katsikas, G. Quirchmayr (Eds.): TrustBus 2012, LNCS 7449, pp. 238–239, 2012.

allowing a secure operating system to run next to a rich operating system like Android on the same physical platform in a secure and trustworthy manner.

Features such as secure-pin entry and "see-what-you-sign" are gaining increasing importance with upcoming secure mobile applications. Thus, SEPIA aims to extend the processor security extension concept to the entire system-on-chip platform, securing I/O along with memory.

In a world where users are permanently online it is important to protected their privacy. Authentication is one particularly critical operation where interests between users and service providers may clash. Service providers have a legitimate interest in knowing who they are dealing with, while users have an equally legitimate interest in preserving their privacy while interacting with service providers. Unfortunately, cryptographically strong anonymity and privacy protection of users and their devices is uncommon on present mobile platforms due to the resource-demanding nature of the involved algorithms.

The platform proposed in SEPIA changes the situation significantly: Critical parts of privacy protecting algorithms can be executed in a small isolated secure world environment which runs at the same native processing speed as the normal world environment hosting the rich operating system. Thus, it becomes feasible to use anonymous signatures and other computationally expensive cryptographic techniques in a practical setting. Here the SEPIA project contributes efficient hardware and software primitives for securely implementing the required cryptography.

Secure elements complement the on-SoC protection offered by processor security extensions and offer an additional layer of isolation and protection for security critical credentials even when the platform is powered off. SEPIA combines both secure elements and processor security extensions to provide a secure platform which fits the security and privacy demands of all stakeholders of the mobile device *including* the end-user.

One further open question is how to establish trust in the security of mobile devices. A commonly accepted means by industry and consumers for establishing trust in the quality of security mechanisms are security evaluations. Currently, the time and effort required for security evaluations as a basis for trust is too high—unless a hardware/software security evaluation and certification methodology is available that can accommodate the dynamic and rapidly changing environment as it exists for example in the mobile handset industry.

SEPIA strives to improve over the current situation regarding security evaluation of mobile platforms, by investigating the feasibility of using a faster modularised evaluation process. Instead of considering an entire mobile device as a whole, SEPIA tries to decompose the device into smaller partitions which can be evaluated indivdually.

Thus, SEPIA makes a first step in providing a secure infrastructure for consumers and service providers. While SEPIA focusses on mobile devices, these problems are equally pressing other embedded settings, especially in settings involving machine to machine communication, but also in cloud computing. Thus, it will become increasingly important to apply the lessons learned in SEPIA to ensure not just isolated devices in a network, but secure devices in a secure network.

Author Index